The Prairie Primer

Literature Based Unit Studies for Grades 3-6 Utilizing the "Little House" Series

Margie Gray

Cadron Creek Christian Curriculum
4329 Pinos Altos Road
Silver City, NM 88061
Copyright, 1993

©   Copyright, Margie Gray, 1993.

All rights reserved. This book may be photocopied by the original purchaser for personal and household use only. Such reproductions may not be resold. Except for the limited authorization to photocopy, stated above, no part of this book may be reproduced or transmitted in any form or by any means, electronic or mechanical, including photocopying, recording, or by any information storage and retrieval system, without permission in writing from the author.

Seventh Printing, 1999.

Acknowledgements

I would like to thank the Lord who has enabled me to do more than I thought possible. He is the great Provider. He has given me an encouraging, helpful husband, as well as friends and acquaintances that have counseled me. He has given me a godly heritage in my father, Dudley Arnold, whose Ph.D. in Science and Administration was an indispensable resource during the writing of this curriculum. I want also to thank my lifelong friend, Richard Ziriax, a climatologist, who made his expertise available on many topics throughout the work. I am grateful to the numerous homeschoolers across the country who gave feedback and encouragement during the year of this work. Special thanks go to Jean, Debbie, and Sheila who gave me input and held me accountable. To Joetta Witkowski and Sandra Petit who have gone above and beyond the call of any customer to improve future editions, I give my heartfelt thanks.

This work would not have materialized without the enthusiastic cooperation of many people. I am indebted to Pastor Ray Miller for the use of the computer, and to a very patient Celia Frizzell, who spent many long hours at the keyboard. A big thank you to Miriam Gilliom for her formatting skills, and to Bill Riopelle for the use of his scanner. My thanks also to my friend and editor, Mei Leslie, who encouraged me and believed this work would help homeschoolers build Christ's character in our children.

About the Author

My parents taught on a Navajo Indian reservation in Arizona where I was born. At age eight we moved to Barstow, California, and there I finished high school. I had many exceptional teachers there; but I began to see the "social agenda" of the educational system. Public school was the government's tool for changing negative social values, like racism and drug use, while it promoted "positive" values, like family planning. Seeing the problems my parents faced within their profession, I chose a nursing degree. After college, I moved to Mountain Pass, California, where in 1983, I met and married my husband, Owen, a heavy equipment operator.

In 1990 we moved our family of six to Arkansas to be nearer to family. My grandmother lived with us the last three years of her life. After she died, Owen and I longed to move west. So in 1997, with hopes of employment nearer to home and better climate, we moved to Silver City, New Mexico. We have always homeschooled our five girls, ages fourteen, eleven, nine (twins), and three. The academic benefits of homeschooling have been wonderful, but greater joy has been in the strengthening of family relationships. I therefore participate actively in the leadership of local homeschool groups to encourage the hearts of parents toward their children.

In 1993, I self-published the literature-based curriculum, <u>The Prairie Primer</u>. I am currently writing a dual project, <u>Academics and Anne</u> and <u>Anne's Anthology</u>, a unit-study and reference work, respectively, based on <u>Anne of Green Gables</u>.

Table of Contents

Introduction... 7

    Topics Covered in <u>The Prairie Primer</u> 7

    Using <u>The Prairie Primer</u> 10

    Making the Most of <u>The Prairie Primer</u> 12

    Resources Required 14

    Additional 1800's Curriculum 14

    General Activities to Do Throughout the <u>Primer</u> 14

Big Woods 15

Prairie 47

Plum Creek 81

Shores... 115

Long Winter 145

Town 165

Golden Years 193

Farmer Boy 223

First Four.. 253

Appendix: Motivational Gifts, Romans 12 267

Bibliography 285

Introduction

"These commandments that I give you today are to be upon your hearts. Impress them on your children. Talk about them when you sit at home and when you walk along the road, when you lie down and when you get up" (Deuteronomy 6:6-7 NIV).

The Prairie Primer has been devised to help parents impress upon their children the way to walk faithfully with the Lord. It is a tool to encourage the productive exchange between parents and their children in academic subjects and godly development. The "Little House" books by Laura Ingalls Wilder provide a springboard for learning Biblical character qualities in the setting of American pioneer history.

The Prairie Primer is designed for children grades third through sixth, but as with most unit studies it can be adapted for use with those younger or older. It covers a variety of academic subject areas, including: U.S. History in the 1800's, U.S. geography, science, language, practical living, health and safety, nutrition, music, and art. Except for a grammar, spelling, and math program, the Primer is a well-rounded scholastic program.

Above all, The Prairie Primer emphasizes studying the Word of God. There are daily Bible readings with character and word studies. Apart from the "Little House" books, the Bible will be the main text.

Topics Covered in The Prairie Primer:

This complete listing of topics covered in The Prairie Primer is broken down into subject areas only. A Writing Scope and Sequence is presented on page 12, but this list is given without age or grade restrictions of when to cover them. You will find that your child learns progressively, that is, he can be exposed to a topic superficially at first, and later acquire more in-depth details and understanding, and still later, he will develop mastery of that subject. Each step in progressive learning, introduction, development and mastery, is necessary for the child to assimilate and add to his store of knowledge. Some of the topics in the Primer you may just want to introduce to your child. Other topics your child may be ready to master.

In mathematics, concepts build upon previously mastered skills. However, subjects such as history or science can be presented in varied order. You need not always follow a prescribed, rigid sequence. For example, the study of ants is not a prerequisite to the study of grasshoppers. Nor does it truly matter if a child learns about insects in the third grade or in the sixth. The key at any age is to be introduced to a specific topic, be given the tools to develop the new information, and allowed the time and further exposure to master the subject area. Your child will be learning and learning how to learn.

Introduction

Bible Concepts and Building Character

Blessing of Children
Comparing Ourselves
Complaining
Courtship
Debt
Egyptian Plague
Envy
Flattery
Foolishness
Gentleness
Getting Even
God's Provision
God's Umbrella of Protection
Gossip
Holy Spirit
Humbleness

Idleness
Jealousy
Mercy
Motivational Gifts
Patience
Perverse Talk
Preparedness
Pride
Reasons for Suffering
Spanking
Struggle with Sin Nature
Success
Temptation
Uniqueness of Individual
Vanity
Yielding Rights

Bible Memory

Psalm 91
Psalm 8
Psalm 51
Romans 8:31-39
Psalm 34 or Psalm 37

Romans 12
Psalm 27
1 Corinthians 13:1-8
Psalm 4-6, Proverbs 31, or Ecclesiastes 4:9-12

Crafts

Candle Making
Knitting

Quilting
Moccasin Making

Health

Bathing/Hygiene
Body Mechanics (Back Care)
Causes of Diseases
Diphtheria
Effects of Tobacco and Alcohol
Emergency Preparedness
Exercise
Fear
Fever
Fiber
Fire Safety
First Aid—Sprains and Burns
Food Groups

Frostbite
Growth and Development
Immunizations
Malaria
Measles
Meningitis
Nutrition
Prevention of Sexual Abuse
Rabies
Scarlet Fever
Sun Safety
Tuberculosis
Water Safety

Introduction

History, Government, Social Studies, and Geography

American Folk Songs
Apprenticeship
Banks and Bank Failures
California Gold Rush
City History
Civil War
Compromise of 1850
Dred Scott Decision
Family History
France
French Influence on U. S.
Geographical Terms
History of American Education
Homesteading
Impeachment
Indians
John Brown and Harper's Ferry Rebellion
Logging
Louisiana Purchase

Mexican/American War
Mexico
Minnesota Massacre
Napoleon
Paper Production
Pony Express
Postal Service
Prairies
Presidents
Railroad
Reconstruction
States and Capitals
State History
Supreme Court
Territories
Timber Culture Act
U. S. Geography
War of 1812
Woman's Suffrage

History—Biographies

An American Indian
An 1800's Evangelist
Clara Barton
Fanny Crosby
Frederick Douglass
Thomas Edison

Andrew Jackson
Thomas Jefferson
Abraham Lincoln
Samuel Morse
Louis Pasteur
Noah Webster

Literature and Language Arts

Basic Elements of Fiction
Categorizing Works of Literature
Cause and Effect
Composition
Dictionary, Thesaurus, Concordance Skills
Foreshadowing
Homograph
Hyperbole
Metaphor

Oral Reports
Participate in Discussions
Poetry
Point of View
Sequencing
Simile
Symbolism
Understatement
Vocabulary

Living

Art
Conservation
Cooking

Guns and Gun Safety
Manners
Music

Page 9

Introduction

Science

Bacteria and Viruses
Communities of Living Things
Density of Solutions
Distillation
Earth's Rotation
Earth's Water Cycle
Electricity
Energy and Fuels
Food Preservation
Food Chain
Heat Transfer
Light and Prisms
Moon and Sun

Pollination
Potential and Kinetic Energy
Properties of Fire
Rust
Simple Machines
Sound Waves
States of Matter
Telegraph
Trees
Underground Water Tube
Water Purification
Weather

Science—Animal Kingdom

Animal Classification
Animal Tracks
Badgers
Bears
Beavers
Bees
Birds
Butterflies
Chickens
Cows
Fish

Grasshoppers
Horses and Mules
Leeches
Mosquitos
Muskrats
Owls
Panthers
Pigs
Snakes
Wolves

Science—Human Body

Blood
Digestive System
Ear
Eyes and Eyesight
Genetics
Heart and Vascular System

Immune System
Lungs Breathing
Nervous System
Reproduction
Skin
Taste

Using The Prairie Primer:

There are nine units in the Primer—one corresponding to each nine "Little House" books. The Primer follows, on average, a book-a-month schedule. Approximately twenty-five pages of reading are assigned from the "Little House" books daily in addition to other suggested reading. When the daily plan is followed, the entire curriculum can be completed in one school year. *But it is emphasized that you follow a plan best suited to your family's pace.* The daily reading and activities can be halved, and the plan completed in two years' time. It is recommended that the books be studied in the order presented in the Primer. Many times studies will refer to previous assignments. Thus, activities tend to build on one another.

Introduction

It is a good idea to skim through the entire curriculum at the beginning of the year to prioritize which material you want to purchase to enhance the studies. Skimming will also help you to preview the field trips ahead of time, allowing you to be on the watch for certain once-a-month community activities such as a Living History weekend.

Units. At the beginning of each unit is a short introduction. This gives the parent some background information about Laura and her family not contained in the reading, which can be shared with their child; and it provides an overview of the direction the studies will take in that unit. Some units have Additional Reference Material. This information is provided to save the parent research time, especially when the topic is difficult to obtain information on and is pertinent to the study.

The beginning of each unit will also list any General Activities to do throughout the unit. These activities include long-term projects like handicrafts, memory work, a timeline, or reading a biography of a nineteenth century contemporary. The parent needs to make note of these activities and encourage daily progress toward their completion as there are only weekly reminders to do so. These General Activities will give your child the satisfaction of finishing a long-term goal.

Several biographies and autobiographies are listed as suggested reading to enhance history studies and to reinforce positive character qualities. The Bible instructs us to look to godly people as examples as we learn to follow Christ (Hebrews 13:7; Philippians 3:17). Books, like companions, should be carefully chosen. Those who limit their reading to novels and romances will encounter little real knowledge of the world or examples of good character qualities. Reading for amusement or entertainment alone is of little consequence. Encourage your child to read systematically, closely, and thoughtfully analyzing each subject.

Some units will list an optional Group Activity. Group activities add the needed spice, variety, energy, and enthusiasm to your schooling. These activities can be done informally with just siblings or may include neighbors, other homeschoolers, or families that are using the Primer.

Any information given before the start of a study is provided to help the parent plan. It is suggested you read each unit before embarking on any study in order to better anticipate the needs of the activities you choose to do.

Weeks. Each unit is divided into four weeks. At the beginning of each week is a Planning Guide that lists the information and items that need to be gathered for the week's activities. Suggested resources for the information and items are given along with field trip possibilities. A line is provided to add your own resources under the suggested titles. Space is allotted also at the bottom of the Planning Guide for your own notes. Use this page to prepare for the week ahead.

Days. At the beginning of each day, the reading assignment is given according to the chapter(s) or pages from the "Little House" books. Following the reading assignment, the day's plan is then divided into Comprehension Questions and Activities. A week in the Primer consists of four days of assignments. Use the fifth day of the week to catch up on any reading or unfinished activities.

Comprehension Questions. The Comprehension Questions are intended for parents to ask aloud to their child and should be answered orally and in complete sentences. Page numbers are included with some of the difficult questions, but no answer key is given. Parents are encouraged to read the books in order that the question and answer exchange can give rise to the development of good communication and thinking skills. Let the dialogue with your child during this time be relaxed, and enjoy getting to know their opinion and their skills in logic and observation.

Activities. The Activities cover academics and Bible studies that relate to the chapters or pages read. An academic category is given in the margin next to each assignment to help you choose, record or balance your child's studies. *Choose those Activities that are age, ability, and interest appropriate for your child.* Many of the Activities may take more than one day to complete depending on your family's interest and

Page 11

Introduction

time. Make note of any Activity that is inappropriate due to the season of the year or the readiness of your family, and complete it when the time and conditions are better.

Frequently, there are more Activities assigned in a day than one student could possibly complete. If many activities are interesting and important to you, slow your pace and take the time to explore. If more than one student is using the Primer, have one student pursue an Activity while another chooses a different one. At the end of the week, have them share with the other what they have learned.

For the ease of the parent, many of the Activity questions have answers, hints, or explanations written in italics. These helps should decrease your research time.

Making the Most of The Prairie Primer:

<u>Bible</u>. Almost all of the daily assignments have Bible Activities. Use a Bible version your child is comfortable reading, but not one that is too easy or that the meaning is unclear. Many of the studies will require the use of a Bible concordance or a topical Bible.

The most successful method in teaching the Bible studies is to preview the scriptures beforehand and allow the Spirit of God to quicken the scriptures to you. If certain scriptures come alive to you, you can in turn give your child fresh "milk and meat from the Word." One of the best ways to encourage a child to taste the Word is for the parent to feed them what they themselves have been "chewing upon" or thinking about. If you share with them "living words," they will experience the fact that God's Word is relevant and meaningful to our daily lives.

Also, because of differing attention spans and assignments, there may be more verses given than can be absorbed. By previewing the scriptures, you can choose to use only those that will emphasize the point you wish to make. Some scriptures are doctrinal by nature. These are listed without comment, so that you can help your child interpret the Word of God according to your belief. Sometimes, real life is such that there may be little or no time to meditate on the scriptures before presenting them. In this case, you and your child will discover the Word of God together.

<u>Writing</u>. The Primer has a variety of writing assignments. Using additional helps, such as <u>You CAN Teach Your Child Successfully</u> by Ruth Beechick, <u>Learning Grammar through Writing</u> by Bell and Wheeler, and/or <u>If You Are Trying to Teach Kids How to Write, You've Got to Have This Book</u> by Marjorie Frank, can aid you to maximize your child's writing potential. Be sure to encourage your child in the editing and rewriting process. This will serve to motivate them to learn the rules of punctuation, spelling, and grammar.

Some written activities refer to previous assignments. It is suggested that your child keep a notebook of their written work. In order to find assignments for future reference, the notebook can be organized according to unit with a table of contents or index.

Use the following writing scope and sequence as a guide in your daily writing assignments to help you strengthen these skills in your child.

Third Grade Level

Write and relate original stories, reports, etc.
Use simple punctuation
Recognize and use complete sentences
Use some prefixes and suffixes

Use logical sequence when writing or telling
   stories, reports, etc.
Identify nouns and verbs

Page 12

Introduction

Fourth Grade Level

Participate in discussion
Write simple stories, poems, reports, etc.
Use simple punctuation correctly—period, comma, question mark, and exclamation point
Use period after abbreviations and initials
Use comma in word series, dates, greetings, and closing of letters
Use apostrophe in contractions and in possessives
Group related sentences to form paragraphs
Write simple letter and address envelope
Capitalize initials
Use correct verb forms—present, past, and future

Fifth Grade Level

Use punctuation correctly including quotation marks around titles and direct quotations
Underline titles
Write notes, invitations, book reports, prose, and poetry
Proofread and edit their own written work
Identify nouns, verbs, adjectives, and adverbs
Identify subjects, predicates, and direct objects
Recognize subject-predicate agreement
Use adjectives and adverbs in writing
Use verbs correctly
Recognize agreement between pronouns and antecedents
Recognize regular plurals
Diagram subjects and predicates, direct and indirect objects, adjectives and adverbs, prepositions and conjunctions
Recognize indirect objects

Sixth Grade Level

Use plural possessives and contractions
Recognize and write compound sentences
Write outlines
Write using correct punctuation including quotation marks, indentation, colons, and semicolons
Write compositions, dialogues, simple poetry, short research paper, and book reports
Write business and friendly letters
Write with unity and coherence
Proofread and revise work
Recognize and use simile and metaphors
Use card catalog in the library and other reference material
Organize information from reference materials for reports
Write research paper including bibliography

(From Christian Home Educator's Curriculum Manual for Elementary Grades by Cathy Duffy, pages 63-64. Copyrighted 1990 by Home Run Enterprise. Used by permission.) Some of the skills listed by Cathy Duffy are not contained in the Primer and are, therefore, not included in the above list. Also refer to topics covered in The Prairie Primer, "Literature and Language Arts," on page 9.

<u>Art</u>. The drawing assignments in the Primer will increase the comprehension of the reading material, as well as increase retention and contemplation of difficult subject matter. It will allow the student to strengthen their nonverbal communication abilities, too. The book Drawing with Children by Mona Brookes can help sharpen your child's drawing skills. Each month as you begin a new "Little House" book, try to concentrate on learning a different art skill. Focus on skills such as lines, shapes, overlapping, perspective, shading, color, color tone, and positive and negative space. Use different media to achieve variations in effects: colored pencils, markers, water colors, charcoal, tempera, india ink, and metal tooling. Experiment with combinations of media for different results.

Page 13

Introduction

<u>Vocabulary</u>. Children should make a vocabulary list of words they cannot read or do not understand. These words should be looked up for both their dictionary respelling (pronunciation) and definition. Included in the text are vocabulary words that most students may not understand. A few of the words are difficult to find in a modern dictionary, but may be found in the <u>American Dictionary of the English Language</u> (the 1828 edition by Noah Webster).

<u>Music</u>. For the musically inclined, the <u>Primer</u> has included page numbers corresponding with the <u>Laura Ingalls Wilder Songbook</u> by E. Garson.

Resources Required:

Use your local library as your main resource. You will need access to good encyclopedias, a dictionary, Bible concordance, and a thesaurus. The <u>Primer's</u> pages correspond with the "Little House" paperback edition, illustrated by Garth Williams, published in 1953. The "suggested sources" given at the beginning of each week are only suggestions. Please use anything comparable that you have on hand. The Bibliography at the end of the <u>Primer</u> is a vendor list where some of the suggested materials can be obtained. The materials are noted according to the frequency of their use in the <u>Primer</u>.

Additional 1800's Curriculum:

<u>Ray's Arithmetic</u> is a nineteenth century math program that was most likely used by Laura and her peers. This program is available today in its unrevised form. It stresses the importance of learning principles and drilling.

For teaching handwriting, the <u>Spencerian System of Practical Penmanship</u>, developed in 1874, was widely taught during this period. "This book describes the teaching methods used in the days of beautiful penmanship, and it details the theory that Spencer thought should be in the mind of every student." (See the Bibliography for the vendors carrying these programs.)

General Activities to Do throughout the <u>Primer</u>:

1. The books of the "Little House" series fall into the category of autobiographical fiction. Written works are categorized as fiction or nonfiction. Fiction includes everything from true-to-life stories to fantasy to historical fiction, where a work of the author's imagination is enhanced by a factual setting. Nonfiction books include reference books, biographies (factual literature written about another person), and autobiographies (factual literature written by and about one's own life). As an ongoing activity, have your child keep a list of all books read this year and separate them as fiction or nonfiction. If a book is fiction, categorize it further by identifying it as historical fiction, fantasy, mystery, romance, science fiction, adventure, etc.

2. Write or type all memory work onto 3 x 5 cards. Place them in a file box for future activities.

3. Begin an historical timeline of the 1800's using butcher block paper, computer paper or construction paper to record famous people studied this year. A similar project for the presidents will be introduced in "Town." This may be kept separate or combined using the format suggested in "Town."

4. Make an individualized list of vocabulary words. These should be words that the child either cannot pronounce or does not understood.

Page 14

Big Woods

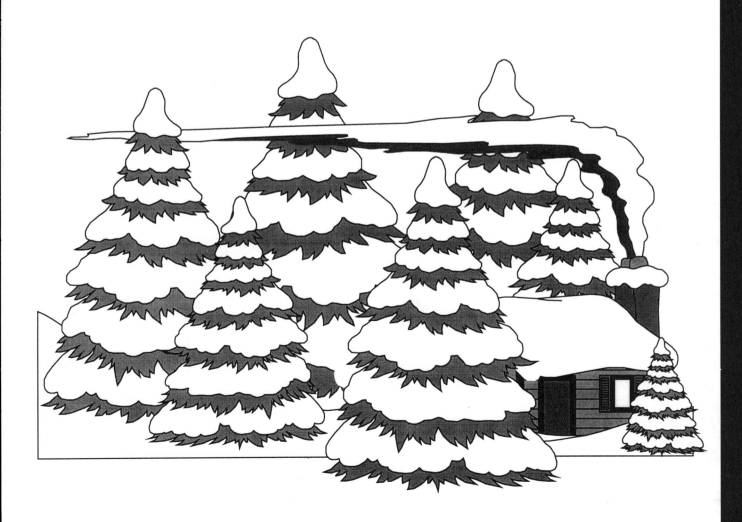

Little House in the Big Woods

Laura Ingalls Wilder was born on February 7, 1867. Her first memories were of the snug cabin in the "Big Woods" near Pepin, Wisconsin. Little House in the Big Woods was Laura's first book published in 1932. Children enthusiastically wrote Miss Wilder asking for more stories. She did not know then that the "Little House" series would be favorites for generations and that they would find their place among the best children's literature.

The "Little House" series is a work of autobiographical fiction. These stories are recollections of events in Laura's, and later in Almanzo's, life but the time sequence and/or names of the characters are sometimes altered. The period of each book usually spans approximately a year in the lives of the characters, but in reality not all the events occurred in one year or at one event. For example, baby Carrie is present in Little House in the Big Woods; however, she was actually born during the time of the second book. The events in Little House in the Big Woods with Carrie occurred after the Ingalls returned there from Indian territory. This series is autobiographical in that it relates true events in the characters' lives, but it remains fiction in that the events recorded are reconstructed for the sake of storytelling.

We see United States history and human nature through Laura's eyes. When she writes of herself, she remains honest in revealing her own soul to us. This transparency helps us to identify with her struggles—struggles common to all mankind.

Additional Reference Material:

Throughout the "Little House" series Laura mentions the foods prepared and eaten. This general nutrition information is provided to be applied in "Big Woods" and at various times throughout the Primer whenever food and food preparation is discussed.

Nutrition

Recommendations, Tastes, and Habits. If a survey were taken asking people's nutritional habits, most would respond that they have healthy diets. How many people do you know that purposely eat unhealthy foods and are proud of it? Not many. Similarly, not many parents deliberately set out to train their children to eat poorly. Yet nutritionists continue to tell us that Americans receive 40% of their calories from fat, instead of the recommended 30%. Few people eat the recommended 30 grams of fiber the body needs daily. Nutritionists broadcast this message continually: "Eat a diet low in fats, especially saturated fat, and high in fiber." Yet many people do not heed this advice because they were not trained to select the proper foods.

One's diet is formed by tastes and habituation. People eat what they are accustomed to eating. If you are exposed to a food often enough, you can acquire a taste for it. Because preferences grow from habit, you must gradually allow your taste buds to learn the correct foods to eat.

Calories and Nutrients. In order for your body to function, it must have energy. Calories are the energy units supplied by foods. Some foods are more calorie-dense than others. For instance, a cup of fat contains many more calories than a cup of parsley. If calories were all your body needed, and your system could process 100% of its calories from fat without harm to the body, then the best food choice might be the cup of fat. However, your body needs many other nutrients to rebuild itself and battle disease. The basic nutrients needed are water, protein, carbohydrates, vitamins, minerals, and fats from appropriate sources.

Big Woods

Since your body needs varied amounts of each nutrient daily, and since foods differ in the amounts and kinds of nutrients they contain, keeping track of nutrient intake can become a complicated task. Fortunately, to simplify the process of eating a well-balanced meal without having to quantify the amounts of nutrients in each food, a grouping of foods with similar benefits to the body was developed.

"Food Guide Pyramid." In 1992, the U.S.D.A. released the "Food Guide Pyramid" (See Fig. 1). This guide lists the recommended daily servings from the basic food groups and thus eliminates the difficulty in counting grams of nutrients. The base of the pyramid consists of bread, cereal, rice, and pasta, with a recommended 6 to 11 servings a day. Next in the pyramid is the vegetable and fruit group. You should have 3 to 5 servings of vegetables and 2 to 4 servings of fruit daily. After this, whatever calcium, iron and protein needs have not been met by eating from the first groups may be obtained from eating 2 to 3 servings from the meat and milk group. Beans and nuts are included in the meat group because they contain similar nutrients as meat. Beans are much higher in fiber and generally lower in fat than either meat or nuts. At the top of the pyramid are fats, oils, and sweets. These should be used sparingly.

This pyramid is easy to understand and to follow. It underscores the requirements to eat largely from the bread and cereal group and also more from the fruit and vegetable group. Please note, however, that not all vegetables are created equal. Presently, the emphasis is on eating more vegetables high in beta carotene, such as carrots, pumpkins, and sweet potatoes, and those from the cabbage family such as broccoli. These seem to provide some protection against cancer.

A common habit is to begin eating with foods from the top of the pyramid that are calorie dense, quick-fix or hunger foods. When this happens, very few of the base foods, the ones that are high in fiber, low in fat, and packed with vitamins and minerals, are eaten.

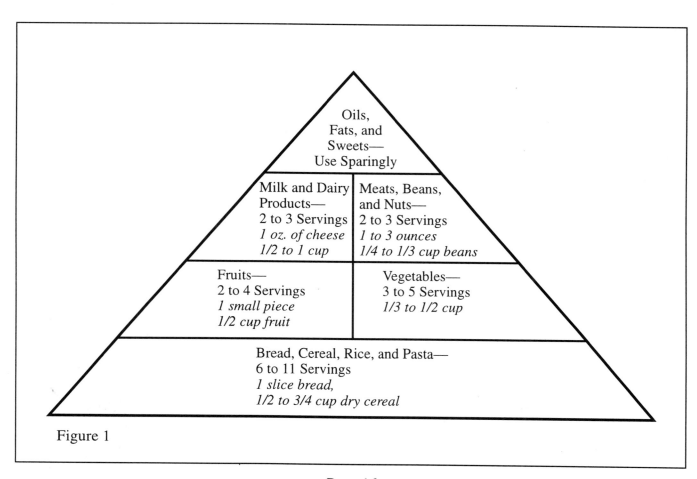

Figure 1

Big Woods

Foods that Build, Foods that Deplete. We must stop viewing certain foods as "neutral." A food either builds or weakens your system. Good, nutrient-rich foods will regenerate cells and the immune system while others will rob the body of needed nutrients. Processed sugar is a culprit. It depletes the body of Vitamin B, zinc, and weakens the immune system while stressing the pancreas and creating an excellent growth medium for bacteria and yeast. Caffeine depletes calcium, Vitamins B and C. Phosphoric acid contained in soft drinks is also a calcium robber. There is evidence that a person's calcium needs increase with an increased intake of meat. Obviously, whatever is put into your body has an effect for well-being or for ill.

Food allergies are a problem for many people. "Every Body Needs Milk" is a catchy slogan but an incorrect nutritional statement. Milk is a common food allergen. Eliminating milk or dairy products from your diet may relieve ear aches, rashes, or other ailments. Other foods such as corn, wheat, and peanuts also cause allergies. A shift in eating habits, where allergies are concerned, may also relieve a child's behavior problems such as short attention span and sleeplessness. You can find out more from your library about hidden food allergies, if you suspect certain foods are a possible problem for you or your child.

Listen to Your Body. Many of us need to retrain our nutritional thinking patterns and instruct our children in proper diet plans. You can instruct your children not to heed the latest food craze on television, but to listen to their bodies. You can train them to feel the way their bodies respond after eating certain foods. Ask them, "Are you more energetic or more sluggish?" Which foods give them prolonged energy, rather than a short spurt followed by tiredness? Children can also begin to recognize the signs and symptoms of nutritional deficiencies. Each body is indeed uniquely created in terms of its nutritional requirements.

The "Little House" Diet. Our modern diet is one of excess compared to the foods and eating habits of Laura's day. We have access to whole, fatty milk, butter, and ice cream. The Ingalls drank skimmed milk if they made butter. The American sugar intake has increased three times what was generally consumed 125 years ago. This remains an alarming statistic when you realize the nutrient depletion occurring.

Laura ate fresh fruit and vegetables grown in nutritionally fertile soil. Our produce today is potentially less nutritious because of overworked land and the expanded time between harvesting and the store shelf. During transport time vitamins in foods lose their potency when exposed to air and light.

Another downfall of the modern diet is, because of ease and advertising, many people have become accustomed to processed, prepared foods. In these foods, not only are naturally occurring fiber, vitamins, and minerals stripped away, but salt, fat, and sugar are added as flavor enhancers. What is eaten may be filling, but our bodies are being nutritionally shortchanged. In Laura's day, food preparation consumed much of the women's time. There were no "convenience foods." Diets were richer in bodybuilding nutrients and naturally better tasting.

Healthy Bodies, Healthy Spirits. The Bible says, "My people perish for lack of knowledge." This can be true physically and also spiritually. Applying these basic nutritional guidelines to your diet will keep the body alive and increase vitality. The goal of physical maintenance is to be able to do the Lord's work. As we develop healthy eating habits for ourselves and our children, we have more energy for service and less sickness. Good nutrition can negate diseases such as chronic mild malnutrition and its ailments: diabetes, heart disease, appendicitis, and gallstones. When children are trained in better eating habits and in feeling the results in strengthened bodies, they will be able to do and give more, and they will recognize it as God's gift in their lives. Because they have been strengthened, they will one day rise up and call us blessed for they will be equipped to carry on the faith for their generation.

Big Woods

Group Activity to Do in This Unit:

1. Plan a Gold Rush party for Week 4, Day 4.

General Activities to Do throughout This Unit:

1. Choose a book on manners or etiquette and schedule to complete it by the end of this unit.

2. Memorize Psalm 91.

3. Begin reading a biography of Louis Pasteur. Schedule to complete it by the end of Week Three. For younger students or less avid readers this may need to be read aloud during a family reading time. If you've quit reading to your older children, this may be a good time to restart the pleasurable time of sharing a book together.

Big Woods
Week 1

Week One Planning Guide

Gather Information on the Following:

(See suggested sources listed)

1. Bears
   —Encyclopedia
   —The Biography of a Grizzly by Earnest Seton
   —A Guide to Animal Tracking and Behavior by Donald and Lillian Stokes
   —Tracking and the Art of Seeing by Paul Rezendes
   —

2. Growth and development
   —Of Children by Guyr Lefraneois
   —

3. Manners
   —Soup Should Be Seen, Not Heard! by Beth Brainard and Sheila Behr
   —Uncommon Courtesy by Gregg Harris
   —

4. Light and prisms
   —Light (Troll)
   —Encyclopedia
   —

5. Rust
   —

6. Owls
   —

7. History of guns
   —

8. The mechanics of a gun
   —

9. Gun safety
   —"Firearms Safety," A-212—a 4-H booklet available through your County Extension Office
   —

10. History of the song "Yankee Doodle"
    —Cassette tape by Little Bear Wheeler, "Songs that Made America Great"
    —

11. Lungs and Breathing
    —Encyclopedia
    —The Human Body by Jonathan Miller
    —You and Your Body: Heart and Lungs (Troll)
    —The Young Scientist Book of the Human Body (Usborne)
    —

12. Rabies
    —

13. Louis Pasteur
    —Louis Pasteur by Tiner (The Sower Series), *for older students*
    —Easy Biographies: Louis Pasteur (Troll)
    —

Big Woods
Week 1

14. Corn husk doll directions
    —The Little Kid's Americana Craft Book by Jackie Vermeer
    —Pioneer Crafts for Kids compiled by Neva Hickerson
    —

Gather These Items:

1. Cracklings (fried pork rinds)
2. A hog's bladder
   —Try a slaughter house or butcher shop
3. Corn cob
4. Items to make homemade butter
   —The Little House Cookbook by Barbara M. Walker
5. Picture of a brindle bulldog
6. File box for memory work
7. 3 x 5 cards
8. Photocopies of "Steps in Making Butter" Sequencing Worksheet if more than one child is using the Primer
9. Items to make molasses-on-snow candy
   —The Little House Cookbook by Barbara M. Walker
10. Materials for a whittling project
11. Pictures of a trundle bed and samples of leather, venison, lard
12. The American Dictionary of the English Language (the 1828 edition by Noah Webster)
13. Disney's video, "Old Yeller"

Suggested Field Trips:

1. Visit an antique store, a pioneer settlement, or a museum that has a butter churn and other antique kitchen equipment.
2. Visit a museum or preferably a person who has an antique gun collection.
3. View a gun safety demonstration.

Big Woods
Week 1
For Use with Day 2

Steps in Making Butter
Sequencing Worksheet

Put the following steps in sequence:

_____ A. Scald the churn dash.

_____ B. Put the milk in a place where it will not be disturbed to enable the cream to separate.

_____ C. Tiny grains of yellow butter begin to appear on the dash.

_____ D. Add carrot coloring.

_____ E. Salt the butter.

_____ F. Cream splashed around the hole.

_____ G. Milk the cow.

_____ H. Place the butter in a mold.

_____ I. Skim off the cream.

_____ J. Wash the butter.

Page 21

Big Woods
Week 1

Read Chapter 1.

Reading Comprehension:

Chapter 1
1. How old was Laura Ingalls Wilder when she wrote this book? Reread the first sentence of Chapter 1 to detect her approximate age.
2. What made Laura feel safe when the wolves were howling (page 3)?
3. Retell what the Ingalls did to preserve the meat. How did Laura help preserve the meat?
4. What was Mary's doll like? What was her name (page 20)?
5. What was Laura's doll like? What was her name (page 20)?
6. What did Laura sometimes do when Susan could not watch? What does this show about her concept of reality?
7. What did Laura and her family do in the evening? To Laura, what was the best time of day?
8. How did Pa keep the coals alive until morning?
9. For what was the hog bladder used?

Activities:

Literature 1. Is this book fiction or nonfiction? Is this a biography or an autobiography? *(It is autobiographical fiction.)* Who is telling this story? *(Laura is both the author, or narrator, and the character. Help your child to distinguish the voice of each. Point out instances where Laura the character speaks, revealing her thoughts, and other times when Laura the narrator gives us information that the characters do not. The "voice" that tells the tale determines the point of view or perspective of the story. Because it is autobiographical, the story is told from Laura's point of view. Discuss the idea that we do not always know what the other characters are thinking, but we do know Laura's thoughts. Discuss how the point of view of a story could change from character to character just as opinions or memories can change from one person to the next.)*

Science/Writing 2. Study bears and their hibernation patterns, habitats, and food. Write a report on what, you have learned. <u>The Biography of a Grizzly</u> is an excellent optional novel

Science 3. The main principle in preserving food is to keep the molds, bacteria, fungi, and yeast from destroying the food. Name some ways that food can be preserved. *(Drying; freezing; salt; sulfur; boiling and sealing which kills bacteria and molds and prevents further growth by cutting off oxygen and exposure to spoilers; smoking which dries the undesirable spores; sugar that lyses the cells.)*

Vocabulary/Living 4. Show or explain each of the following: trundle bed, leather, venison, and lard. Eat venison.

Psychology/Bible	5.	Explain to your child that the ability to understand different Bible concepts comes with growth and development. (See I Corinthians 13:11.) To expound on this idea, obtain Piaget's stages of cognitive development and "test" the development of younger children. This can be beneficial for older children in understanding younger siblings or in baby-sitting.
Bible	6.	Laura's father was an important part of her life. What does Malachi 4:6 say?
Living	7.	Eat cracklings or put them in cornbread.
Art	8.	Make a corn cob doll and play only with it all day.
Living	9.	Make a hog's bladder balloon.
Manners	10.	Laura interrupted Mary; this was poor manners. Read a book on manners and schedule to complete it by the end of Week 3.
Bible	11.	Good manners frequently help a person to carry out biblical principles. Interrupting another person may have the root cause of esteeming oneself higher than others (Philippians 2:3-5). Another verse that addresses interrupting is Proverbs 18:13.
General	12.	Remember this week to schedule and make time for General

DAY 2

Read Chapter 2.

Reading Comprehension:

Chapter 2
1. What did they sometimes do after the chores were finished?
2. When the butter was removed from the churn, what was left (page 32)? What did they do with it?
3. When did Pa have time to play (page 35)?
4. What did Laura enjoy about watching the fireplace and the kerosene lamp?
5. Retell the panther story.
6. What made the girls feel safe (page 44)?

Activities:

Science	1.	Study the densities of various solutions. *(Butter is made from unhomogenized milk. Homogenization mechanically breaks up the fat globules into minute particles that mix with the water particles, thus dispersing the fat permanently throughout the milk and making it impossible to obtain only the cream. The cream is less dense than water per unit volume. The density of water is 1.0. Anything greater than 1.0 will sink; less than 1.0 will float. Try making different solutions, such as*

Big Woods
Week 1

oil mixed with water.) Can you hypothesize the density of oil based on knowing water's density? Do the same experiment using other liquids. Use food coloring to differentiate between clear liquids.

Living	2.	Make butter.
Art	3.	Find a picture of a brindle bulldog. Draw your own illustration.
Science	4.	How does salt in the bottom of a kerosene lamp keep it from exploding? *(Hypothetically, it would decrease the rate of evaporation of the kerosene and therefore decrease the amount available to explode.)*
Art	5.	Illustrate Laura's descriptive imagery of Jack Frost (page 27).
Living	6.	Describe Ma's chore schedule. Does your family have one? What chores, because of modern improvements, do we not do or not do as frequently? *(Churn, iron, bake bread.)*
Writing	7.	Write about the joys of your favorite chore day.
Literature	8.	On page 33, what did Pa call Laura? *(This is a metaphor. Metaphor and simile are literary terms that describe words that compare essentially dissimilar things. Laura is being compared to a cup of cider. In a simile, the comparative words "like" or "as" are used to make the comparison explicit. A metaphor, however, uses no comparative word. The comparison is implied.)* What imagery and insight does this comparison give you about Laura and about Pa's perception of Laura?
Science	9.	Study light and prisms. Why did the fire burn yellow, red, and green? *(Most of the energy from fire goes into heat, but some of it goes into light. Light behaves in many ways like waves. Light waves have a different range of wavelengths. Different wavelengths appear as different colors. White light is a combination of all colors.)* What caused the colors to separate? *(Different chemicals and chemical compounds contained in the wood burn at different temperatures. These different temperatures illuminate different wave lengths of color.)*
Bible	10.	The Bible teaches us how to be safe. Read Proverbs 18:10 and Psalm 91. Set a schedule to memorize Psalm 91. Remember to type or write it on a 3 x 5 card and store it in your memory box.
Music	11.	Sing "Yankee Doodle."
History	12.	Study the history of the song "Yankee Doodle."
Sequencing	13.	Give child(ren) the "Steps in Making Butter" Sequencing Worksheet. *(Answers: A.5; B.2; C.7; D.4; E.9; F.6; G.1; H.10; I.3; J.8)*

Page 24

Big Woods
Week 1

DAY 3

Read Chapter 3.

Reading Comprehension:

Chapter 3
1. What did Pa do before telling stories (page 45)?
2. What was the consequence of not minding Pa (page 46)?
3. Tell about cleaning the gun.
4. In cleaning a gun, why must the water be boiling (page 47)?
5. Why did Pa reload his gun as soon as he had fired it (page 52)?
6. What could happen if Pa did not kill a bear or a panther with the first shot (page 52)?
7. Retell the story of "Pa and the Voice in the Woods."

Activities:

Science/Writing	1.	Study about owls and write a report. Include in your report information about their diet, habitats, and behavior.
Science	2.	What is rust? What does it look like? What causes it to occur?
History/Writing	3.	Research and write a report on the history of guns.
Science	4.	Study the mechanics of a gun.
Safety	5.	Discuss gun safety.
Social Studies/ Speech	6.	Research present gun control laws and pending gun control policies. In a debate format, present some pro and con positions in the currently proposed policies. Use this information to give an oral presentation to your father or another family.
Vocabulary	7.	What is a ravine (page 55)?

Page 25

Big Woods
Week 2

Bible

8. On page 58, what had Grandpa told Pa about listening to his instruction? God places people in authority over us. Bill Gothard said, "The essence of submission is not getting under the domination of authority, but rather getting under the protection of authority." (See Ephesians 6:1-3; Proverbs 6:20-21; Proverbs 15:5.) Discuss with your child the principle of being under parental authority; it's similar to being under an umbrella. It only protects, if the person remains under the umbrella.

Big Woods
Week 1

Read Chapter 4.

Reading Comprehension:

Chapter 4
1. How did they make pictures in the snow?
2. What aroused Laura's interest and kept her from going to sleep (page 67)?
3. If Aunt Eliza would have had a gun what would she have done? Have you ever wrongly rejected that which was sent to protect?
4. Why had Prince been acting so strangely?
5. What did everyone get for Christmas? What did Laura get for Christmas? Why were the other girls not jealous (page 76)? What did Laura call her doll?
6. Why did the children not say anything at the table?
7. What did they use to keep their hands warm? their feet?

Activities:

Literature	1.	The first sentence of the first paragraph on page 60 is a simile. What imagery does this simile evoke?
Science	2.	Study the process of breathing. What is the purpose and main function of the lungs? What controls breathing? Research what exchange takes place in the lungs.
Art	3.	Watch someone whittle or start a whittling project. (Some experts believe that a child under eleven does not have the dexterity for safely whittling.)
Cooking	4.	Make molasses candy.
Vocabulary	5.	What are gaiters (page 76)?
Science/Writing	6.	On page 70, it makes reference to questioning whether the dog had gone mad. What does this refer to? *(Rabies.)* Study and do a written report about the signs and symptoms, the route of transmission, prevention, and treatment of rabies. Be sure to include about vaccinations and when they became available.
Living	7.	Watch the video, "Old Yeller."
Character	8.	The big girls were not jealous of Laura's doll. Look up "jealous" and "jealously" in the American Dictionary of the English Language (the 1828 edition by Noah Webster). Which definition applies to the statement? Discuss with your child what has been learned regarding jealousy.
Bible	9.	What does the Bible say about jealousy (Proverbs 14:30; 27:4)? What does the Bible say should be our response when something good happens to or is given to another person (I Corinthians 12:26)?

Page 27

Big Woods
Week 1

Science

10. One way that poisons are eliminated from the body is through the gastrointestinal track. The longer the toxins stay in the body the less healthy it is. Measure the amount of time it takes for food eaten to come out as stool. This may be done by eating sesame seeds and seeing how long it takes to see them or by eating food dyed. A natural diet will produce a transit time from ingestion to elimination of 35 hours. A diet of refined food may take 70 to 80 hours.

Week Two Planning Guide

Gather Information on the Following:

(See suggested sources listed)

1. Making maple syrup
   —<u>Sugaring Time</u> by Kathryn Lasky

2. Function of sap in a tree and products derived from sap
   —"Know Your Trees"—available through your County Extension Office

3. Animal tracks
   —<u>Tracking and the Art of Seeing</u> by Paul Rezendes
   —<u>Animal Tracking and Behavior</u> by Donald and Lillian Stokes
   —<u>Animal Tracks and Traces</u> by Kathleen Kudlinski

4. Skin and its function
   —<u>Inspector Body Guard Patrols the Land of U</u>, "The Siege of Toeprint Ridge" by Vicki Cobb
   —<u>The Young Scientist Book of the Human Body</u> (Usborne)

Gather These Items:

1. Photocopies of "The Story of Grandpa's Sled and the Pig" Cause and Effect Worksheet if more than one child is using the <u>Primer</u>
2. Real maple syrup and maple-flavored syrup
3. Items to make hasty pudding
   —<u>The Little House Cookbook</u> by Barbara M. Walker
4. Yarn and knitting needles for a small project
5. "Favorite Little House Songs" cassette tape
6. <u>The American Dictionary of the English Language</u> (the 1828 edition by Noah Webster)
7. <u>Laura Ingalls Wilder Songbook</u> by E. Garson
8. Sealing wax or sheets of wax to make rose flower pins

Suggested Field Trips:

1. Arrange to collect sap from maple trees and make into syrup and/or sugar. (This will be available only in early spring in certain regions of the country.)
2. Watch square dancing and/or arrange to have members of a square dancing group instruct a group of children on square dancing or a simple reel.
3. Arrange for a park service interpreter to do a program on tracking.

Notes:

Big Woods
Week 2
For Use with Day 1

The Story of Grandpa's Sled and the Pig
Cause and Effect Worksheet

Match the cause with the effect in the following:

Causes:

_____ A. Nothing could be cooked on Sunday.

_____ B. That week their father had them working hard cutting down trees in the Big Woods.

_____ C. They finished the sled at sundown.

_____ D. A hog was in the road. There was not time to stop or turn.

_____ E. They passed the house with the pig squealing.

_____ F. The Sabbath was over.

Effects:

1. They had no time to work on the sled until Saturday afternoon.

2. The sled picked up the hog.

3. They ate a cold breakfast.

4. They could not slide down the hill even once.

5. Their father was standing in the doorway looking at them.

6. Their father spanked them.

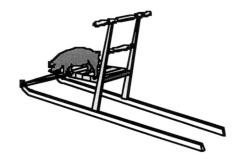

Big Woods
Week 2

DAY 1

Read Chapter 5.

Reading Comprehension:

Chapter 5
1. From where did the water for their Saturday bath come?
2. Tell what Laura did on Sundays.
3. How much free time did Grandpa have per week?
4. Why did Grandpa walk to church?
5. What were Sundays like when Grandpa was a boy?
6. In Grandpa's time, how must little girls behave?
7. What had Mary made for Laura?
8. What was special about Monday? How old was Laura?
9. What is a darkey (page 100)?

Activities:

Writing	1.	Write your favorite true story about your grandmother or grandfather.
Writing	2.	Pa showed mercy to Laura. Look up mercy in the <u>American Dictionary of the English Language</u> (the 1828 edition by Noah Webster). Read James 2:13. Write a poem or half a page on mercy.
Bible	3.	Sunday was a day set apart in Laura's home. What does Isaiah 58:13 say about the Sabbath? Pray and meditate how Sunday can become more special in your home. Are Sundays and the Sabbath Day the same thing?
Cause and Effect	4.	Give the child(ren) "The Story of Grandpa's Sled and the Pig" Cause and Effect Worksheet. *(Answers: .A.3; B.1; C.4; D.2; E.5; F.6.)*
Dictionary Skill	5.	Identify each of the following in the dictionary:

    a. **Guide Words**—The two words at the top of the dictionary page tell the first and last words on the page.

    b. **Entry Word**—The base form of the word printed in bolded letters.

    c. **Forms of the Word**—The base word changed by suffixes.

    d. **Dictionary Respelling**—The pronunciation divided into syllables. (Note: <u>The 1828 Webster Dictionary</u> does not have dictionary respellings.)

    e. **Parts of Speech**—The classes into which words are grouped according to their uses in a sentence.

    f. **Definition**—The meaning of the word.

    g. **Example Sentence**.

Big Woods
Week 2

Music   6.   Sing from <u>Laura Ingalls Wilder Songbook</u>, pages 72 and 138.

General   7.   Remember this week to schedule and make time for General Activities.

DAY 2

Read Chapters 6 and 7.

Reading Comprehension:

Chapter 6
1.   Why did Pa go to town?
2.   Why did he not take his gun?
3.   What had Laura and Mary never seen (page 102)?
4.   What did Ma do when they went to milk the cow?
5.   On page 106, Ma told three things that Laura did which enabled them to get away from the bear. What were they?
6.   How did the house seem without Pa (page 107)?
7.   Retell your favorite bear story.

Chapter 7
8.   On page 117, what sounds did Laura hear?
9.   Why were the buckets made from cedar and white ash (page 121)?
10. Why was it called sugar snow?
11. When would Grandpa use the store sugar (page 127)?
12. What would happen on Monday?

Activities:

Memory   1.   Have you ever heard the prayer that Laura prayed that night? If your child does not already know it, have them memorize it.

Language/Art   2.   On page 119 the last paragraph, Laura used three words to describe Pa. What were they? Pick three words to describe your father. Draw or paint a portrait of your father and use your descriptive words in the caption.

Living   3.   Research collecting maple syrup.

Science/Writing   4.   Study about tree sap. What function does sap provide to a tree? What products originate from the sap of trees? Write a report about what you have learned.

Living   5.   Arrange a field trip to collect sap, and make it into syrup or sugar.

Living/Nutrition   6.   Purchase both real maple syrup and maple-flavored syrup. Compare the taste, ingredients, the price, and the nutritional value. What are the advantages and disadvantages of each?

Big Woods
Week 2

Living 7. What store-bought item was thought to be better than homemade? Think of items that you feel are better quality when store-bought. Which items are better homemade than store-bought? *(Cakes, bread, clothes, etc.)*

Bible 8. Which bear story was scarier—the real or the imagined? In Psalm 64:1, David prays for protection from the fear of the enemy. Psalm 53:5 and Psalm 73:19 speak about the ungodly becoming consumed with fear. Luke 21:26 speaks of the fear associated with the Second Coming of Christ. Does the fact that fear was caused by something real or imagined matter? What tactic was used to thwart the rebuilding of the temple (Ezra 4:4)? Think of a time that an imagined fear has kept you from doing what you needed to do. What did Pa do? What did David do? What did those building the temple do?

Dictionary Skill 9. In the dictionary there are words that are spelled alike but have different meanings, origins, and sometimes pronunciations. These words are called homographs. Look up "primer" as in The Prairie Primer. Note the numbered entry words. Note the dictionary respelling. Are they pronounced the same? Which definition and, therefore, pronunciation fits The Prairie Primer? Another homograph with different pronunciations would be "sow." Look this word up and decide which entry word and definition could be used to describe what ended up on Grandpa's sled.

Music 10. Sing from Laura Ingalls Wilder Songbook, pages 63 and 132.

DAY 3

Read Chapter 8.

Reading Comprehension:

Chapter 8
1. Why did they do their chores by lamplight (page 131)? Have you ever prepared that early to go on a trip?
2. In what war do you think Uncle George was a drummer boy (page 137)? *(The year this book refers to is 1870.)*
3. When Uncle George played the bugle, what additional sound was heard (page 137)? *(Echo.)*
4. How were socks made (page 139)?
5. What did Grandma and George do? Who won?
6. Why did the children watch anxiously when Grandma ladled the syrup?

Activities:

Writing 1. Reread Laura's description of her Grandmother's living room on page 134. Write a description of your living room.

Science 2. Study about animal tracks. Make imitation tracks in snow, playdough, or putty and have another person guess what animal's tracks they are.

Cooking 3. Make hasty pudding. See The Little House Cookbook.

Page 33

Big Woods
Week 2

Bible	4.	What were the two girls arguing about (page 143)? This argument was foolish. Foolishness lives in the hearts of young children and must be removed (Proverbs 22:15). Read the following verses regarding fools: Proverbs 18:6-7; 26:4; 20:3. Look up "contention" in the <u>American Dictionary of the English Language</u> (the 1828 edition by Noah Webster).
Living	5.	Contact a local square dance club and go to watch them dance, or gather a group of friends and have club members teach a simple square dance or reel to your group.
Vocabulary	6.	What is a hearth (page 138), a basque and flounces (page 140)? Use the dictionary respelling to pronounce each word.
Craft	7.	Teach your child to knit and have them knit a simple project such as a muffler. Have them work on this project during family reading time. Contrast the thickness of yarn for a muffler to that of a sock. Contrast the details involved in each.
Craft	8.	Wrap small sheets of wax around a straight pin to make wax roses.
Music	9.	Sing from <u>Laura Ingalls Wilder Songbook</u>, page 58.

Read Chapter 9.
Reading Comprehension:

Chapter 9
1. What changes did Laura see in the spring?
2. What did they play under the two oak trees?
3. What could Laura and Mary not play well?
4. What had Pa seen that day?
5. Why would there be no more fresh meat until all the little animals had grown up? What did this show about Pa?
6. How did Ma curl their hair (page 161)?
7. When Laura saw the town, how did she feel (page 164)? Explain what Laura meant when she said she understood how Yankee Doodle felt when he could not see the town for the houses. (Refer to song on page 37.)
8. What did the girls do while Pa went to town to talk with the other men (page 172)?
9. What "dreadful" thing happened to Laura?
10. What made Laura feel safe? What had Laura put her faith in?

Big Woods
Week 2

Activities:

Science/Writing 1. On the first warm day, why could they only go to the woodpile and back in their barefeet? *(Their feet were soft and uncalloused from wearing shoes all winter. Calluses are formed from an accumulation of dead skin. This thickened layer of skin gives padding to the feet.)* Study the layers of skin and the function of the layers. *(Skin is the first barrier against infection, temperature control, etc.)* Write a report, with illustrations, on this body system.

Living 2. Why did it impress Laura that the wash was out to dry (page 166)? From your experience visiting other families, name some different ways that other families do common household things.

Vocabulary 3. Look up galluses (page 170).

Bible 4. On pages 174 and 175, Laura compared herself unfavorably with Mary. Read what the Bible states about comparing ourselves among ourselves (II Corinthians 10:12). Laura had measured herself against Mary and found herself lacking. Self-rejection breeds self-criticism (Isaiah 45:9) and wishful comparison with others. This keeps us from desiring to be Christlike (Romans 8:19- 20). The bitterness which springs up becomes directed toward God (Ephesians 4:29 and Job 40) and causes difficulty in loving others (Matthew 19:19). This root sin unrepented will cause other sins to grow. Who made Laura the way she was? *(God created Laura to look the way she did.)* Watch in future chapters for the effect of this root sin.

Bible 5. What frightened Laura (page 163)? Read Isaiah 40:6-31 to see man's greatness compared to God's.

Page 35

Big Woods
Week 3

Week Three Planning Guide

Gather Information on the Following:

(See suggested sources listed)

1. Nutritional information on cheese

2. Nutritional information about honey and sugar

3. Moon
   —<u>Destination Moon</u> by Astronaut James Irwin

4. Yellow jackets

5. Oats

6. Hat weaving

7. Sumac (information and picture)

8. Horsepower

9. The California Gold Rush
   —<u>The California Gold Rush</u> by May McNeer
   —<u>The California Gold Rush</u> by Ralph Andrist
   —<u>The Great American Gold Rush</u> by Rhonda Blumberg
   —<u>The California Gold Rush</u> by Catherine Chambers (Adventures in Frontier America Series)
   —<u>By the Great Hornspoon</u> by Sid Fleischman

10. Medicinal usage of herbs, especially fever decreasing herbs

11. Meat substitutes (nutritional information)

12. Anaphylactic shock
    —Family medical book

13. —Salt
    —<u>about Salt</u> by Dorothy Telfer

Big Woods
Week 3

Gather These Items:

1. Honey
2. Items to make cheese
   —The Little House Cookbook by Barbara M. Walker
3. Materials to weave hats
4. Hulled corn (hominy) and milk
5. Items to make johnnycakes
   —The Little House Cookbook by Barbara M. Walker
6. Nuts to crack
7. Rent the video, Paul Muni in "The Story of Louis Pasteur." This is an old classic. *(Try video stores with a large classic selection or a public television studio.)*
8. Different forms of oats such as oat groats, oat bran, quick oats, oatmeal, Cheerios
9. A grubbing hoe or a picture of a grubbing hoe, rennet, and whey
10. Laura Ingalls Wilder Country by William Anderson
11. Laura Ingalls Wilder Songbook by E. Garson

Suggested Field Trips:

1. Arrange to watch cheese being made.
2. Visit an apiary and watch a beekeeper take honey from his hives.
3. Arrange to see oats harvested or processed.
4. Watch wheat being threshed. Observe which part of the grass is removed to reveal the grain.

Notes:

Big Woods
Week 3

DAY 1

Read Chapter 10.

Reading Comprehension:

Chapter 10
1. Why was Mrs. Peterson's house always clean (page 177)?
2. Tell about their conversation. Have you ever talked like this?
3. What does Laura think about her hair? What does this stem from? *(Comparison and Self-rejection.)*
4. What were the wood chips used for? *(In cool weather, it was considered unmannerly to enter the house without bringing in some kindling.)*
5. What was Laura spanked for? What was the root of her action? How did Pa cause her to identify something positive with her hair? (Proverbs 16:24)
6. What is green cheese?
7. What did some think about the moon?
8. What caused Grimes to dry up and blow away?
9. What did Pa say about Mrs. Grimes? about Ma?
10. Tell about making cheese.
11. What were the girls' summer chores?
12. What had Pa found? How had Pa collected the honey? Did Pa take all of the honey? What might have happened if he had?
13. What type of mood are bears and panthers in during the summer?

Activities:

Bible	1.	What does the Bible say about spanking? (Read Proverbs 22:15; 13:24; 29:15; Hebrews 12:5-11.) What is the product of proper punishment? *(Harvest of righteousness and peace.)*
Vocabulary	2.	In the dictionary, look up rennet, grubbing hoe, and whey, or show your child these items. What is the purpose of each?
Math	3.	How could the cookies have been divided equally (page 179)?
Science	4.	Study about the moon. Write about what you have learned.
Nutrition	5.	Research the nutritional differences between honey and sugar.
Bible	6.	What does the Bible have to say about honey? (Proverbs 24:13; 25:16; 25:27.)
Living	7.	Taste honey.
Living	8.	Watch a beekeeper take honey from a hive. What color of clothes did he wear? Was there a reason for that? What steps has he taken to protect his hive?
Living	9.	Make cheese. See The Little House Cookbook.

Page 38

Big Woods
Week 3

Nutrition	10.	What nutrients does cheese have? What percent of calories come from fat? Which of the cheeses are lower in fat? Would you consider cheese a food low or high in fat? Does cheese have cholesterol? *(Cholesterol is present in anything that is a fat from animals. Everybody produces cholesterol. Our body uses cholesterol to form bile salts for fat digestion. It also helps to form hormones and gives the water-resistant quality of the skin. Cholesterol forms the insoluble cell membrane, making the cells stronger. Yet, too much cholesterol in the blood is linked to heart disease. Some feel these elevated levels occur because too many animal products have been eaten. However, our bodies make cholesterol from the fat consumed, especially saturated fats.)* Consider the amount of nutrition and fat in cheese and decide in which food group it belongs.
Nutrition	11.	List the foods you eat that contain cholesterol.
Bible	12.	How did Ma feel about Pa's provision for the family (page 193)? This is a godly attitude of a wife toward her husband. Read I Peter 3:2 (Amplified), and Titus 2:4-5. Did Ma give respect to her husband in front of the children?
Music	13.	Sing from <u>Laura Ingalls Wilder Songbook</u>, page 68.
General	14.	Remember this week to schedule and make time for General Activities.

DAY 2

Read Chapter 11.

Reading Comprehension:

Chapter 11
1. What did the children play while at Aunt Polly's?
2. What was the purpose of putting the oats in shocks (page 202)?
3. Retell the story of Charlie.
4. How had Charlie been a liar?

Activities:

Science	1.	Study about oats. What are uses for oats? To what plant family do they belong? How are oats processed?
Living	2.	Eat oats in different forms—oat groats, oatmeal, oat bran, Cheerios.
Science/Writing	3.	Study about yellow jackets. Are they solitary or social insects? Where do they build their nests? How do they differ from bees?
Health	4.	What is the body's response to a wasp sting? *(A bee or wasp sting is caused by a puncture of the skin by the insect's stinger and the injection of venom. Immediately after the sting an intense burning pain occurs at the site. Minutes later swelling, redness, and itching occur.)* What is the

Page 39

Big Woods
Week 3

treatment for insect stings? *(The honeybee and some wasps leave part of the stinger and poison sacs in the wound to give more venom. The stinger should be carefully removed by scraping it off with a knife blade, the side of tweezers, or a fingernail. Do not grasp the stinger, because this releases the remaining venom into the wound. Since bee venom is an acid, apply ammonia or baking soda to the wound. Wasp venom is alkaline or neutral and should be treated with lemon juice or vinegar. Also, a paste made with unseasoned meat tenderizer is effective in breaking down the protein in the bee venom and decreasing its harmful effects. An ice pack may help with the swelling and pain. Sometimes antihistamines may be given. If the pain or swelling persists or if the sting is on the tongue or in the mouth, a physician should be consulted at once. Symptoms of severe allergic reaction, such as collapse, or swelling of the body, indicate anaphylactic shock.)* If someone in your family is very allergic to bees, research and briefly describe the risk of anaphylactic reaction and what must be done. How were the wasp stings treated in the book? *(The mud may have been beneficial both as a cooling agent and for treatment if the soil was acidic.)*

Living | 5. | The Ingalls used herbs for treating fevers. Research what herbs are known for their fever decreasing ability. *(Virginia snakeroot, wormwood, hyssop, and garlic are a few herbs that have been used for fevers.)* What is presently given for fever? *(Aspirin, Tylenol, etc.)*

Character | 6. | In Proverbs 20:11, it says that a child is known by his deeds. What character qualities did Charlie exhibit?

Bible | 7. | Read Proverbs 10:5. How did Charlie cause shame?

Bible | 8. | Read Proverbs 10:23; 15:21 and 26:18-19. How was this true with Charlie?

Bible/Art | 9. | Apply Proverbs 17:12 to the situation with Charlie. It warns against being in the company of fools in their folly. Make a warning poster for this verse. A warning poster may be made using bold lettering, scriptural references, and appropriate illustrations. Try using poster paint, ink, or markers.

Bible | 10. | How does having a foolish son or daughter affect the parent? (Proverbs 17:21; 17:25; 19:13.)

Bible | 11. | By not doing what his father had instructed, Charlie had stepped out of God's protection and covering for himself. If he were a child of God, apply Hebrews 12:5-11 to the incident. If a healthy fear of the Lord resulted, then the following could have been the harvest of righteousness: Proverbs 9:10-11; 16:6; 10:27; 14:27. What is the fear of the Lord? Read Proverbs 8:13.

Big Woods
Week 3

DAY 3

Read Chapter 12.

Reading Comprehension:

Chapter 12
1. Tell how Ma made straw hats.
2. What was Laura and Mary's autumn chore?
3. Could Laura and Mary leave uneaten food on their plates?
4. Why was the "wonderful machine" better than threshing wheat with flails?
5. What did Pa think of progress?
6. What made Laura proud of her Pa?

Activities:

Crafts	1.	Make straw hats or, for an easier project, a straw mat.
Conservation	2.	When the girls made hats, they utilized all of the materials. Think of ways that all of a product could be used to conserve materials and money.
Science/Art	3.	Look up and draw sumac. What is the difference between sumac and poison sumac? Is either in your area? If so, use your picture to identify it in your area.
Living	4.	Crack nuts, enough to include in at least one thing—for example, chocolate chip cookies.
Character	5.	List Pa's character qualities shown in this book.
Cooking	6.	Eat hulled corn (hominy) and milk.
Cooking/History	7.	Make johnnycakes. See <u>The Little House Cookbook.</u> To which war does the name of this refer?
Science	8.	The thresher was powered by eight horses. Laura called it an "eight-horsepower machine." What does this expression mean today?
Bible	9.	Laura thought well of her father. Exodus 20:12 is the first commandment with a promise. What is it? Laura lived to be 90 years old.
History	10.	Watch the video, Paul Muni in "The Story of Louis Pasteur."
Cooking	11.	Make pumpkin pie or stewed pumpkin.
Nutrition	12.	Refer to the Food Guide Pyramid on page 19 in <u>The Primer to</u> organize the foods listed on page 226 in the different food groups.

Big Woods
Week 3

DAY 4

Read Chapter 13. This Finishes the Book. Also read <u>Laura Ingalls Wilder Country</u>, Chapter 1, "The Big Woods of Wisconsin."

Reading Comprehension:

Chapter 13
1. What had Pa done to attract deer?
2. What happened when Pa went hunting?

Activities:

History/Writing	1.	From the book and/or the video, write a two-page report about Louis Pasteur.
Science	2.	Physicians of Pasteur's day did not believe in the germ theory. Another theory scoffed at was the link between tobacco use and cancer. Can you think of any current theories that are not accepted, but may be years from now? The Yeast Theory made famous by Dr. Crook may be one such example. If it interests you, you may want to research this further.
History	3.	What event in American history inspired the folk song, "Oh, Susanna" to be written? How many years earlier did the gold rush begin?
History	4.	Begin reading a book about the California Gold Rush; schedule to complete it by the end of Week Four.
Science	5.	Study about the importance of salt in our diet and history.
Psychology	6.	From reading the last paragraph in this chapter, what concept of time did Laura have?
Nutrition	7.	The Ingalls family would not have meat for a while. Name three nutrients that meat provides. What foods, other than meat, could be eaten and still provide proper nourishment for their bodies?
Nutrition	8.	How many servings of meat are recommended per day? How many servings of meat are contained in a McDonald's Quarter Pounder?
Bible	9.	Read Proverbs 15:17. How does this apply?
Music	10.	Sing from <u>Laura Ingalls Wilder Songbook</u>, page 46.

Big Woods
Week 4

Week Four Planning Guide

Gather Information on the Following:

(See suggested sources listed)

1. Uses for gold

2. Processing of gold

3. Different methods used in mining, especially gold or minerals

4. Fiber content of foods

Gather These Items:

1. Props for an oral report on the gold rush
2. Bible concordance
3. Yellow paper
4. Small prizes

Suggested Field Trips:

1. Visit a plant that refines metals.
2. Visit a deserted mining town.
3. Visit a mine.

Notes:

Page 43

Big Woods
Week 4

Activities:

History	1.	Read selected pages about the California Gold Rush. Note ideas to use in an oral report to be given at the end of the week.
Writing	2.	Discuss with your child his earliest memories. Write one or two pages about one significant memory—for example, a vacation, a birthday, or a hospital visit.
Bible	3.	Using a Bible concordance, study what the Bible says about gold. (Psalm 19:9,10; 119:127-128; Rev. 1:12-13; 9:20; II Kings 10:28-29; Genesis 13:2; Exodus 25; Esther 8:4, 15.)
Nutrition/Math	4.	The forty-niners, who came by land, crossed the Rocky Mountains. Pretend that you are ascending the Rocky Mountains. To climb to the top, you must eat thirty grams of fiber for three consecutive days. Using graph paper, plot each day's fiber consumption. Which foods are highest in fiber? (Depending on your family's nutritional status, this may be a long term project.) To make it even more fun, each family member can race to see who can reach the top first. (More fiber may change your stool consistency. Stools should not sink but float. Ideally, a person should have at least two bowel movements a day. If the climb of fiber mountain is taken too quickly, gas and bloating may occur. If this happens, slow the increase in fiber.)

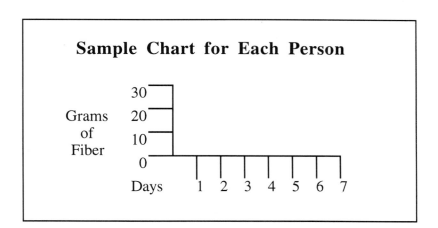

General	5.	Remember this week to schedule and make time to conclude General Activities.

Big Woods
Week 4

DAY 2

Activities:

History	1.	Read selected pages about the California Gold Rush.
Writing	2.	After parental editing, rewrite yesterday's assignment, Activity 2, if needed; expound on and clarify your descriptions.
Art	3.	Draw at least two pictures illustrating your significant memory.
Science	4.	Study the processing of gold.
Bible	5.	Use a Bible concordance to find verses about those who get rich quick. (Proverbs 10:2, 4-5.)

DAY 3

Activities:

History	1.	Read selected pages about the California Gold Rush.
Writing/Art	2.	In your neatest handwriting, rewrite Day 2, Activity 2, with final corrections leaving space in the appropriate places for illustrations. Splice in illustrations. Add depth and shading to them.
Science	3.	Study about the present-day uses for gold.

Big Woods
Week 4

DAY 4

Activities:

History/Reading	1.	Finish reading about the California Gold Rush.
Speech	2.	Prepare and give an oral report on the California Gold Rush. Use any visual aids available. (Costumes, maps, mining tools.)
Science	3.	Study the different methods of mining gold.
Fun	4.	Have a Gold Rush Party. Divide your house into claim areas (every room is its own claim) and hide in each claim "gold nuggets" (Bible references you've been memorizing on crumbled up yellow paper). Each miner must file for a claim (pick a room) and look for gold. For every scripture the miner can recite correctly, he wins a prize. Eat only golden, yellow foods from the Food Pyramid—for example, cornbread, pears, bananas, yellow squash, honey, lemonade, etc. OR eat cornbread, pork 'n' beans and jerky.

Finish Any Undone Activities!

Prairie

Little House on the Prairie

Laura was two years old when the family left for Kansas prairie country. Baby Carrie, mentioned in <u>Little House in the Big Woods</u>, had not yet been born. Originally, Laura Ingalls Wilder had only planned to write one book. She did not complicate her story with the fact that they had lived in Pepin for two years, then moved to Indian Territory, only to return to live again in Pepin. The response from the children reading her stories was so phenomenal that it encouraged her to write an eight-volume historical novel for children covering her life on the American frontier.

Therefore, the events of this book took place before many events in <u>Little House in the Big Woods</u>. Since Laura was only two when they made the journey to Kansas, much of this book is from stories she was told. One thing that did leave a lasting impression on little Laura was the Indian war chants. The chants were so clearly audible to them because Pa and Ma had unknowingly settled on the Osage Diminished Reserve. This did not make either the Osage people or the United States government happy.

Background Information:

History of the Osage Indians

The French explorers, Jacques Marquette and Louis Jolliet, first explored the Mississippi River in 1673. During the next decades, other Frenchmen explored the rivers flowing into Kansas. Charles Claude du Tisne journeyed on the Missouri River in 1719 and encountered both the Osage and Pawnee Indians. In 1744 French fur trappers built a stockade near Leavenworth to further their fur trade with the Osage. In 1803 the United States purchased the Louisiana Territory, which included Kansas.

From 1678-1803 the Osage Indians performed a feat that no other American tribe duplicated. They stopped the westward expansion of the Euro-American people and tripled the size of their domain. The Osage occupied parts of Missouri, Arkansas, Oklahoma, and Kansas. Because of the Osage Nation, neither France nor Spain had been able to control the Middle Waters area (the area west and central to the Mississippi River).

In times of peace, the Osage traded with neighbors and helped them. During times of war, they tried not to take life unnecessarily. Frequently, instead of killing an enemy they would sell them to other tribes as slaves. Early visitors always mentioned how well mannered the Osage were. They did not interrupt each other in speech and treated each other with courtesy.

The differences in Osage and the Euro-American culture caused friction. The Osage saw the superiority of Western trade goods as compared to their own, but they considered the other cultural aspects of western civilization to be inferior. A culture that obtains most of its food from hunting has a different idea of land ownership than a culture that gets its food from agriculture. A similar conflict occurred later between the open range cattle ranchers and the farmers that fenced the land. All of the Indian land was owned communally. Personal ownership of land and control of passage over the land was not understood by a hunting people.

The Osage land policy created a situation where the inhabited people either were adopted as individuals or groups, were merged with existing groups, or were forced to evacuate. Yet the desire for trade with the Euro-Americans caused a need for another land policy. This allowed for trading posts. Periodic raids were used to limit the size of the Euro-American settlements. The Osage land title was held by occupation, conquest, and their ability to enforce the claim. Intruders who plundered the resources or who, without

Page 47

Prairie

invitation, settled on Osage land were killed on or near the spot of the violation. Generally their decapitated heads were placed on a stake to serve as warnings.

The United States government land policy was that all land not physically occupied by Indians was considered United States property. All Osage lands were used; they were seldom vacant and unoccupied land produced game animals that were used for food. The Osage lived on their land in villages and hunting camps.

The Osage economy was not as sophisticated as western civilization's. Their food supply came from hunting, gathering nuts, wild potatoes, persimmons, berries, prickly pear cactus, milkweed sprouts, herbs, leaves, and bark for the preservation of food. They performed some supplemental farming, producing pumpkins, corn, beans, and squash. They only did simple manufacturing such as tanning and bow and handle-making. Instead of money, the Osage used a barter system that offered less flexibility in trade.

In 1804 President Jefferson sent the Lewis and Clark expedition to explore newly-purchased Louisiana Purchase. Lewis and Clark wrote highly of this delightful land. After the expedition, more Euro-Americans came into Osage domain in Missouri. The Osage considered the intruders to be rude and offensive in odor. Many of these were not upstanding Americans. Greed for land and personal possessions was not a new experience for the Osage, but they had never seen it on such a grand scale. The strain of trying to shun these contacts to avoid open warfare greatly affected the Osage.

The United States government had four views in dealing with the Indians. One was to annihilate them. A second was to confine them to reservations. A third was to create an Indian State and a fourth was to incorporate them into the general population. All these occurred to the Osage.

The intruding Euro-Americans took property such as game, furs, hides, livestock, and the plunder from Osage burial grounds. Many exaggerated claims were filed against the Osage. These "unfounded" claims were paid by treaty provisions. Only rigid restraint by their leaders, known as the Little Old Men, prevented all-out war against the intruders.

Until 1815 the Indians had enough power and sovereignty to have the treaties enforced. After that time, the Indian nations gradually became subordinate to the United States government. Between 1808 and 1839 seven treaties were made with the Osage. Each treaty made it seem that the United States was desiring to benefit the Indian. Through the wording, the Osage gave up some rights to land. For example, in 1825 continued trading with Mexico caused the United States government to sign a treaty with the Osage guaranteeing safe passage through Indian Territory along the route from Missouri to Santa Fe. This trail later became known as the Santa Fe Trail.

These conditions caused turmoil and anger. Many bands of Indians began to leave Missouri. The clash with the Euro-Americans caused the Osage to accept a buffer zone between themselves and the intruding settlers. The Treaty of 1825 provided for a twenty-five-mile-wide and fifty-mile-long strip of land between the Osage villages and the western boundary of Missouri. In the late 1820's and the early 1830's, the Osage were largely left alone and continued to live as they always had. Gradually, however, the neutral lands were violated by non-Indian settlers. This strip was called Osage Neutral Lands until it was given to the Cherokees and became the Cherokee Neutral Lands. The buffer zone experiment did not work because Euro-Americans settled on the land and the United States government made no effort to enforce the treaty agreement.

Beginning in 1829 the defeated Indians from the East (Shawnee, Delaware, Wyandot, Miami, Ottawa, Pottawatomie, Kickapoo, Chippewa, Iowa, Sac, and Fox) were forcibly removed and settled on huge tracts of land in Osage territory in Kansas. This caused much suffering among the Indians. Within two years about half the immigrant Indians died because of exposure, lack of proper food, and differing climatic conditions. While other Indians were forced to give up their land to settlers, the Osage were forced to give their land to other Indians.

In the 1850's more settlers trespassing on the reservation caused problems. In 1854 the buffer zone became open to settlers. Hundreds of settlers ignored the reservation restrictions and settled on Indian Territory. In

Prairie

1859 the Indian agent called in Federal troops to remove the squatters. However, many were overlooked or returned when the troops went home.

Pressure from settlers eased during 1861 when the Civil War began. Interestingly, the Civil War affected the Indian tribes. Indians from the Five Civilized Tribes were slave owners and fought on the side of the Confederacy. (Cherokees, Creeks, Choctaws, Chickasaws, and Seminoles had adopted white man's ways and were called the Five Civilized Tribes because of their advanced societies.) Several Osage warriors fought in skirmishes against civilians sympathetic to the Union cause. But most of the Osage did not back the Confederacy. Some attempted to fight with the Union but resigned due to the discipline and drill required by the army.

At the end of the war, the Five Civilized Tribes were compelled to sign a punitive treaty because of their support of the Confederacy in the Civil War. One part of the treaty stipulated that other "friendly tribes" would be relocated to the western part of their reserve. That same year the Osage signed another treaty giving up more of their land. The government's attempts to eject the squatters were ineffective.

The coming of the railroads in the late 1860's destroyed the way of life for the Plains Indians. Hunters killed the buffalo merely for their hides, while sportsmen slaughtered the animals for pleasure from the windows of trains. Outraged at seeing their source of food disappear and their way of life threatened, the Indians fought back by attacking isolated homesteads. As a result, in the late 1860's the United States Army built additional outposts including Fort Dodge. During 1868 and 1869 two-hundred settlers were attacked and killed in Kansas. Some of these raids were probably caused by the invasion of white hunters into Indian hunting grounds.

In 1869 the Ingalls family moved to Kansas. That same year a new Indian agent, Isaac Gibson, was sent to provide honest administration sympathetically to the Osage. Gibson convinced the tribe that their best course of action was to move south into Indian Territory rather than fight for their land in Kansas.

Some Osage leaders had considered trying to oust the intruders by force, but they decided to join a meeting scheduled for August 1870 (the month that Carrie was born). The meeting was postponed one month so that the Osage could hunt buffalo. It was at this meeting that they reluctantly signed a treaty where they purchased land from the Cherokee and sold their land to the settlers for $1.25 an acre. One of the Indian's demands on signing the treaty was that they would be able to leave the reservation to hunt buffalo. The buffalo herds disappeared in 1875.

According to a local newspaper, on the day after the removal treaty was signed in 1870, "the air was filled with the cries of the old people, especially the women, who lamented over the graves of their children, which they were about to leave forever." Most of them left their Kansas homes in the late fall for the semiannual buffalo hunt and returned to the new reserve in the early part of 1871. A few, however, did not settle there until 1874.

References:
Terry P. Wilson, Indians of North America: The Osage, Chelsea House Publications, 1988.

Zachary Kent, American the Beautiful—Kansas, Childrens Press, 1991.

The History of the United States Postal Service

For the first 120 years the postal system in the American colonies was primitive, slow, and uncertain. There was little communication between the people of one colony and another. Most correspondence was between England and the colonies. Private citizens, wishing to communicate with one another, depended upon friends who happened to be traveling in the general direction or upon reliable Indians. In 1657 the Colonial court of Virginia passed a law providing for the transmission of letters from one plantation to another. Each planter was required to provide a messenger to dispatch the letter to the next plantation. If they failed to do so, they were fined tobacco. This law applied only to official mail.

Prairie

In 1692 the crown granted a patent to Thomas Neale to set up a postal service in the colonies. Instead of being profitable, this patent lost him money. Some problems encountered were the varying coinage between colonies, the lack of usable roads making the transportation expensive and slow, and the lack of volume of mail. Possibly only half of the total volume of mail went through the postal service, which deprived the struggling service of revenues. The other half was transported by private individuals. In 1711 the crown attempted again to establish an official colonial post, but it appeared to many that the crown was more concerned with raising revenues for England's wars than improving the system. Virginia felt strongly that this was taxation without representation. The travel time for a letter from Williamsburg, Virginia, to Boston during poor weather was shortened to four weeks. In good weather it took half that time.

Tavern keepers were the usual "postmasters" in the colonies. Letters being left at their businesses attracted potential customers. Also, the government often waived the excise tax on beverages sold as recompense for the innkeeper's postal work. This savings allowed the innkeeper to undersell his competitors.

In 1737 Benjamin Franklin was appointed Postmaster General in Philadelphia. He swiftly and energetically made reforms; he made new surveys of the routes, shortening some and improving others; he also persuaded legislators to build usable roads and repair existing ones. He cracked down on dishonest postriders. The practice was for postriders to solicit business on their own. As a result, many postriders carried in their bags only a few letters on which postage had been paid and many others from which only they received the profit. Although Benjamin Franklin profited little from his postal service, it did enable him to have his newspaper delivered to the public at no expense. It increased the demand for his newspaper and the advertisements within.

Franklin lost favor with the crown and on January 3, 1774, was dismissed. It would have been madness to retain a man of Franklin's political sympathies in control of the only effective system of communication existing in the increasingly rebellious colonies. The colonial post never amounted to much after Franklin was dismissed.

By 1766 Sons of Liberty were disrupting the postal service in the colonies, calling them a grievous instrument of taxation. Ship captains were forced to deliver mail to coffeehouses instead of the legal post offices.

On July 26, 1775, a committee of the Continental Congress established an official American postal service. This service had multiple problems, but with reforms suggested by the committee, effective service was established. Legislation passed forbidding anyone to be paid to carry private letters. This legislation established the sanctity of the mail by stating that, except in time of war, no private letters could be opened or destroyed without an act of the Congress or the President.

George Washington insisted upon the necessity of improving the lines of communication between the states and with the settlements on the frontier. He felt that the settlers needed to be supported or else they might turn away from the United States. In 1794 Congress had doubts whether the Ohio River postal route should be continued. Fighting the Indians along the route was expensive, but the route remained open. As one postal surveyor general wrote, "Nothing can be more fatal to a republican government than ignorance among its citizens. They will be easy dupes of designing men, instead of supporting the laws, the reason and policy of which they are ignorant." George Washington's prediction that the postal service would become an impetus by which citizens would be loyal to the central government was becoming a reality.

In 1794 the first letter carriers appeared in American cities. They received no salaries but were permitted to collect two cents for every letter they delivered. Since the addressees had the option of accepting this service or picking it up at the post office, the letter carriers never became rich.

The Act of 1847 began the use of adhesive postage stamps in the United States. For a while two systems were at work. One either prepaid with stamps or paid the letter carrier directly. However, in 1856 adhesive stamps became obligatory and prepayment became the national system. This made the postal service much more convenient for the average citizen. Postal volume doubled within four years.

Prairie

From 1831 to 1861 the postal agency had grown from a minor office of the government, affecting a few people indirectly, to a major social, economic, cultural, and political agency of a nation. The railroad dominated postal transportation, but horseback and stagecoach completed the system.

The most exciting service in postal history was the operation of the Pony Express. It involved danger, daring riders, and a race against time. But the Pony Express died for three reasons. Congress eliminated the possibility of continuing the service on a profitable basis by legislating the surcharge from $5.00 per half ounce to $1.00, and stating that each rider must carry five pounds of government mail free of charge. Secondly, the cost of fighting the Indians to keep its routes and stations free from interference was enormous. Thirdly, the completion of the transcontinental telegraph line dissipated the need for the Pony Express.

Another postal improvement began the day after the Battle of Gettysburg; free letter carriers began delivering mail in 49 of the largest cities. Each letter carrier walked approximately twenty-two miles a day, every day of the year. It worked so well that it showed a tenfold profit. Delivery of mail to California cost 30 times more to deliver than revenues obtained, but mail routes were kept open.

From the time of Benjamin Franklin onward, the appointment of postmaster was politically and financially expedient. Many changes in the system may not have been best, but they were politically correct. Garfield's assassination by "a disappointed office seeker" stimulated the public demand for civil service reform.

Reference:
Gerald Cullinan, The United States Postal Service, Prager Publishers.

Group Activity to Do in This Unit:

1. Plan an Indian party for Week 3, Day 4.

General Activities to Do throughout This Unit:

1. Memorize Psalm 8 (especially verses 3-9).

2. Study simple machines. Do 1-2 pages daily from Work & Machines (Milliken) or Pocket Science: Simple Tools and Machines by Dinah Zike and Jan Hutchings

3. Read a biography or autobiography of an Indian. Two suggested titles are My Indian Boyhood by Luther Standing Bear and Indian Boyhood by Harles Eastman.

Prairie
Week 1

Week One Planning Guide

Gather Information on the Following:

(See suggested sources listed)

1. Your family's history during the 1870's

2. Mustangs

3. Nutritional value of molasses

4. Process for making molasses

5. Treatment for sprains

6. Health hazards of chewing tobacco

7. Simple machines
   —Encyclopedia
   —Science Pocket: Simple Tools and Machines
   —Work and Machines (Milliken)
   —Force and Motion (Eyewitness Science)

8. Blood components (purpose of each)
   —Encyclopedia
   —Inspector Body Guard Patrols the Land of U, "How Your Body Fights a Cold" and "How Your Blood Clots to Stop Bleeding," by Vicki Cobb
   —Life's Liquid: How Our Body Makes and Uses Blood (Provision Media)

9. History of the United States Postal Service
   —How They Carried the Mail by Joseph Walker

10. Tales of the Pony Express
    —The Pony Express by Samuel Adams
    —The Pony Express Goes Through by Howard Driggs
    —The Pony Express by Joseph Dicerdo

11. Different types of Indian houses
    —The Indian How Book
    —The Book of Indians by Holling C. Holling

12. How the Indian hunted and used buffalo
    —The Indian How Book
    —The Book of Indians by Holling C. Holling

13. Prairies
    —Encyclopedia

Page 52

Gather These Items:

1. Pictures of your relatives who lived in the 1870's
2. Pictures of mustangs
3. The American Indian Story by May McNeer and Lynn Ward
4. Bible concordance
5. Molasses and pancakes
6. Items to make stewed rabbit with dumplings
7. United States road map
8. The American Dictionary of the English Language (the 1828 edition by Noah Webster)
9. Photocopies of United States Map "Laura and Her Friends' Travels" if more than one child is using the Primer
10. Laura Ingalls Wilder Songbook by E. Garson

Suggested Field Trip:

1. Observe molasses being made.

Notes:

Prairie
Week 1

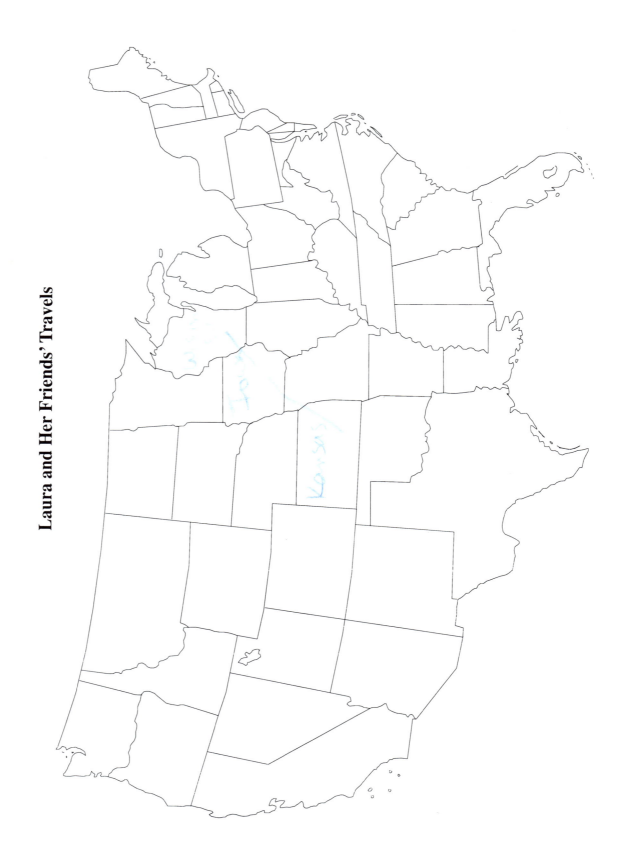

Laura and Her Friends' Travels

Prairie
Week 1

Read Chapters 1 and 2.

Reading Comprehension:

Chapter 1
1. Why did Pa leave? Describe where they were going.
2. Why did they not take their beds, tables, or chairs?
3. What did they cross which was iced over?
4. How did they get Pet and Patty? What type of horses were they?

Chapter 2
5. How could Pa tell he was at the ford?
6. Why did Ma cover the girls with the blanket (page 22)?
7. What could have changed the outcome crossing the creek (page 24)?
8. What happened to Jack? How did Laura imagine Jack felt?

Activities:

History/Writing	1.	Research your family's ancestors living in the 1870's. Show pictures, if possible. Write a brief biographical account of one ancestor.
Geography	2.	On the United States map provided, trace a hypothetical trail of the Ingalls' journey. Refer to this map throughout the <u>Primer</u> to mark Laura and her friends' travels.
Bible	3.	Although Laura ceased to complain outwardly, she felt she was still naughty. What does the Bible say about this? Read Mark 7:1-23 and Matthew 5:27-30.
Science	4.	Study about mustangs. Find a picture of one. What are the advantages of this breed of horse?
Vocabulary	5.	What is a ford (page 17)?
Bible	6.	On page 27, what did Pa say to answer Laura's question about Jack going to heaven? What verse was he referring to? Use a concordance to look for the reference. Is this using the verse in the correct context?
General	7.	Remember this week to schedule and make time for General Activities.

Prairie
Week 1

DAY 2

Read Chapters 3 and 4.

Reading Comprehension:

Chapter 3
1. How did Pa make a firebreak?
2. What made the land appealing to Pa?
3. What caused Pa not to shoot first, but to check out the approaching animal? *Hint: the horses' reaction (page 34).*
4. What sounds did Laura hear that night?

Chapter 4
5. Why did Ma not like Indians?
6. Who helped Laura and Mary get dressed?
7. How did Laura forget her manners? What did she do wrong (page 40)?
8. What did Laura and Mary want to catch and take to Ma (page 44)?
9. How did they approach the "hunt" differently?
10. What did Ma get instead? How did Ma react (page 45)?
11. What was dinner (page 46)? What did Laura think of dinner?
12. Were they in Indian Territory? Did they think it mattered?

Activities:

History	1.	Schedule to finish reading The American Indian Story by the end of this week. The first 22 pages refer to Indian religion. Preview this subject before allowing your child to read the section.
Art	2.	Draw Pet and Patty on their picket lines.
Writing	3.	On page 29, what did Pa say about being safe? Write about a time that you should have followed this advice or a time you used this principle to avoid trouble.
Literature	4.	What aspect of this chapter is an example of autobiographical fiction? (*Carrie was born while the Ingalls were in Indian Territory, not prior. Also, do you think that Laura remembered what was eaten each day?*)
Nutrition	5.	Compare the nutrient value of molasses to sugar.
Living	6.	Describe the process of making molasses or make molasses or sorghum.
Living	7.	Eat pancakes with molasses for breakfast or cornbread and molasses for lunch.
Art/Science	8.	Draw meadow larks, dickcissels, prairie chickens, mockingbirds, Phoebe birds, and gophers. Label and write an interesting, informative caption on the bottom of each drawing.
Geography	9.	Find Independence, Missouri, on a road map. With a compass mark a forty-mile radius.

Page 56

Living	10.	Wash clothes by hand in a tub and hang them out to dry.
Bible	11.	Study what the Israelites did with the inhabitants when they arrived in the promised land. Also, read Psalm 44:1-9. What was their "foreign policy?" Compare this to American foreign policy. Should the policy be the same? Why or why not? Discuss.
History	12.	Study the history of the United States relations with the Osage. (See background information.)

DAY 3

Read Chapter 5.

Reading Comprehension:

Chapter 5
1. What frightened Laura (page 54)?
2. What did the Ingalls family think was providential?
3. What are the steps that Pa took in building their house?
4. How were they able to finish the house? What are the advantages of trading labor?
5. How did the night end?

Activities:

Living	1.	Make stewed rabbit with dumplings.
Vocabulary	2.	In the <u>American Dictionary of the English Language</u> (the 1828 edition by Noah Webster), look up "providential." This word is seldom used anymore. What word has commonly replaced it? *(Luck.)* Look up "providential" in a modern dictionary. The Bible says to "give honor to whom honor is due" (Psalm 96:8; Romans 13:7-8.) What does God think about us attributing things to luck?
Bible	3.	On page 54, how did Laura feel being left alone without the wagon on the high prairie? The psalmist also experienced this feeling in Psalm 8 (especially verses 3-9). Memorize this Psalm to recite by the end of this unit.
Health/ First Aid	4.	What happened to Ma's ankle? What is a sprain? *(A sprain is a wrenching or twisting of a joint, with partial rupture of its ligaments. Ligaments are fibrous tissues connecting bones or cartilages, used to support and strengthen joints. Sprains may damage blood vessels, muscles, tendons, and nerves. Severe sprains are so painful that the joint may not be used.)* What color did Ma's ankle turn? Why? *(Severe sprains have much swelling, with red to blue discoloration coming from the bleeding within the tissue. The yellow and green colors come from the by-product of broken blood cells called bilirubin.)* How did Ma treat her sprain? What is the recommended treatment today?

Page 57

Prairie
Week 1

Science	5.	Research the components of blood and their functions. *(Blood is composed of plasma, blood cells, and platelets.)* For what purpose was each component created? Where are red blood cells made? *(The kidneys stimulate the red bone marrow of the ribs, sternum, skull, pelvic bones, and the ends of the long bones of the arms and legs to make red blood cells. These are stored in the spleen. The average life of a blood cell is four months. It then disintegrates and is removed by the spleen and the liver.)* Please explain that blood can also carry diseases. Try to avoid coming in contact with another's blood. If it unavoidably happens, wash skin immediately with soap and water to remove any remaining particles. Two diseases that can be transferred from **infected** people this way are AIDS and hepatitis. Becoming blood brothers by mixing blood can be deadly.
Art/Science	6.	Illustrate the cycle of a red blood cell by drawing each organ within the body through which it travels and labeling the organs according to their function.
Health	7.	Why is chewing tobacco an unhealthy habit?
Living	8.	Trade labor to accomplish a large task. Some ideas could be weeding, trimming trees, painting a house, making jelly, or canning.
Science	9.	Pa needed help lifting the heavy logs. Study the six types of simple machines: lever, wheel and axle, pulley, inclined plane, wedge, and screw. Pick one a day to demonstrate and discuss. Look for these in use in daily life and in the books you are reading.
Geography	10.	Read about prairies. What are the characteristics of a prairie? What are other geographic regions in the United States? the world?
Music	11.	Sing from <u>Laura Ingalls Wilder Songbook</u>, page 66.

Read Chapter 6.

Reading Comprehension:

Chapter 6
1. What was served for breakfast? Why do you think this was eaten?
2. Where did Pa think the Indians were?
3. What did Pa use for a temporary roof? What forethought did this take?
4. Why did Pa not finish the house?
5. Why did Pa feel he could be content to live here the rest of his life?
6. Why did Pa want a well?

Prairie
Week 1

Activities:

History/Bible   1.   Study the history of the United States Postal Service. (Refer to Background Information.) Much work and money have gone into perfecting the postal service. Read Proverbs 26:6. Was this a good expenditure of resources?

History   2.   Read several accounts of the Pony Express. Have your child retell their favorite one in their most exciting storytelling fashion. Have a pony express storytelling contest or party.

History/Economics   3.   What economic factors inspired the Pony Express? What factors caused it to go out of business? Research past inventions or business ventures that are now obsolete.

Social Studies   4.   Study the different types of Indian homes, particularly homes of the Plains Indians such as the Osage.

Social Studies   5.   Study how the Indians hunted the buffalo. How were the different parts of the buffalo used? Explain how the buffalo was a central part of Indian economy.

History   6.   The Indians are frequently heralded as living in harmony with nature and using all parts of an animal. Compare and contrast the Ingalls' interaction with their environment to that of the Indians. What items do you or your family partially use? How could they be used completely?

Literature   7.   Find the simile on page 79. What impression of does this give? (Refer to "Big Woods," Week 1, Day 2, Activity 8 for a discussion on metaphor and simile.)

Page 59

Prairie
Week 2

Week Two Planning Guide

Gather Information on the Following:

(See suggested sources listed)

1. Mules
   —Encyclopedia

2. Malaria
   —Encyclopedia

3. Wolves
   —Encyclopedia
   —Tracking and the Art of Seeing by Paul Rezendes

4. Mosquitoes
   —Encyclopedia

5. Goldenrod
   —Rodale's Illustrated Encyclopedia of Herbs
   —Encyclopedia

6. Poisonous snakes native to Kansas
   Physical characteristics of poisonous snakes
   Purpose of snakes flickering their tongues
   —Snakes A Golden Guide (Golden Press)
   —Encyclopedia

7. Safety design of fireplaces

8. Indian life-styles
   —The Book of Indians by Holling C. Holling
   —My Indian Boyhood by Luther Standing Bear
   —Indian Boyhood by Harles Eastman

9. Indian hair style, dress, cleanliness, and hospitality
   —The Indian How Book

10. Results of excessive exposure to the sun and methods to decrease sun exposure risk

11. Nutrients found in milk and alternate sources for these nutrients

12. The use of calcium in the body

13. Underground water table, wells, and aquifers

14. The sun
    —

15. Quicksand
    —The Quicksand Book by Tomie de Paola
    —

Gather These Items:

1. Items to make a model door as described on pages 101-103
2. A pattern and calico material to make sunbonnets
3. Empty aquarium, sand
4. A hole punch
5. Photocopies of "Building a Fireplace" Sequencing Worksheet if more than one child is using the Primer
6. Southern by the Grace of God by Michael Andrew Grissom

Suggested Field Trip:

1. Visit an Indian museum.

Notes:

Prairie
Week 2
For Use with Day 2

Building a Fireplace
Sequencing Worksheet

Put the following steps in sequence:

_____ A.   Laid a row of rocks around three sides.

_____ B.   Began making the chimney.

_____ C.   Spread the mud over the rocks.

_____ D.   Mixed clay and water to thicken mud.

_____ E.   Hauled saplings from the woods.

_____ F.   Plastered the notched saplings with mud.

_____ G.   Cut a hole in the wall with an ax.

_____ H.   Cleared a space by the house wall.

_____ I.   Made the mantel shelf.

**Prairie
Week 2
For Use with Day 4**

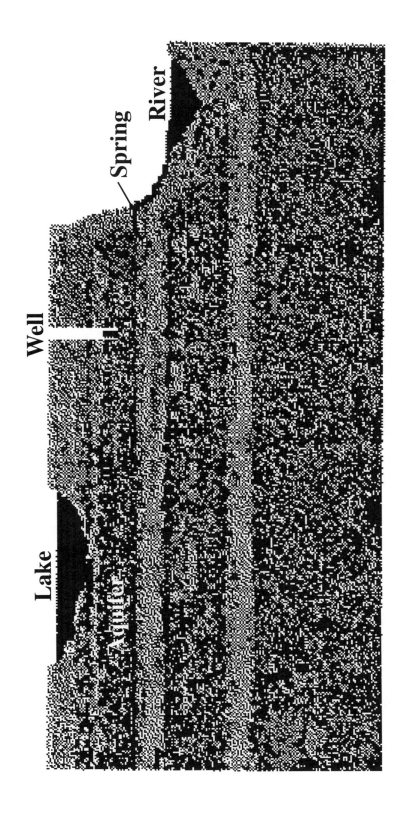

Prairie
Week 2

DAY 1

Read Chapter 7.

Reading Comprehension:

Chapter 7
1. Tell about the neighbors Pa met on his scouting trip.
2. How did Pa care for his neighbors?
3. Why did Pa think that the wolves did not attack?
4. Why did the house not feel safe (page 94)? What surrounded the house?

Activities:

Science 1. What are the characteristics and physical traits of a mule?

Science/Writing 2. Study about wolves. Include their habitat, social structure, character, and feeding habits. Read about the ecological history of the wolf from near destruction to his present protection under law. Write a report about wolves.

Science 3. The Ingalls' neighbors had fever 'n' ague. This was malaria. What did they (the Ingalls) think was the cause? What is the real cause? What are the symptoms? *(Chills, fever of 104-106 degrees, and sweating. Other symptoms are headache, body pains, and after the attack, exhaustion and anemia. Symptoms reoccur for about two weeks. If untreated, attacks can occur at sporadic intervals for several years. Quinine is the general treatment used for malaria. Quinine is a bitter substance that is taken from the bark of the cinchona tree in South America. Indians used the bark as medicine even before the 1500's. Some herbs associated with attempts to treat malaria are: goldenrod, Virginia snakeroot, coffee, and angelica. Malaria is rare in the United States because infected people are treated promptly before the parasite-carrying mosquito can transmit the disease to someone else. Decreases in the number of mosquitoes by eliminating stagnant water, where they breed, and the use of pesticides deters the transmission of the disease.)* How was their theory of fever 'n' ague related to the true cause?

Writing 4. Write a fictitious first-person account about malaria, how you contracted the disease, the symptoms you experienced, and your road to recovery.

Bible 5. Pa rushed home to beat the wolves to the homestead to protect his family and animals. A father's role is to defend and protect his family. That is why in Psalm 82:3 God is called the defender of the fatherless. Use a concordance to read a few verses referring to God the Father as our protector or defender. Meditate on this attribute of God. (Job 22:26; Psalm 7:10; 89:18; 59:9, 16-17; 94:22.)

History 6. Schedule to finish an Indian biography or autobiography by the end of Week 4.

General 7. Remember this week to schedule and make time for General Activities.

Prairie
Week 2

DAY 2

Read Chapters 8 and 9.

Reading Comprehension:

Chapter 8
1. How did the horses react to the presence of the wolves? Compare this to how they acted when Jack arrived from his struggle with the river.
2. What did Pa use for nails for the door?
3. What did Pa make instead of a door knob? How was the door "locked?"
4. Why must they lock their horses at night?
5. How did Laura assist her father in building the door?

Chapter 9
6. Tell about their trip to the creek. How did each girl react differently?
7. What did Laura like about the prairie (page 113)?
8. What did Pa do to his hair to make himself more appealing to Ma while they were courting (page 115)?
9. To make the house homey, what was placed on the mantel? on the table? on the beds?
10. Where was Laura's napkin while she was eating? What table manners did she use (page 119)?

Activities:

Craft/Reasoning	1.	Using popsicle sticks, toothpicks, and string, create a model of the door Pa created.
Science/Writing	2.	Study mosquitoes. Write a report about mosquitoes including the role they play in the transmission of disease.
Bible	3.	God created the universe. Since we are made in God's image, there is a desire in us to be creative also. What did Pa create? Was this satisfying? Do you have the desire to create anything?
Living/Art	4.	Laura saw goldenrod growing on the prairie. Draw this herb and research its uses.
Safety	5.	Many people have died attempting to heat their home or tent with a barbecue cooker. What safety features does a fireplace have that a barbecue does not? Why does smoke inhalation cause death? *(Smoke contains the by-products of burning fuel, one of which is carbon monoxide. Inhaling smoke has the same effect on your lungs as sitting in a running car in a closed garage. Instead of oxygen, our red blood cells will wrongfully attach to carbon monoxide, thus starving the tissues of oxygen.)*
Art	6.	Make a warning poster to prevent death by smoke inhalation.
Science	7.	What poisonous snakes could be present in the area where Laura lived?

Page 65

Prairie
Week 2

Art
8. Make a "scale" model of a snake. Using a hole-punch, cut out scales from construction paper and arrange with glue on an outlined drawing of a snake. Make them overlap from tail to head. Draw a picture and label with name and informative facts at the bottom. What are some physical characteristics of poisonous snakes versus nonpoisonous?

Sequencing
9. Give child(ren) the "Building a Fireplace" Sequencing Worksheet. (Answers: A.3; B.5; C.4; D.2; E.6; F.7; G.8; H.1; I.9.)

DAY 3

Read Chapters 10 and 11.

Reading Comprehension:

Chapter 10
1. What were Mary and Laura busy doing during the daytime?
2. What did they like about Mr. Edward's character?
3. How did Pa keep from wasting the nails? How did the girls help him in this endeavor?
4. How did Pa split the wood?
5. What does "We'll cross that creek when we come to it" mean?
6. How was the hearth made? How did Pa fill the cracks in the wall?

Chapter 11
7. What made Jack sad? What did Laura and Mary do to comfort him?
8. Who was their surprise company? Were they friendly? Why do you think they came?
9. How did they smell and why?
10. Laura chose to override Pa's command because the situation had suddenly changed. How did Mary possibly save the family and Jack from Laura's disobedience?
11. What did Pa say sweetened the cornbread (page 143)?

Activities:

Sewing
1. Make sunbonnets.

Health/Writing
2. What harm comes from excessive exposure to the sun? *(Sunburn may be an immediate effect. A long term effect may be the development of skin cancer and cataracts. Some researchers are linking excessive ultraviolet exposure to a decrease in the immune system.)* Study about ultraviolet light. Write down steps one can take to decrease the harmful effects of the sun's rays.

Science
3. Study about the sun.

Character
4. On page 124, what did Pa say about being beholding? What must Pa do to continue this way of life? Do you think that this is a good goal to strive for? If so, name some ways in which you could implement this in your relations with others. Apply Romans 13:8-10.

Page 66

Prairie
Week 2

Science	5.	Why do snakes flick their tongues? Study the various sense organs of snakes such as: eyes, pits, and the Jacobson's organ.
Bible	6.	Read Proverbs 24:3-4 and apply it to the Ingalls.
Living	7.	Split wood. Straighten nails. How easy is this to do?
Vocabulary	8.	What is a puncheon (page 129)?
Social Studies	9.	Research Indian dress, hair, cleanliness, and hospitality. How did each aspect of their hygiene and customs work well in their life-style?
Bible	10.	What did Pa say the girls needed to do so that no harm would come to them? Remember the story from <u>Little House in the Big Woods</u> with the same theme. What was the Biblical principle behind this? (Refer as needed to Week 2, Day 1, "Big Woods.") Also read Romans 13:1-3 and Romans 12:2-3. Apply this to Laura. How did her actions exhibit that she was thinking more highly of herself than she ought?

Read Chapters 12 and 13.

Reading Comprehension:

Chapter 12
1. What part of the well did Pa do by himself?
2. Why did he need help to finish? How was he able to get help to finish?
3. What was the purpose of sending the candle down the well?
4. What happened to Mr. Scott?
5. How did Pa get rid of the gas?
6. What safety rule did the Ingalls have regarding the well?
7. What did Laura think of well water?

Chapter 13
8. What did Laura hear as she went to bed?
9. Initially, what would be Pa's pay for helping the cowboys keep the cows out of the ravines? Was it easy work?
10. What did Laura wish she could be and why (page 167)?
11. What did Pa bring home besides his meat? Why did the cowboys give them to Pa (page 168)?
12. What did the cow do to Pa? How was Pa able to milk the cow? Who got the first milk?

Prairie
Week 2

Activities:

Science

1. Pa dug a well. Where does the water for a well come from? *(Well water comes from an aquifer, that is, soil or rock saturated with water. This water comes from rain, snow, and streams and filters through the soil to the aquifer.)* To demonstrate this, take an aquarium and fill it with 2 inches of water. Then fill the tank with sand until half full. The top of the sand represents the ground soil. Dig a hole in the sand until you hit water. The water represents the water in the aquifer. What is an artesian well? *(An artesian well is a well in which the water rises to the surface of the well without pumping. The water pressure in the aquifer is large enough to lift the water to the surface. An artesian aquifer has a confining layer above the water table that keeps the water from the surface.)* What is a spring? *(A natural hole in the confining layer of the artesian spring.)* See illustration on page 74.

Science

2. Mr. Scott did not light the candle to test the air. What could have caused him to pass out? Study about the naturally occurring gases derived from geologic formations in the earth's crust. *(The earth's interior has several gases present. These gases will displace the atmospheric gases when released through digging, drilling, or seepage. Some possible gases that are naturally occurring are carbon dioxide, carbon monoxide, and natural gas, which could have caused a large explosion when Pa sent the "bomb" down. Sulfur dioxide smells while hydrogen sulfide is almost immediately deadly.)*

Health

3. What was wrong with Mr. Scott's skin? Was there anything that he could have done? From our previous study on sun exposure what does he run the risk of developing? To decrease the amount of time spent in the highest intensity of the sun's rays when would have been the best "shift" to dig, the morning or the afternoon? When did he dig?

Living/Exercise

4. Climb a rope hand over hand as Pa did. How easy was this? What simple machine could have aided Pa in his climb out? What aided them in getting Mr. Scott out?

Living/Math

5. Are there private wells where you live? Find out the average cost of digging a well in your area. Calculate the number of days your father would need to work to pay for a well. Pa made a bedstand for Ma. What would it cost to do this today? How many hours would your father need to work to pay for one? Pa worked at home rather than away. He did not need to hire someone to come dig or build. In those times and economic system, families were forced to be more self-sufficient because goods and services were not available. Today families are not self-reliant in this way. Compare the advantages and disadvantages of each system. Include in your comparison the effect on the family when the father is present or absent most of the time.

Bible

6. Mr. Scott acted foolishly by not using safety precautions. Apply these verses to Mr. Scott: Proverbs 12:15; 1:22-23; 17:12; 13:16; and 23:12. Although Pa had to risk his own life, he saved Mr. Scott. Read Ephesians 4:9-12 and apply to the experience of digging the well. Mr. Scott was not a true fool. He admitted he was wrong. When they dug his well, do you think he forgot to light the candle?

Page 68

Prairie
Week 2

Vocabulary	7.	Look up these words: windlass, quicksand, and scalawag. (Use both dictionary and encyclopedias to research these words. For "scalawag" refer to <u>Southern by the Grace of God</u>, page 168. Mention that you will be studying about the Civil War when you read <u>Little Town on the Prairie</u>.)
Nutrition/Health	8.	Because the Ingalls did not have a cow, they had not had milk since they left the Big Woods. What nutrients are conveniently found in milk? *(Milk is a ready source of calcium.)* From what other foods could these nutrients be obtained? What are the important, different ways calcium is used in the body? What foods inhibit the absorption of calcium? *(Foods high in fat, high in protein, coffee, soft drinks containing phosphoric acid, salt.)* What aids the absorption of calcium into the bones? *(Vitamin C and weight-bearing exercise.)* List exercises that are weight-bearing *(running, walking, jumping rope, ballet)* and non-weight-bearing *(swimming, bicycling, rowing).*
Art	9.	Make a poster warning against calcium "robbers."
Nutrition/Living	10.	The Ingalls did not have butter since leaving the Big Woods. Do not use butter on or in any food for a week. If your family does not eat butter, try going without something you use everyday such as margarine, peanut butter, or oils.

Page 69

Prairie
Week 3

Week Three Planning Guide

Gather Information on the Following:

(See suggested sources listed)

1. Fever (purpose and treatment)
   —Inspector Body Guard Patrols the Land of U, "How Your Body Fights Chicken Pox" by Vicki Cobb
   —Why you feel hot, Why you feel cold—Your Body's Temperature by James Berry

2. Foods the Indians ate
   —Food the Indians Gave Us by Wilma R. Vernon

3. Oak, sycamore, and cottonwood trees (pictures)

4. Osage and French relations

5. Indian methods of travel and trails

6. Indian games

7. Indian ceremonial headdresses

8. Indian sign language

9. North American panthers or mountain lions
   —Tracking and the Art of Seeing by Paul Rezendes

Gather These Items:

1. Groceries to make an Indian dinner
   —Foods the Indians Gave Us
2. Salad macaroni, food coloring, and yarn to make craft project, Week 3, Day 1
3. Moccasin-making kit with beads
4. Items to make bean porridge
   —The Little House Cookbook by Barbara M. Walker
5. Items to make salt rising bread
   —The Little House Cookbook by Barbara M. Walker
6. Items to make stewed dried fruit
   —The Little House Cookbook by Barbara M. Walker
7. Items to make a ceremonial headdress
8. Laura Ingalls Wilder Songbook by E. Garson

Suggested Field Trips:

Prairie
Week 3

DAY 1

Read Chapters 14 and 15.

Reading Comprehension:

Chapter 14
1. Where did the girls go?
2. What did they see?
3. What could Pa tell about the Indians from the camp?
4. What did the girls gather?
5. What did Mary do with her beads? What did Laura do? What was Laura's attitude?
6. What did Laura feel good about?

Chapter 15
7. What did Ma and Laura gather at the creek? What did they do with them?
8. What did Pa do in an attempt to keep the mosquitoes away?
9. How did the mosquitoes get in the house?
10. What was wrong with the girls?
11. Who was able to get Mary a drink of water?
12. What was Jack's reaction to their illness?
13. What do you think Dr. Tan gave Laura?
14. Who had found them ill?
15. When the doctor was away, who cared for them? When did she go home?
16. What did Mrs. Scott think caused the illness?
17. Explain the common saying "It's an ill wind that doesn't blow some good." What good came from the malaria (page 197)?
18. What did Pa think caused the malaria (page 197)?

Activities:

Bible 1. Ma praised her girls for being unselfish. Laura did not want to be giving. Apply the following verses to Laura: I Samuel 16:7b; II Corinthians 9:7.

Craft 2. Make an Indian beaded belt or necklace. Dye uncooked salad macaroni by soaking in red, blue, or green food coloring and enough water to cover macaroni. Soak for two to three minutes. Spread to dry on a cookie sheet overnight. String with yarn. Tie several strands together to make a belt or necklace.

Social Studies 3. Study about the different foods that the Indians have given us.

Cooking 4. Cook an Indian meal for dinner.

Writing 5. Begin a daily journal, writing as if you were an Osage Indian. In your first journal entry write about why you are leaving your camp and where you are going.

Literature 6. Instead of saying plainly, "There were a lot of mosquitoes," Laura the author is careful to paint a descriptive word picture telling us the amount. Find and read aloud five sentences that emphasized the amount of mosquitoes there were.

Page 71

Prairie
Week 3

Writing	7.	By dictation, write a few sentences describing the malaria. Correct your copy with the book. Or, after reading Laura's description of malaria, improve your account about malaria written on Week 2, Day 1.
Bible	8.	What did Mrs. Scott say about her nursing them? What does the Bible say about neighbors? (Proverbs 27:10; Matthew 22:39.) Think of some ways you can be neighborly.
Bible	9.	Did Dr. Tan arrive at the Ingalls' house by chance or divine appointment? For an example from Scripture of a divine appointment, read Acts 8:26-39.
Health	10.	What is the average normal body temperature? *(98.6 degrees F.)* What is a fever? What purpose does a fever serve? What steps should be taken when a fever is present?
General	11.	Remember this week to schedule and make time for General Activities.

Read Chapters 16 and 17.

Reading Comprehension:

Chapter 16
1. How differently did Pa handle the hay in this climate?
2. Why would Pa not go to town when the weather was so hot?
3. Where did Pa go? Why did he not shoot a deer? a turkey?
4. What happened while Pa was gone? Could it have been prevented?
5. What was each girl's reaction to danger?
6. Why did Pa need to go to town?

Chapter 17
7. Why did Mary and Laura not go to town?
8. Who did Jack "tree?" Why had he come?
9. What was Mrs. Scott's opinion of the Indians and their land (page 211)?
10. How did Laura contradict Mary?
11. What did Mr. Edwards say about the Indians?
12. What slowed Pa coming home? Why did he not stay in Independence?
13. What surprise did he bring home? What was Ma's reaction?
14. Of what were the girls able to have a spoonful?

Activities:

Science	1.	Identify or draw a picture of an oak, sycamore, and cottonwood tree. Or collect the leaf and seeds of these trees, if found in your area, and mount them for display.

Prairie
Week 3

Health   2.   Why did the Ingalls need more quinine? *(It is the treatment and prevention of malaria. Since malaria is a parasite, the body does not become immune and may be reinfected. A maintenance dose of quinine keeps reinfection from occurring.)*

Social Studies   3.   Pa did not needlessly kill game. What was the Osage opinion and reaction to those who needlessly slaughtered game? What effect would the needless slaughter of animals have on the Osage? What might have happened to the Ingalls if Pa's character were different?

Vocabulary   4.   What is a massacre?

Writing   5.   In your Indian Journal, write about your reaction to settlers coming to Kansas.

Music   6.   Sing from <u>Laura Ingalls Wilder Songbook</u>, pages 96 and 155.

DAY 3

Read Chapters 18 and 19.

Reading Comprehension:

Chapter 18
1. Who came to visit the Ingalls?
2. What did Pa say about getting along with the Indians?
3. What almost happened to Jack?
4. Why was Jack chained during the day? at night? What did chaining him do to his disposition?
5. What did Pa trap and hunt?
6. What did the Indians who barged into the house do? Why do you think they dropped the furs?
7. Why had Ma and Pa gone to Indian Territory to live?
8. Did Pa and Ma feel it was wrong to be in Indian Territory?

Chapter 19
9. Why were the girls disappointed when they went to bed?
10. Who came early in the morning?
11. Retell the Santa Claus story. Why did Santa not have his reindeer?
12. Tell about their gifts.
13. What special thing did Mr. Edwards bring for dinner?

Activities:

Science   1.   Pa trapped and hunted wolves, foxes, beaver, muskrat, and mink. Why did he do this in the winter? Study the habits of one of the animals Pa trapped or hunted. From your newly-gathered information, devise a plan to trap or hunt that animal.

Bible   2.   What was Pa's justification for being on Indian Territory? Was it right for Pa to go where the government had previously agreed settlers would not go? See Proverbs 21:2.

Page 73

Prairie
Week 3

History	3.	The Ingalls' house was next to an Indian trail. Study about the Indians' methods of traveling and of Indian trails that later were used by the white men.
History	4.	Pa thought the Indian had spoken French. What kind of relationship had the Osage had with the French? *(The Osage were known for their expert fur tanning ability and frequently traded with the French.)*
Cooking	5.	Make at least two items from the Ingalls' Christmas dinner for a special dinner.
Writing	6.	In your Indian Journal, tell how you hunted or trapped an animal for its fur.
Craft	7.	Make moccasins.
Music	8.	Sing from <u>Laura Ingalls Wilder Songbook</u>, pages 92.

DAY 4

Read Chapters 20 and 21.

Reading Comprehension:

Chapter 20
1. What woke them in the middle of the night?
2. What did Pa think it was? What did he do about it? Was Pa a good neighbor?
3. Who actually made the noise?
4. What did Pa do the next several days? Why did he work so hard at hunting the panther?
5. Why did he stop?

Chapter 21
6. Where had Pa gone? Why?
7. What were the girls playing outside?
8. What treat did Pa bring from town?
9. What made Pa happy (page 269)?
10. What did the Indians think of the settlers?

Activities:

Science/Writing	1.	Write a report about panthers. Are there any in the United States presently? Trace a map of the United States. Color the habitat range of the panther.
Cooking/Nutrition	2.	Make bean porridge. What food groups does bean porridge contain?

Page 74

Prairie
Week 3

Social Studies	3.	How did Pa communicate with the Indian? The Indians had a universal sign language that was developed to communicate among the differing tribes. Study Indian sign language. Pick an Indian name for yourself and learn the corresponding sign. Introduce yourself and sign a simple story in a presentation to family or friends. Dress in Indian clothing.
Bible	4.	Pa was a cheerful giver. Discuss how God is also a gracious giver *(John 3:16)*. *Just as Pa takes pleasure in his family, so Father God takes pleasure in us (Psalm 149:4).*
Living	5.	Play hopscotch.
Social Studies	6.	Indians enjoyed playing games. Research Indian games and their purpose; learn one or two to play.
Craft	7.	Make an Indian ceremonial headdress. It could be as simple as making it from construction paper or as elaborate as using leather and feathers.
Writing	8.	From information read in The American Indian Story, write in your Indian Journal a recounting of Indian relations with the white man.
Fun	9.	Have an Indian party. Incorporate Activities 3, 6, and 7. Serve Indian foods as refreshments. Use sign language in games of charades.

Prairie
Week 4

Week Four Planning Guide

Gather Information on the Following:

(See suggested sources listed)

1. Minnesota massacre (1862)
   —Encyclopedia
   —America the Beautiful—Minnesota

2. Competition of homesteaders for Indian Territory
   —Encyclopedia

3. United States forts in your area and the part they played in western expansion

Gather These Items:

1. Laura Ingalls Wilder Country by William Anderson
2. Laura Ingalls Wilder Songbook by E. Garson

Suggested Field Trips:

1. See "living history" reenactments depicting Indian or frontier life. Check with the state park districts.
2. Visit a restored fort in your area.

Notes:

Prairie
Week 4

DAY 1

Read Chapters 22 and 23.

Reading Comprehension:

Chapter 22
1. What were the possible reasons for the prairie fire?
2. Who spotted the fire?
3. How did the Ingalls fight the fire?
4. If the backfire would not have worked, what would the Ingalls have done?
5. Why were the Indians gathering?
6. What did Mr. Edwards, Mr. Scott, and Pa each think of the Indians?

Chapter 23
7. What did the Ingalls' family have to endure?
8. How did the stress affect each family member?
9. Who rode past the house in the moonlight?
10. Why did the Indians leave?
11. Who had spoken for the white settlers?
12. What effect did this man have on the Ingalls' life?
13. What Indian did Pa think was a good Indian?

Activities:

Science	1.	How did the backfire save the Ingalls' homestead?
History	2.	Briefly study about the Minnesota massacre.
History	3.	Study about the race of homesteaders into other Indian Territories.
Writing	4.	In your Indian Journal, describe how you felt the night before a buffalo hunt. What did you prepare for the hunt? Describe the hunt itself.
Reasoning	5.	Why do you think the Osage chief spoke in defense of the settlers?
Bible	6.	On the bottom of page 292 and the top of page 293, find and read aloud the passage describing the intensity of the terrible night compared with a nightmare. For those that are not living for the Lord, there will also be a great and terrible day. There will be no waking up. Read Revelation 6:15-17.
Field Trip	7.	American forts played an important part in the western expansion. Visit a fort in your area or study about the role it played in your area.
Vocabulary	8.	What is a stockade (page 289)?
General	9.	Remember this week to schedule and make time to conclude General Activities.

Page 77

Prairie
Week 4

DAY 2

Read Chapters 24 and 25.

Reading Comprehension:

Chapter 24
1. Who was the first Indian in the procession?
2. From the background information, where were the Indians going?
3. What was different in the way the Indian rode his pony from the way the settlers rode theirs?
4. What did Pa do to Jack for the first time?
5. What sign of respect did Pa give the Osage chief?
6. What of the Indian way of life intrigued Laura to the point that she wished she was an Indian (page 307)?
7. For what did Laura cry and ask Pa to get for her (page 308)?

Chapter 25
8. What were the Ingalls busy doing during the daytime?
9. What did they plant?
10. What made Pa mad?
11. Who did he give the cow to and why?
12. In the context of the story, explain this saying, "There's no great loss without some small gain."
13. How was a whole year gone? What was gained? How would you feel?

Activities:

Reading
1. Laura wished to be an Indian. Many children of the settlers were captured by and raised as Indians. Two books that tell of such an incident are Captured by Indians by Lois Lenski and Captive Treasure by Milly Howard (BJU Press). These are optional reading for those interested.

Writing
2. In your Indian Journal, write about how you felt as you traveled in the procession going by the Ingalls' homestead. Where were you going? What would you do?

Nutrition
3. The Ingalls ate meat and bread. Which food groups were missing? What nutrients were they probably deficient in?

Bible
4. The Americans appeared to have the upper hand in their relationship with the Indians. Superior technology and communication were important factors. Yet, the Indians also felt that there was another reason for their defeat: Americans had large families. Read Psalm 127:3-5; 128:3-4; Proverbs 14:28; Deuteronomy 6:3; and Job 12:23. For further study read about how God opens and closes the womb—Abraham and Sarah, Hannah, Elizabeth, David and Michal.

History
5. Without the Americans and Indians ever fighting, the Indian population decreased. When the Europeans came to America, they brought disease. Although these diseases killed some Europeans, they brought devastation to the Indian tribes, whose immune systems had never been built up against these diseases. Name some of these catastrophic diseases.

Page 78

Prairie
Week 4

DAY 3

Read Chapter 26. This Finishes the Book. Also read <u>Laura Ingalls Wilder Country</u>, Chapter 2, "Kansas Prairie Country."

Reading Comprehension:

Chapter 26
1. What had to be left? How would they get another one?
2. Why was Laura excited (page 327)?
3. What mistakes had the "tenderfeet" made?
4. What were they taking out of Indian Territory that they did not bring in?
5. Who would eat their garden?
6. How did Laura decide to end this book? What makes it a good ending?

Activities:

Field Trip   1.   Visit a "living history" museum in a state park where they reenact how Indians or pioneers lived.

Speech   2.   From your Indian biography entertain your family with a story (Week 2, Day 1, Activity 6).

Bible   3.   What were the tenderfeet's hearts set upon? Read Matthew 6:25-34.

Literature   4.   Why do you think Laura wrote this story as if she were older than she was when the events occurred?

Bible   5.   Recite from memory Psalm 8.

Music   6.   Sing from <u>Laura Ingalls Wilder Songbook</u>, pages 46 and 117.

DAY 4

Finish Any Undone Activities!

Page 79

Plum Creek

On the Banks of Plum Creek

After leaving Indian Territory in 1871, the Ingalls returned to Pepin, Wisconsin. Pa's desire to move West caused the family to move again in the spring of 1873. When the covered wagon stopped, they were near the village of Walnut Grove, Minnesota. Charles and Caroline bought 172 acres of fertile soil surrounding the banks of Plum Creek. Laura and her family were surrounded by nature's beauty and severity. They worked and fought to create their livelihood.

Throughout <u>On the Banks of Plum Creek</u>, Laura's awareness of God begins to develop. She begins to realize how godly principles affect her life. She is confronted often with temptations. Each of Laura's episodes in disobedience are systematic, timeless illustrations of ways Christians are instructed to avoid sin. She also begins to perceive God's provision and to trust God's care for her family.

Additional Reference Material:

Classification of Living Things

This study will also emphasize the classification of living things. All living things are divided into five kingdoms. The two best known are the plant and animal kingdoms. The other three kingdoms are fungi, monera, and protista. Kingdoms are divided into a classification's pattern from largest to smallest categories. As an example, the animal kingdom categories are: Kingdom, Phylum, Class, Order, Family, Genus, and Species. Each plant or animal is specifically identified by its genus and species name. This is called binomial nomenclature. For a more in-depth reference, look in an encyclopedia under "Animal/A Classification of the Animal Kingdom" and "Plant/A Classification of the Plant Kingdom."

Refer to this breakdown of the kingdoms as you do the General Activities for this unit.

Nonliving—rocks, minerals, etc.
Living—things that grow and reproduce.

Kingdoms:

Plant—They generally make their own food by using sunlight and water.

Animal—They generally have body parts, mobility, and can respond to their environment.

Protista—They are single celled organisms that have a nucleus and organelles. Examples: paramecium, kelp, and most algae.

Monera (Bacteria)—They are single, simple cells without a nucleus or chloroplast. Bacteria receive their nutrients from other organic material. They are divided into two main groups: aerobic (requires oxygen to live) and anaerobic (does not require oxygen). Bacteria are decomposers.

Fungi—They do not produce their own food, but live off other organic matter. Fungi are decomposers. Examples: mushrooms, puffballs, and toadstools.

Plum Creek

The Animal Kingdom:

Phylum   **Chordata**—These animals have backbones.

    Class   **Mammals**—These animals have hair, give birth to live young and nurse their offspring, and are warm blooded (always maintaining a constant body temperature). Example: beaver.

    Class   **Birds** (Aves)—These animals have feathers and hollow bones. Example: crows.

    Class   **Reptiles**—These animals are cold-blooded (body temperature changes with the surroundings and therefore they are less active in cold weather), have scales, and lay eggs. Example: lizards.

    Class   **Amphibians**—These animals live on both land and water. They are cold-blooded with smooth, moist skin. The egg hatches into larvae that breathes with gills and then develops into the adult stage. Example: egg->tadpole->frog. (The adult frog has lost its tail and gills. It can only breathe air.)

    Class   **Fish**—These animals breathe with gills, live only in water, and may or may not have scales.

Phylum   **Arthropoda**—These animals have jointed legs and an exoskeleton (a shell on the outside of the body) which usually must be shed in order to grow.

    Class   **Insects** (Insecta)—These have three body parts (head, thorax, and abdomen), and six legs. Example: grasshoppers.

    Class   **Arachnids**—These animals have eight legs and the head and the thorax are fused leaving two body parts. Examples: tarantula, ticks.

    Class   **Crustaceans**—These have gills, two sets of antennae, and a thick exoskeleton made of chiton. As they grow, they lose their exoskeleton by molting. Examples: crabs, crayfish, shrimp.

    Class   **Millipede**—These have segmented bodies with pairs of legs from each segment. They usually feed on decaying plant life; some will attack crops grown in moist soil.

    Class   **Centipede**—These have narrow bodies divided into many segments, each with a pair of legs. They have a pair of antennae on their head. The first pair of legs behind the head is used for fighting. A gland from the head fills these legs with poison.

Phylum   **Annelida** (Segmented worm)—These animals have long bodies divided into many segments. Usually they move about with bristles. Examples: earthworms, leeches.

Phylum   **Mollusca**—These are soft bodied animals. Most are covered by a hard limy shell. Example: snails, clams, oysters, octopus, squid.

The Plant Kingdom:

Division   **Spermatophyta** (Seed Bearing Plants)

    Class   **Angiosperms**—These are true flowering plants. Most plants fall into this category. They reproduce by cross pollination. Examples: plum trees, tumbleweeds, ragweed, wheat.

    Class   **Gymnosperms**—These plants have seeds in cones. They are usually evergreen and have needles for leaves. Examples: pines, firs, cedars.

Division   **Ferns** (Pterodophyta)—These plants reproduce by spores and are flowerless. They have fronds. The rhizome stems are close to the ground. They contain vascular tissue—xylem and phloem, which transport food and water. Example: Boston Fern.

Division   **Mosses** (Bryophyta)—These plants reproduce by spore capsules. Since they lack vascular tissue, they grow close to the ground or other moist places.

Plum Creek

Background Information:

Grasshoppers and "Grasshopper Weather"

The plants and animals living in the same habitat are called a community. There exist many varieties of habitats on the earth and many kinds of communities within them. Each member of a community fills a place within the food chain of that habitat. A food chain is the path that food travels in a community. Most food chains include a plant, a plant eater, and one or more predators. Decomposers, like fungi and bacteria, are also a part of every food chain. The grasshopper was a very destructive member of the living community at Plum Creek.

In 1873-1877 the great plague of migrating grasshoppers in the United States was a national calamity resulting in a multi-million-dollar loss of wheat, barley, corn, oats, and rye. After the crops were destroyed, the grasshoppers ate grass, leaves, and barren trees. The swarms began in the plains east of the Rocky Mountains in Montana, Wyoming, and Colorado. After destroying everything in these lands, they left a trail of destruction eastward to the Mississippi River and southward into Texas.

There are many reasons for an over abundance of grasshoppers in certain years. Nature must provide favorable conditions for the tiny grasshoppers to flourish. Grasshoppers must have time in the fall to lay their eggs before the cold weather comes. Warm weather late in the fall is one type of "grasshopper weather." A cool fall shortens the egg-laying time. The nymphs hatching in the spring must have plenty of food nearby and warm weather for feeding. After hatching, if the weather turns suddenly cold, many nymphs will perish. Proper feeding cannot take place below a temperature of 70 degrees F. Grasshopper weather also occurs, when the early spring is cool and moist, and is then followed by weeks of warm, dry weather.

Rainfall also affects the grasshopper's survival. If heavy rainfall occurs during hatching or immediately after, many of the delicate nymphs cannot survive. Also a week or more of cloudy, wet weather encourages certain diseases that kill many grasshoppers.

Grasshoppers are members of the food chain. Therefore, the number of grasshoppers that survive the summer also depends on the grasshopper's predators. Bee flies, blister beetles, and ground beetles lay their eggs in the soil close to the grasshopper egg pods. Their hatching larvae can destroy as many as half the grasshopper eggs. Flesh flies, spiders, ground squirrels, and field mice eat grasshoppers. Most birds feed on grasshoppers; some even scratch the ground for their eggs.

When conditions are favorable for the grasshopper over several years and when for various reasons the number of natural predators is reduced, the insects become more numerous. The increase in numbers may not be noticed until they are in plague proportions. This series of conditions set the stage for the destructive grasshopper plague that hit Plum Creek in 1875.

Plum Creek

General Activities to Do throughout This Unit:

1. Have your child jot down a list of new objects appearing in each chapter. While doing the Daily Activities, take the list and together classify the objects according to Kingdom, Phylum, and Class. For example, lizards-> living-> animal-> chordata-> reptile. By the end of this study the child should have a simplified understanding of classification. Below is a list of some objects that could be classified: lizards, crabs, leeches, grasshoppers, panthers, wolves, cows, muskrats, otters, minks, plums, willows, ragweed, tumbleweed, turnips, Jack, Pa, Ma, horses, oxen, wheat, grass, gray rock, hens, butterflies, and Charlotte (doll).

2. Set a schedule to have Psalm 51 memorized by the end of this unit. It was one of Laura's favorite Psalms to pray when she had sinned.

3. Read a biography of Noah Webster.

4. Sew a nine-patch quilt square. Frame it when done.

Plum Creek
Week 1

Week One Planning Guide

Gather Information on the Following:

(See suggested sources listed)

1. Willows (pictures and habitat)
   —Trees A Golden Guide (Golden Press)

2. Diagram of the parts of a tree
   —Encyclopedia
   —Studying Plants (Milliken)

3. Sources of heat exchange (conduction, convection, and radiation)
   —Encyclopedia
   —Heat (Troll)

4. Morning glories (pictures and blooming cycle)
   —Flowers A Golden Guide (Golden Press)

5. Water safety
   —Swimming and Diving Skills (Usborne)

6. Badgers

7. Lichens

8. Butterflies
   —Moths and Butterflies (A Bantam Book)
   —Life of the Butterfly by Heiderose and Andreas Fischer-Nagel
   —Pets in a Jar by Seymour Simon

9. Scythes
   —The Story Book of Wheat by Petersham
   —Wheat the Golden Harvest by Dorothy Henshaw Patton

10. Bees
    —The Fascinating World of Bees by Angels Julivert

11. Characteristics of Germans, Swedes, and Norwegians

12. The human body's response to fear (release of adrenalin)
    —Inspector Body Guard Patrols the Land of U, "Fear to the Rescue" by Vicki Cobb
    —The Young Scientist Book of the Human Body (Usborne)

13. How to preserve fruit by drying
    —How To Dry Foods by Deanna DeLong

Page 85

Plum Creek
Week 1

14. Water purification
   —The Magic Schoolbus at the Waterworks by Joanna Cole
   —

15. Mammals
   —Encyclopedia
   —

16. Thanksgiving
   —

Gather These Items:

1. Horehound candy
2. Items to make parched corn
   —The Little House Cookbook by Barbara M. Walker
3. Microscope
4. United States road map
5. United States topographical map
6. The American Dictionary of the English Language (the 1828 edition by Noah Webster)

Suggested Field Trip:

1. Visit a water purification plant and/or read about water purification.

Notes:

Page 86

Plum Creek
Week 1

DAY 1

Read Chapters 1, 2, and 3.

Reading Comprehension:

Chapter 1
1. What was Laura's nickname? How did it fit her?
2. What did Pa pay to buy the house and the land (page 5)? How much did your parents pay for their house?
3. Why did Pa like the land (page 6)?
4. What hope for the land did Pa have?
5. How old was Laura?
6. How did Laura feel when Pet and Patty were sold? What made Laura feel better?

Chapter 2
7. Explain how the ceiling was made (page 11).
8. How did Laura bring water to the house (page 13)?
9. What did Pa say about Laura (page 14)?
10. What did Pa say about grumbling?
11. What did Ma like about where they were living (page 17)?
12. What did Laura want?

Chapter 3
13. What were Mary and Laura's chores? What are your morning chores?
14. Tell about Mary and Laura playing outdoors.
15. What did Mary and Laura discover about rushes?
16. What safety rule did they have?

Activities:

Science
1. Take pond or creek water, add some grass, and place in a window or other warm place for a day or two. Take a sample and view it under a microscope. What do you observe?

Health
2. The Ingalls obtained their water from the creek. Why is it not recommended that we drink creek water? What diseases can be gotten? *(Cholera, dysentery, hepatitis.)* Why do you think they could drink the water?

Health
3. Visit a water purification plant and find out the steps taken to ensure public safety of drinking water.

Health
4. Find out how to purify water at home. *(Boiling, chlorine tablets.)* In what situations would you need to purify your water at home?

Geography
5. Look at a topographical map of the United States and make a trail following the path the Ingalls probably took from Pepin, Wisconsin, to Walnut Grove, Minnesota. From a road map determine the mileage and the present-day travel time.

Page 87

Plum Creek
Week 1

Science	6.	Find a picture of a willow tree. What habitat do they like? Draw a picture of a willow. Include parts of a tree and label: roots, bark, phloem, cambium, xylem, and leaves.
Science	7.	What are the three methods of heat transfer? *(Conduction, convection, and radiation.)* The Ingalls lived in a dugout for a time at Plum Creek. Using your information about heat transfer, what are the advantages of having an underground home?
Writing	8.	The Ingalls traded Pet and Patty for the dugout and oxen. Write about a time your family sold a car, an animal, or another item that you were attached to. Include why this event was necessary in your family.
Art	9.	Draw a picture of morning glories and blue flags *(blue irises)*. Use shading techniques to make them more realistic.
Science	10.	Morning glories are said to be equinoctial. Look up this word and explain how these flowers got their name.
Bible	11.	What happened to the Israelites when they complained (Numbers 11:1-6 and Numbers 11:18-20)? What was Laura's complaint (page 16)?
General	12.	Remember this week to schedule and make time for General Activities.

DAY 2

Read Chapters 4, 5, and 6.

Reading Comprehension:

Chapter 4
1. What happened when Laura went into deep water?
2. What must Laura not do?

Chapter 5
3. What was Laura's first step to sin?
4. What did Laura do wrong in this chapter?
5. What did God send to cause her to turn?
6. Who knew that she had done something wrong?
7. Who did she tell?
8. What did Pa lose in Laura?
9. What was Laura's punishment?
10. What did she learn?

Chapter 6
11. Why was Johnny's face red and his hair bleached white?
12. What came home with Pa and the girls?
13. How did Pa pay for her?
14. What did it mean for the family?
15. What had Laura learned to do by example?
16. According to Ma, what did she do wrong?

Page 88

Plum Creek
Week 1

Activities:

Geography   1.   Which of the following geographical terms best fits the description of the "table land" (page 22)?

      a.   **Butte**—a small area up to an acre.

      b.   **Mesa**—an area with a one to two-mile diameter.

      c.   **Plateau**—an area encompassing a four to fifty-mile diameter.

      d.   **Plain**—the largest expanse of level land on which the slope cannot be seen.

Bible   2.   Apply I John 1:8-9; James 5:16; and Proverbs 28:13 to Laura's need to tell her Pa about the swimming hole adventure.

Bible   3.   Laura sinned. At a time such as this what would be a good Psalm to pray? *(Psalm 51.)* Read and/or recite Psalm 51. Continue working on memorizing this Psalm.

Geography   4.   What countries are Swedes, Germans, and Norwegians from? Locate these countries on a map. How do these countries compare to Minnesota in latitude? What do these people look like? Explore their characteristics and culture.

Science/Writing   5.   Do a report on butterflies. Include which characteristics of an insect it has. Also, include the life cycle of a butterfly.

Science   6.   Watch a caterpillar grow into a moth or butterfly.

Science/Writing   7.   Do a report on lichens. Collect lichens and include them with your report. *(Lichens live in symbiosis with algae and fungi; that is, they coexist for their own benefit, but are not detrimental to each other. An example of lichen would be to take a mass of white thread, representing fungi, and pour a layer of salt on it, representing algae.)*

Health/Safety   8.   Discuss water safety rules. Compare the added dangers of river swimming to pool swimming.

Science   9.   Research and give an oral report on badgers. Are they nocturnal or diurnal?

Bible   10.   The Ingalls felt the badger's appearance was providential. See if these scriptures support their theory: II Thessalonians 3:3 and Psalm 25:20. Can you think of other scriptures?

Plum Creek
Week 1

DAY 3

Read Chapters 7, 8, and 9.

Reading Comprehension:

Chapter 7
1. What was Laura and Mary's new chore? When must they rise to do their chore?
2. What happened to their roof?
3. Could anything have stopped it?
4. What happened to Laura because of the incident?

Chapter 8
5. Why must the little girls not play with the scythe?
6. Laura and Mary knew they had done something wrong. What was it? What did Pa say? What effect did their playing in the straw have on Pa?
7. What did the girls do after they were told not to?
8. What was Pa doing when he turned his back (page 160)?
9. Who else could have suffered because of their sin?
10. What is the purpose of having the straw stacked?

Chapter 9
11. What type of work did Mary prefer? Laura (page 64)? Which work of the two do you prefer?
12. What is the trick to shaking the plum tree?
13. What was the weather like at Thanksgiving?
14. What do you think "grasshopper weather" is?

Activities:

Research	1.	Read about wheat. To what family does wheat belong? *(Grass.)* What are other members of this family? Find a picture of a scythe. Describe how to thresh wheat.
Bible	2.	One step into sin is to question the law (Lord) or to tell half truths, excusing oneself by a technicality (Genesis 3:5). Read about Abraham and Sarah (Genesis 12:10-20). How was Laura's excuse still a sin?
Bible	3.	Laura led Mary astray. Children must be very careful what they lead their friends and siblings into (Matthew 18:6 and James 3:1).
Science/Writing	4.	Study and write about bees and bumblebees. These are social insects. What does this mean? Can you think of another social insect? *(Ants.)*
Living/Science	5.	Eat plums. Dry plums or another kind of fruit such as apples. What type of dried fruit do you normally consume? What is the purpose of drying plums? *(Preservation.)* What would happen if they were not dried? *(Spoilage from bacteria, fungi, and molds would occur.)* What is removed during the drying process?
Science/Living	6.	There are different varieties of the same fruit. What is the advantage of having several varieties? *(Differences in pestilence resistance, differences in flowering time that could be protective in late frosts or droughts, and*

Page 90

Plum Creek
Week 1

differences in ripening times allow time to gather fruit and a longer availability of fresh fruit.) Visit a grocery store and note the number of varieties of apples, plums, and grapes available.

Literature   7.   Foreshadowing is a literary device in which a previously mentioned idea or event is repeated later in a story. The mention of grasshoppers in Chapter 8 is a significant one. It foreshadows the grasshopper plague described in Chapter 25. Be on the lookout for other events in the story that may foreshadow a more significant happening.

DAY 4

Read Chapters 10, 11, and 12.

Reading Comprehension:

Chapter 10
1. Why did Mary and Laura stay home? How old were they? How long would Ma and Pa be gone?
2. How did Ma recycle Laura's old dress?
3. What is an ox goad?
4. What happened to the hay?
5. On page 70, it says Mary was too scared to move and Laura was too scared to stand still. What does this tell about their personalities?
6. How did the girls protect the hay?
7. Where was Johnny?
8. What would have happened if the girls had not been there?

Chapter 11
9. How did Pa save Ma and Carrie?
10. What did the wheat crop mean to them?

Chapter 12
11. What worried Laura?
12. What did Pa want?
13. Who did they say Santa Claus was (page 85-86)?
14. What extra thing did Laura pray that night?
15. Did the Lord answer her prayer?

Activities:

Character/   1.   Look up "idleness" in the <u>American Dictionary of the English Language</u>
Vocabulary   (the 1828 edition by Noah Webster). It states, "To be idle, is to be vicious" (Rambler); and, "Idlement is the parent of vice." Apply this to Laura's attitude before spotting the cows.

Cooking   2.   Make corn dodgers. See <u>The Little House Cookbook</u>.

Page 91

Plum Creek
Week 1

Science	3.	What is the human body's response to fear? *(The flight or fight response.)* How did Laura and Mary display this response (page 70)?
Bible	4.	Apply these verses to Johnny: Proverbs 20:11; 27:23, 27; Proverbs 6:9-11.
Living/Cooking	5.	Eat horehound candy. Make and eat parched corn.
Science	6.	How long is the time from planting the wheat until harvest? What factors influence the duration from sowing until harvest? *(Rainfall, temperature, latitude, strain of wheat.)*
Bible	7.	What scriptural principle did Laura apply when she prayed for the Lord to give her a heart to be happy without toys so Pa could have a horse? (I Corinthians 3:18; James 1:5; Matthew 7:7-11.)
Science	8.	Read about mammals in the encyclopedia. What are the characteristics of a mammal? Zoologists divide the Class of mammals into Orders of related species. What are the Orders listed in the encyclopedia? What are the characteristics of each? Name some animals and place them into the correct Order.
History	9.	Research the Pilgrims first Thanksgiving. How was Laura's account different from the actual event? *The Festival of Booths was the Israelites' Thanksgiving. They stayed in booths for a week to remember that God made the children of Israel dwell in booths when He brought them out of the land of Egypt. (Leviticus 23:39-43). One of the first Thanksgiving observances in America was entirely religious and did not involve feasting. When the Pilgrims arrived at Berkely Plantation on the James River on December 4, 1619, they had a day of Thanksgiving. The group's charter required that the day of arrival be observed yearly as a day of thanksgiving to God. After nearly half the Pilgrims died the first winter in Massachusetts Governor Bradford declared a time of thanksgiving to God. The Pilgrims prepared a large feast and invited the Indians. The custom of Thanksgiving Day spread from Plymouth to other New England colonies. During the Revolutionary War, eight special days of thanks were observed for victories and for being saved from dangers. In 1789, President George Washington issued a general proclamation naming November 26 a day of national Thanksgiving. For many years, the country had no regular Thanksgiving Day. Then President Abraham Lincoln proclaimed the last Thursday in November 1863, as "a day of thanksgiving and praise to our beneficent Father."*

Plum Creek
Week 2

Week Two Planning Guide

Gather Information on the Following:

(See suggested sources listed)

1. Leeches
   —Ponds and Streams by John Stidworthy
   —Encyclopedia

2. Blue herons (pictures)
   —Birds A Golden Guide (Golden Press)

3. Noah Webster
   —Noah Webster by David Collins (The Sower Series)

4. The history of paper production

Gather These Items:

1. Antique buttons
2. Items to make vanity cakes
   —The Little House Cookbook by Barbara M. Walker
3. The American Dictionary of the English Language (the 1828 edition by Noah Webster)
4. "Beauty and the Beast" video
5. Photocopies of "Laura on the Playground" Sequencing Worksheet if more than one child is using the Primer
6. Laura Ingalls Wilder Songbook by E. Garson

Suggested Field Trips:

1. Go fishing in a pond or stream that has buffalo fish, pickerel, catfish, shiners, and bullheads.

Notes:

Plum Creek
Week 2
For Use with Day 3

Laura on the Playground
Sequencing Worksheet

Put the following steps in sequence:

_____ A.   The school girls played Uncle John.

_____ B.   The school girls played ring-around-a-rosy.

_____ C.   With both hands, Nellie grabbed Laura's hair.

_____ D.   Nellie was in the schoolhouse crying.

_____ E.   Nellie tossed her curls and flounced her skirt because she thought she had her way.

_____ F.   Christy began singing "Uncle John . . ."

Plum Creek
Week 2

DAY 1

Read Chapters 13, 14, and 15

Reading Comprehension:

Chapter 13
1. What did the girls make for Carrie? Why was it special?
2. Did the girls look forward to making the gift?
3. What surprise gift did they get for Christmas?
4. What were the girls able to do Christmas morning?

Chapter 14
5. What did Laura do?
6. Why was Mary surprised at Laura?

Chapter 15
7. Describe what happened to Laura in this chapter.
8. Why did Ma not punish Laura?
9. What lesson had Laura learned (page 106, last paragraph)?

Activities:

Living   1. Look at antique buttons. Compare them to buttons made today.

Art   2. Make a button string.

Literature   3. Uncle Tom gave the Ingalls <u>Millbank</u> written by Mary J. Holmes and published by Hurst & co. *This book is out of print and generally available only in used bookstores.* This is not a children's book. This book and author made such an impression on Laura's memory that she mentioned it in the Little House books which have stood the test of time. Besides the Little House books, which books stick in your mind as favorite family read alouds and why? Following is a brief summary of the plot of <u>Millbank.</u> An old man who had two sons by two different wives, just died. His oldest son was dead, but had left a son. The old man's grandson was about the same age as the younger son. Frank, the grandson, and Roger, the son, were both teenagers. On the train ride home to his father's funeral, Roger sat beside a lady with a baby girl. She asked him to watch her while she did something, but she never returned. Roger took the child home and raised her. The will left everything to Roger, with only a tiny amount for Frank. It was contested because Frank's mother insisted the father had revised it and left all to Frank, because Roger's mother had been unfaithful. The revised will could not be found, so Roger owned everything. Roger helped Frank frequently, because they were good friends. The boys grew up, and so did the baby girl. Both boys fell in love with the girl. Finally, the revised will was found and Roger found out what really happened to his mother. Frank married. Roger and the girl marry and live happily ever after. The part about Roger's mother may be questionable reading.

Art   4. Draw a picture of the girls going to the creek.

Page 95

Plum Creek
Week 2

Language 5. On page 98, Laura describes the flood. Identify what words describe which of the five senses. For example, "icy" identifies the sense of touch.

Writing 6. Write a paragraph using descriptive words that appeal to the five senses.

Bible 7. In Chapter 15, Mary was surprised that Laura was so different from herself. How unique is each person and why were people created? Read the following verses: Isaiah 43:7; Psalm 139:13-16; and I Corinthians 12:12-30.

Bible 8. In Chapter 15, compare the lure of temptation (drugs, sex, greed, or other dangers) to Laura's enticement and entrapment in the water. Then read and apply Isaiah 53:6 and James 1:14-15 to Laura's adventure with the water.

Bible 9. Joseph knew not to play with sin or tempt himself. Read the story of Potiphar's wife (Genesis 39:1-13). Identify the four steps Joseph used to resist temptation:

   a. He realized the wrong it would cause his master (verses 7-8).

   b. He realized that he would be sinning against God (verse 9).

   c. He said "no" repeatedly (verse 10).

   d. He quickly removed himself from the situation (verses 10, 12).

   Just saying "no" is not sufficient to resist sin. Apply I Corinthians 10:13. In what previous episodes in this book did Laura allow herself to be lured by temptation? *(The two incidents with the creek and the haystack.)*

General 10. Remember this week to schedule and make time for General Activities.

DAY 2

Read Chapters 16, 17, and 18.

Reading Comprehension:

Chapter 16
1. What were the Christmas horses called?
2. Why did Pa say that the land was dry (page 107)?
3. What was Pa too tired to do?
4. What besides wheat did Pa plant?
5. What does give your work "a lick and a promise" mean? Have you ever done this?
6. What did Pa put on the outside of the house (page 110)?
7. What type of broom did they have?
8. What were both Mary and Laura scared to do? Laura was afraid but pretended not to be. Have you ever been afraid and not shown it?

Page 96

Plum Creek
Week 2

Chapter 17
9. What did each girl have in her box (page 123)?
10. What one thing did Laura think was wrong with her room (page 123)?
11. What noise did Laura realize she had missed?

Chapter 18
12. What did Mary and Laura find in the water?
13. When Laura went into the muddy water, what got on her?
14. Why could Mary and Laura now go to school (page 132)?

Activities:

Art 1. On page 108, Laura tells of all the flowers she saw. Draw or paint the picture she describes.

Bible 2. What does the Bible say about debt? See Proverbs 22:7.

Living 3. What insulates your house? Look in the attic, the exterior, the flooring, etc. What makes a good insulator? *(Poor conductors.)*

Crafts 4. Make the star light catchers as described on page 121. Directions: Fold lengthwise a 2" wide by 12" long paper into 1" accordion folds. Trace a 1" star-shaped pattern and cut out, leaving two points of the star uncut where the paper folds. Unfold and hang in a window.

Writing 5. Write a descriptive paragraph on the noises heard at night at your house.

Science 6. Research leeches, including past medical uses, classification, and the proper way to remove them. *(Pour salt on them.)*

DAY 3

Read Chapters 19, 20, and 21.

Reading Comprehension:

Chapter 19
1. What was Pa making (page 134)?
2. How did Laura help?
3. What did Laura think she would miss by being at school?
4. Explain how and why the trap worked.
5. How often did they have fish to eat?
6. What did Ma praise Charles for?
7. Why did Pa not hunt in the spring? What does this tell you about his character?
8. What did Pa do with the fish that he could not eat?

Page 97

Plum Creek
Week 2

Chapter 20
9. How far must they walk to school?
10. Why did Laura put her sunbonnet back on (page 143)?
11. How would they know when they arrived in town?
12. How would they know where the school was?
13. Why were the girls called snipes?
14. Who protected Laura and introduced herself? What did Laura and this girl have in common?
15. What did Laura notice about Nellie?
16. Were the Ingalls girls in shoes?
17. What did the teacher do when someone was naughty?
18. How did they share a book for study?
19. Could anyone else in school not read?

Chapter 21
20. How did Mary carry the money to the store (page 154)?
21. Did Willie and Nellie obey?
22. What kept Laura from being as mean as Nellie?
23. What did the dime not buy?
24. Where did they get the extra penny to buy chalk?
25. What do we use instead of slates and slate pencils for daily work? What are the advantages to both? *(Less waste versus permanence and ease.)*
26. What did Laura feel kept her from being like Nellie? Apply what you learned from the study of Joseph.
27. How did Laura honor Pa?

Activities:

Writing	1.	From the material gathered yesterday on leeches, do a two paragraph report about this creature.
Language	2.	Identify the simile on page 134. A simile is using the word "like" to compare two things not usually equated. Think of other similes to describe family members.
Art/Science/Living	3.	Find pictures of fish listed on page 139. Draw a picture of each. If possible catch and eat the different varieties.
Vocabulary	4.	What is a knoll? a snipe?
Science	5.	Find a picture of a blue heron. What type of habitat does it prefer? How is its body suited to where it lives?
Reasoning/History	6.	Why was the daily use of paper prohibited? What factors have made paper commonplace?
Bible	7.	Apply these verses to Nellie: Proverbs 12:1; 13:1; 13:24; 15:5, 12; 22:15; 28:23.
Art/Environment	8.	Illustrate the inside of the Oleson's store. How were items packaged? How does it compare with the way items are packaged today? Which method results in better stewardship of the earth's resources?
History	9.	In this chapter, Laura begins to read. One who contributed much to American education was Noah Webster, the author of the American Dictionary of the English Language (the 1828 edition by Noah Webster).

Plum Creek
Week 2

Begin reading his biography and schedule to finish it by the end of Week 4. This is a good book to read aloud to slower readers or younger students.

Language   10.   Laura went to school. In the <u>American Dictionary of the English Language</u> (the 1828 edition by Noah Webster) read the definition of "school" and compare it to the definition of "education." How have these words changed their meaning?

Play   11.   Play Uncle John as described on page 159.

Sequencing 12.   Give child(ren) the "Laura on the Playground" Sequencing Worksheet. *(Answers: A.5; B.1; C.2; D.6; E.3; F.4.)*

Music   13.   Sing from <u>Laura Ingalls Wilder Songbook</u>, page 74.

DAY 4

Read Chapters 22 and 23.

Reading Comprehension:

Chapter 22
1. Was Nellie a good hostess?
2. How did she embarrass Laura?
3. What did Laura do for the first time today?
4. What did Laura do wrong?
5. Why was Jack lonesome?
6. What did Ma suggest?
7. What did Laura tell Christy (page 168)?

Chapter 23
8. How did Laura get even with Nellie?
9. What was Ma's definition of vanity? Who in this story is vain?

Activities:

Manners   1.   Go over rules of being a good host(ess).

Vocabulary 2.   What is a velocipede?

Bible   3.   Look up the following verses and apply them to Laura's wish for getting even: Proverbs 25:21-22; 20:22; 14:22; 6:16, 18; 10:23; 24:17-18, 29; 26:18-19; Romans 12:19; Matthew 5:39; Matthew 18:22.

Bible/Art   4.   Make a warning poster about not getting even—not repaying evil for evil.

Cooking   5.   Make vanity cakes. See <u>The Little House Cookbook</u>.

Page 99

Plum Creek
Week 2

Writing

6. Look up "vanity" in the <u>American Dictionary of the English Language</u> (the 1828 edition by Noah Webster) and references to vanity or conceit in the Bible. Write a one-page report on vanity.

Character

7. Watch "Beauty and the Beast." Discuss the implications of vanity in this film.

Plum Creek
Week 3

Week Three Planning Guide

Gather Information on the Following:

(See suggested sources listed)

1. The history and origin of American folk songs
   —
2. Ragweed
   —<u>Weeds</u> A Golden Guide (Golden Press)
   —
3. Tumbleweed
   —<u>Weeds</u> A Golden Guide (Golden Press)
   —A desert magazine with pictures of dried tumbleweeds
   —

Gather These Items:

1. <u>Favorite Little House Songs</u> by Waring (cassette)
2. Turnips
   —Grocery store
3. Photocopies of "Charlotte" Cause and Effect Worksheet if more than one child is using the <u>Primer</u>
4. Materials and directions to sew a nine-patch quilt square
5. <u>Laura Ingalls Wilder Songbook</u> by E. Garson

Suggested Field Trips:

1. Visit a state park or preserve where there are firebreaks. Find out if your local forest preserves have prairie fire demonstrations.

Notes:

Page 101

Plum Creek
Week 3
For Use with Day 3

Charlotte
Cause and Effect Worksheet

Match the cause with the effect in the following:

Causes:

_____ A. The Nelsons were from Norway.

_____ B. Ma had not seen Laura play with Charlotte.

_____ C. Anna ripped the paper doll. The girls wanted to protect their paper dolls.

_____ D. They were expecting a letter from Pa.

_____ E. Anna had tossed Charlotte away.

_____ F. Anna began to cry when she was to leave Charlotte.

Effects:

1. Anna did not speak English.

2. Ma gave Charlotte to Anna.

3. The girls wanted to be good hostesses. The girls allowed Anna to play with Charlotte.

4. Laura had gone to check for mail at the Nelsons.

5. Laura found Charlotte frozen in the mud.

Page 102

Plum Creek
Week 3

DAY 1

Read Chapters 24 and 25.

Reading Comprehension:

Chapter 24
1. What was Ma excited about?
2. What was different about the girls' hair? What determined the color of ribbon they were to wear?
3. What preparations did Pa make before their trip (page 180)?
4. How did they go to town?
5. How was town different on Sunday? How is the town in which you live different on Sundays?
6. Why did Rev. Alden only come once a month (page 188)? What did they do when he did not come?
7. What did Pa need?
8. Why did he walk to town?
9. What did he do with the money for his boots?

Chapter 25
10. Why did the walls drip with sticky pine juice?
11. How did the grasshopper's coming change their lives?
12. What was Pa's reaction? Ma's? What things did the girls do to make it easier on their parents (pages 203-204)?
13. Why did they not go to school anymore?

Activities:

Vocabulary	1.	What is a belfry? a cravat?
Bible	2.	Apply these verses to the observance of Sunday: Isaiah 56:2; Hebrews 5:9-10; Exodus 20:8-11.
Bible	3.	Should Pa have given his shoe money for the bell? From reading these scriptures what do you think God thought about his sacrifice? Does God require such sacrifice from us for salvation? See Romans 6:23; Psalm 4:5; Romans 12:1; II Corinthians 10:7.
Writing	4.	Pretend that you are an Israelite. Write a descriptive story about the grasshopper plague on Egypt. (Exodus 10:1-20).
Science	5.	Draw a food chain cycle using the grasshopper. Identify elements within the community that could cause the grasshopper population to become out of control. What effect did the grasshoppers have on the community's balance?
Science	6.	Could another grasshopper plague happen in the United States? What methods to control grasshoppers do we have today that they did not have in the 1870's? *(Pesticides, tractor plows to decrease the number of eggs that can hatch, conservation methods to protect natural enemies.)*

Plum Creek
Week 3

Bible 7. What is God's opinion of man's attempt to control His judgments expressed in natural phenomena? What does the Bible tell you about future plagues and pestilence coming upon the earth? Read Psalm 9:19; Job 42:2; and Revelation 6, especially verse 8 (NAS version). It is not wrong to control nature with pesticides or flood walls, etc., but these will be futile against God's power in His Day of Judgment.

Bible 8. Laura recommended reading Psalm 46 when facing a crisis. Read this and think about how this Psalm could have comforted Laura at this time.

Music 9. Sing from Laura Ingalls Wilder Songbook, page 108.

General 10. Remember this week to schedule and make time for General Activities.

DAY 2

Read Chapters 26, 27, and 28.

Reading Comprehension:

Chapter 26
1. What had Laura observed (page 207)?
2. What had Pa observed?
3. How did Laura know something was wrong when she saw Pa?
4. How did the girls honor their Pa (page 210)?
5. On page 209, what reason did Pa give that they were better off than lots of folks?
6. What was Pa's solution to provide for his family?
7. Where would he go and how would he get there?

Chapter 27
8. Where was the only shade?
9. How did Ma get water for the family?
10. When they read the Bible, how could they relate to the story? Did Laura believe it?
11. What do you think about Ma having the girls dressed properly when it was so hot and no one else was around?
12. What did the rain do?

Chapter 28
13. What worried the girls?
14. What did the letter say?
15. Why were the boots an important part of the letter?

Activities:

Math 1. Use the information on page 208 to calculate how many potential grasshoppers were in each square foot of ground.

Page 104

Math	2.	If a person can walk 4 miles per hour, how long would it take to walk 250 miles? How many days would it take, if one were to stop 8 hours a day to rest?
Nutrition	3.	What food groups were missing from the meal on page 210? Why were they missing?
Bible	4.	The author recommended reading Psalm 121 when traveling. Read this and see how it could have spoken to Pa.
Bible	5.	Pa was a good provider. What does the Bible say about providing for one's family (I Timothy 5:7-8)?
Bible	6.	Proverbs 24:16 distinguishes the fall of the righteous from the fall of the wicked. What is the difference? Also, read Psalm 57:1.

Math/Reasoning 7. How many gallons of water does your family use in a day? (Look at the water bill and divide.) Compare this to how many gallons the Ingalls family used. What can be attributed to the difference?

Language 8. On page 219, Laura is describing the drought. Write the five senses across the top of a page. Under each sense list the words Laura uses which require that sense to experience. ("Moo"—hearing; "wood smell"—smelling.)

Science 9. Knowing about the underground water table, why did the well go dry? *(The water table fluctuates according to the amount of water that seeps into the ground from rainfall and/or streams plus its rate of use.)*

Science 10. What causes heat waves to be visible? Why are they generally visible during times of low humidity? *(As the sun heats the ground, the ground becomes hotter than the surrounding air. When the warm rising air from the ground meets the colder air above, the temperature differences bend the light. Just as light bends when it passes through water or a prism, so the temperature differences cause the long waves of radiant heat to bend the shorter waves of the sun's light and we see a wavy pattern in the air. These visible waves of heat usually occur during times of low humidity. When there is a minimal difference between ground and air temperatures, heat waves will not occur. The moisture within the ground moderates the rise and fall of ground temperature.)*

Music 11. Sing from <u>Laura Ingalls Wilder Songbook</u>, pages 24 and 48.

DAY 3

Read Chapter 29, 30, and 31.

Reading Comprehension:

Plum Creek
Week 3

Chapter 29
1. What is a thresher?
2. Did Laura do what was right when she brought Charlotte home? What would you have done?
3. What was the first problem that Pa solved when he came home (page 239)?
4. Why do you think that Pa had not bought presents?

Chapter 30
5. What did Mary get?
6. What did Laura think about Mary getting new shoes? Was this right? Have you ever felt like this?
7. What did Laura get that was new?
8. Where was Ma's gray challis? Pa's overcoat? Why were these decisions made?

Chapter 31
9. What did Pa trap? Why did Pa trap them?
10. Why would it still be "grasshopper weather?"
11. What schedule did the Ingalls girls follow for homeschool (page 245)?
12. Tell the process of taking a bath in Laura's day (page 247). Compare it to taking a bath in your house.
13. What safety rule did Laura almost break?
14. What surprise awaited them at the church? How was it decorated?
15. What was Laura's special gift that God provided for her?

Activities:

Bible	1.	When Laura wanted Mary's new shoes, which of the ten commandments was she breaking (Exodus 20)?
Bible/Art	2.	Make a warning poster about envy, using one of the following verses: Job 5:2; Proverbs 14:30; I Timothy 6:3-5; Titus 3:3-5; James 3:16.
Bible	3.	God is so good. He supplied what Laura secretly wanted. Any coat would have kept her warm, but this one showed how God cares even for the details in life. Choose a verse to memorize: Philippians 4:19; I John 5:14-15; or Psalm 23:6.
Safety	4.	What car safety rules does your family have? *(Wearing seatbelts,* locking doors, not opening doors, not putting hands outside the window in traffic, etc.)
Music	5.	Sing folk songs like the ones listed on page 245.
History	6.	Research and read about the origin and history of American folk songs.
Cause and Effect	7.	Give the child(ren) "Charlotte" Cause and Effect Worksheet. *(Answers: A.1; B.2; C.3; D.4; E.5; F.2.)*
Writing	8.	Write a description of a doll or toy that captured your heart at a young age. Describe why it was special and how it became worn through certain events.
Music	9.	Sing from <u>Laura Ingalls Wilder Songbook</u>, page 82 and 142.

Plum Creek
Week 3

DAY 4

Read Chapters 32, 33, and 34.

Reading Comprehension:

Chapter 32
1. How long did the grasshopper walking last (page 265)?
2. What bothered Ma and Pa (page 265)?
3. What could no one tell Pa?

Chapter 33
4. Why did Pa leave whistling (page 269)?
5. What did Laura know was coming?
6. What caused the fire?
7. How did they fight the fire?
8. Who helped? How did he know they needed help?

Chapter 34
9. Why did the girls not wear their mittens while digging in the garden on a cold day?
10. What was the salve for their hands made of (page 277)?
11. What did the girls do to calculate Pa's arrival?
12. Why did Pa arrive earlier than calculated?
13. Review the literary device of foreshadowing as mentioned in Chapter 9 with the event of the grasshoppers. What happened in Chapter 34 that may be a foreshadowing of a future event?

Activities:

Art
1. Draw a picture of the most impressive part of the migration of grasshoppers.

Language
2. Copy, or by dictation write down, your favorite descriptive paragraph. Compare the two copies and make changes. Underline the verbs. Discuss each verb and tell what picture it conveys.

Writing
3. Review and rewrite your assignment about the grasshopper plague (Week 3, Day 1). Substitute any verbs or adjectives with more descriptive words.

Bible
4. Apply Joel 2:25-26 to the grasshopper problem at Plum Creek.

Science
5. Look up and make a drawing of ragweed and tumbleweed (Russian Thistle). Write two or three sentences about each plant at the bottom of each of your illustrations.

Living/Cooking
6. Find turnips in the store. Prepare and eat turnips.

Bible
7. Tell how Proverbs 27:10 proved true. What else could this verse mean?

Page 107

Plum Creek
Week 3

Science

8. Study the properties of fire:

a. **Kindling temperature**—the point that the fuel and oxygen present will start burning. Different materials have different kindling temperatures.

b. **Fuel**—anything that combines with oxygen to break down and give off heat.

c. **Oxygen**—needed for fuel to combust. A component of air.

By knowing these three properties, how can fires be extinguished?

a. *Take away oxygen—such as smothering with a blanket.*

b. *Remove the fuel—such as using a firebreak.*

c. *Decrease the kindling temperature by dousing with water.*

Knowing these properties, why does a firebreak work?

Living

9. Make note of postmark dates on letters and see how long it takes for mail to arrive from different destinations.

Plum Creek
Week 4

Week Four Planning Guide

Gather Information on the Following:

(See suggested sources listed)

1. Beavers
   —Ponds and Streams by John Stidworthy
   —A Guide to Animal Tracking and Behavior by Donald and Lillian Stokes
   —Tracking and the Art of Seeing by Paul Rezendes
   —Beavers by Elin Kelsey (Nature's Children Series)

2. Quilt patterns (particularly nine-patch and bear's track patterns)

3. The hazards of tobacco use
   —The American Cancer Society

Gather These Items:

1. Laura Ingalls Wilder Country by William Anderson
2. Laura Ingalls Wilder Songbook by E. Garson

Suggested Field Trips:

Notes:

Page 109

Plum Creek
Week 4

Read Chapters 35 and 36.

Reading Comprehension:

Chapter 35
1. What did Pa want to do?
2. Which of Ma's character qualities were given on page 285? How would you describe your mother's character qualities?
3. Which of Pa's stories prompted the girls to carry in the wood?
4. Who could carry more wood at one time? Who was faster?
5. Was it good that there was wood in the house?

Chapter 36
6. How did Pa find his way to the stable and back with limited visibility?
7. Why did Pa milk the cow, although he would make it back with little milk?
8. With what did Pa compare the previous places they had lived?
9. What did the girls do during the day?
10. What did the girls do with their slate?
11. What type of quilts were the girls working on (page 296)? Whose quilt was more difficult?
12. What did they do on Sunday? Why did they not go to church?

Activities:

Language   1. This book is written in the third person. Instead of saying, "I knew it was true (page 284)," what was said? If Laura Ingalls Wilder had not written this book, what personal insight would be lost?

Writing   2. Choose a character other than Laura and rewrite an episode from their perspective. When a story is told in the first person, we learn about the events from that character's point of view. Point of view or perspective changes from character to character. To rewrite an episode from another character's perspective you must imagine how that person feels and perceives their world and how they would react to the events happening around him/her. Examples of events to rewrite in the first person:

       a. How Pa felt when walking back East to look for work.
       b. What Ma thought while Pa was gone to town.
       c. What Carrie thought when her sisters started carrying wood or when the oxen ran away.

Science   3. Research and classify beavers. Talk about their diet.

Plum Creek
Week 4

Science   4.   From understanding living communities, why were so few beavers left? *A reduction in number could have resulted from:*

            a. *An increase in the number of predators (more trappers, because of an increase in population).*

            b. *Lack of water (drought).*

            c. *Lack of food (fewer shoots of willows and cambium layers of trees from the grasshopper destruction).*

Living   5.   Look at and enjoy pictures of the quilt patterns the girls were working on.

Craft   6.   Sew a nine-patch quilt square. Frame it when done.

Health   7.   What are the health hazards of tobacco use? *(Increase in heart attacks, cancer, and emphysema. For pregnant women: low birth weight and premature infants.)* With all the evidence against smoking, what are the factors that encourage young people to initiate smoking? *(Advertising, peer pressure, false sense of immortality, yielding to temptation.)*

Art   8.   Make an antismoking poster.

Bible   9.   Apply these verses to tobacco use: Proverbs 14:12; John 10:10.

Bible   10.   On page 291, what did Laura think would happen when they were older? Discuss this concept with your child. *(Foolishness is bound up in the heart of a child. See Proverbs 22:15. With proper raising foolishness is removed in childhood. Yet even the best men make mistakes as adults. Therefore, to make as few mistakes as possible, it is wise to have godly counsel for major decisions. See Proverbs 15:22. Also we must always honor our parents even after we are grown. See Proverbs 6:20-21.)*

Music   11.   Sing from <u>Laura Ingalls Wilder Songbook</u>, page 144.

General   12.   Remember this week to schedule and make time to conclude General Activities.

DAY 2

Read Chapters 37 and 38.

Reading Comprehension:

Chapter 37
1. What chores did Ma do in the barn?
2. Why did Ma put a lamp in the window?
3. What did Laura sneak down and see Ma doing?
4. What did Ma do to Carrie's pajamas?
5. What came down the stovepipe? What do you think caused it?

Plum Creek
Week 4

Chapter 38

6. What character qualities did the girls show while Ma was doing Pa's chores?
7. What happened when Ma went out to do the chores? Do you think that she wanted to do the chores?
8. What did Laura think about crying?
9. Why did Ma not leave the lantern in the window the second night?

Activities:

Living/Play   1.   Play bean-porridge hot (page 309), and pussy in the corner (page 317).

DAY 3

Read Chapters 39, 40, and 41. This Finishes the Book.

Reading Comprehension:

Chapter 40

1. What did all the snow mean for the wheat crop?
2. What had Pa bought in town? How did each help him when he was stranded?
3. Why could Pa not stop walking? What kept Pa from having a sense of direction in the storm?
4. How did God provide for Pa?
5. How close was Pa from home?
6. What was the girls' reaction to Pa eating their candy?

Chapter 41

7. What did they do for Christmas Eve?
8. Which is your favorite song that they sang?
9. What did Laura say was so good about this Christmas?

Activities:

Play   1.   Play cat's cradle.

Bible   2.   Pa knew he had to keep walking and not give up. Read Proverbs 24:10; Isaiah 40:29; Romans 8:31-39; Psalm 27:5. What gave him strength to continue?

Writing   3.   Write a two-page report on Noah Webster.

Music   4.   Sing from Laura Ingalls Wilder Songbook, pages 63, 76, and 128.

Page 112

Plum Creek
Week 4

DAY 4

Read <u>Laura Ingalls Wilder Country</u>, Chapter 3, "Walnut Grove and the Banks of Plum Creek" and Chapter 4, "Little Hotel in the Village."

Activities:

Play   1.   Play the classification game. Tape a name of an animal on your child's back. They are to ask only "yes" or "no" questions. For example: Am I an arthropoda? No. Am I a chordata? Yes. Am I a mammal? Yes. Other questions that may be asked at this time are: Do I have claws? hoofs? Am I vegetarian? Am I carnivorous? Am I nocturnal? See if they can guess what you have taped to them.

Bible   2.   Recite from memory Psalm 51!

Finish Any Undone Activities!

Shores

By the Shores of Silver Lake

In the fall of 1875, Pa returned home and moved Ma and the girls into a rented house in Walnut Grove. On November 1, 1875, Charles Frederick Ingalls was born. When the 1876 crop ruined, Pa felt he could no longer remain in Walnut Grove. Friends from their church urged them to become their partners in a hotel business in Burr Oak, Iowa. Pa agreed. En route to Iowa, while visiting Uncle Peter and Aunt Eliza Ingalls, illness struck Laura's only brother. On August 27, 1876, less than a year after his birth, little Freddie died.

Along with possibly 200 other wagons, the Ingalls arrived in Burr Oak, sad and tired from the events of their journey. The Ingalls quickly went to work caring for the guests. Laura, at age ten, went to school with Mary. It was during their year long stay in Burr Oak that Grace Pearl Ingalls was born.

After a year in Burr Oak, the Ingalls returned to Walnut Grove. While living in town, Pa supported his family with a variety of jobs as a carpenter, a clerk, a butcher, a storekeeper, and a miller. Then in 1879, the opportunity to move westward happened and Pa was again on the move.

Background Information:

The Dakota Territory

In the 1850's the fur trade flourished in the Dakotas. With the high quality furs came fur trading posts and river transportation. Both Catholics and Protestants built missions and the United States government opened post offices in growing settlements.

The Dakota Territory was created by President James Buchanan in 1861. The status of territory was preparation for statehood and created the need for temporary government. Lincoln appointed Dr. William Jayne, a campaign manager and family doctor, to be the first territorial governor of the region. The ten Dakota governors that served the span of time from territorial status to statehood were described as unpopular with the people. Most were Easterners who had no interest in the country. Their only concern was salary or political advancement.

After creating the Dakota Territory, Congress passed the Homestead act of 1862, which gave free land to people who would settle on it and plant crops. Beginning January 1, 1863, settlers who promised to cultivate and live on the land could have up to 165 acres. At the end of five years they had to prove they had fulfilled the conditions. Few people filed or made claim on the land until the 1870's.

Another bill that affected settlement of the area passed in 1864. It gave the railroad over fifty million acres of land on which to lay track. It was for work on the Dakota Central Division of the Chicago and Northwestern Railroad that brought the Ingalls family to the Silver Lake Camp.

It was not until 1870 that wheat began to make a big impact on the Dakota economy. In that year two Minnesotans developed a new milling process for spring wheat. In the new process, flour made from spring wheat was considered superior to flour made from winter wheat. Spring wheat became a major crop.

Shores

During the 1880's, several efforts were made by territorial residents to admit Dakota to the Union. None were successful. Special-interest groups such as the railroads and flour mills opposed statehood. They wanted to keep a form of government that could easily be persuaded to look after their interests.

In 1887 the voters split the Dakota Territory into North and South Dakota. Both had far exceeded the 60,000 minimum residents required for statehood. In 1889 after Congress passed the Omnibus Bill, which authorized the drafting of constitutions for North Dakota, South Dakota, Montana, and Washington, these territories elected delegates for a constitutional convention.

On November 2, 1889, President Benjamin Harrison signed documents making North Dakota and South Dakota two states. He closed his eyes while signing, in order not to know which one was signed first. As a result, both states claim to be the thirty-ninth state. Officially, North Dakota is first because it is first alphabetically.

Reference:
Margaret Herguth, America the Beautiful—North Dakota, Childrens Press, 1990.

General Activities to Do throughout This Unit:

1. Do the following bacteria collection experiments (see Week 1, Day 1, Activity 7). Add one tablespoon of agar to one cup of water. Boil in a sauce pan for five minutes stirring constantly. Add one teaspoon of sugar and stir to dissolve. Pour mixture 1/2 inch deep into sterilized bowls or petri dishes. Cover with plastic wrap. Repeat as necessary to complete the experiments.

   a. Pick three different sites to obtain bacteria. (Examples: garbage can, clean plate, hands, or food.) Stick a piece of tape to it. Pull the tape up and stick it back down once or twice. Remove the plastic wrap, press the sticky side down onto the gel surface, remove it, and immediately re-cover the gel. Label with the site where obtained. Repeat with different sites, using separate dishes. Place dishes on a cool shelf out of the sun. Make a hypothesis about the amount of bacterial growth. Compare at three, seven, and ten days. Compare results to your hypothesis.

   b. On the bottom of an agar dish, mark its diameter with tape or a marker. Collect a cellophane tape bacteria sample from a chosen site. Place the tape sample across the diameter of the agar dish so that some of the sample is on both sides of the dish. Remove the bacterial tape. With a clean Q-tip, smear a little antibiotic ointment on only one side of the dish (use Neosporin or Bacitracin). Cover the dish and place on a cool shelf out of the sun. Watch for a week or two. Note the results of both sides of the dish.

      Reference:
      John Cassidy, Explorabook, Klutz Press, 1991.

2. Memorize Romans 8:31-39.

3. Memorize each state with its corresponding capitol in the sequence in which they entered the Union. To finish by the end of this unit, three states a day will need to be memorized. (As an alternative, use Learn Your States and Capitals Wrap Ups.) As these are memorized, draw them on the United States map provided and mark the capital with a star.

Shores

	State	Captial	Admitted	
a.	Delaware	Dover	1787	1
	Pennsylvania	Harrisburg	1787	2
	New Jersey	Trenton	1787	3
b.	Georgia	Atlanta	1788	4
	Connecticut	Hartford	1788	5
	Massachusetts	Boston	1788	6
c.	Maryland	Annapolis	1788	7
	South Carolina	Columbia	1788	8
	New Hampshire	Concord	1788	9
d.	Virginia	Richmond	1788	10
	New York	Albany	1788	11
	North Carolina	Raleigh	1789	12
e.	Rhode Island	Providence	1790	13
	Vermont	Montipelier	1791	14
	Kentucky	Frankfort	1792	15
f.	Tennessee	Nashville	1796	16
	Ohio	Columbus	1803	17
	Louisiana	Baton Rouge	1812	18
g.	Indiana	Indianapolis	1816	19
	Mississippi	Jackson	1817	20
	Illinois	Springfield	1818	21
h.	Alabama	Montgomery	1819	22
	Maine	Augusta	1820	23
	Missouri	Jefferson City	1821	24
i.	Arkansas	Little Rock	1836	25
	Michigan	Lansing	1837	26
	Florida	Tallahassee	1845	27
j.	Texas	Austin	1845	28
	Iowa	Des Moines	1846	29
	Wisconsin	Madison	1848	30
k.	California	Sacramento	1850	31
	Minnesota	St. Paul	1858	32
	Oregon	Salem	1859	33
l.	Kansas	Topeka	1861	34
	West Virginia	Charleston	1863	35
	Nevada	Carson City	1864	36
	Nebraska	Lincoln	1867	37

Shores

	State	Capital	Admitted	
m.	Colorado North Dakota South Dakota Montana	Denver Bismarck Pierre Helena	1876 1889 1889 1889	38 39 40 41
n.	Washington Idaho Wyoming	Olympia Boise Cheyenne	1889 1890 1890	42 43 44
o.	Utah Oklahoma New Mexico	Salt Lake City Oklahoma City Santa Fe	1896 1907 1912	45 46 47
p.	Arizona Alaska Hawaii	Phoenix Juneau Honolulu	1912 1959 1959	48 49 50

4. Make a small notebook about your state and city. Daily assignments are given to include in your notebook. These are under the headings State or Local History. Add important events to the existing timeline or make a separate corresponding timeline for state or local history.

   Use the public library for studying state and local history. Ask the librarian for help in finding books on your state, county, and/or city. From the Yellow Pages find places to visit in your area. Look under Chamber of Commerce, tourist information, historical sites and societies, museums, etc. Also, check national, state, county, and city government listings to find parks and historical monuments.

5. Read a biography on Fanny Crosby

Shores
Week 1

Week One Planning Guide

Gather Information on the Following:

(See suggested sources listed)

1. Causes of diseases
   —<u>The Young Scientist Book of Medicine</u> (Usborne)

2. How germs get in the body and how infections spread
   —<u>The Young Scientist Book of Medicine</u> (Usborne)

3. Bacteria and Viruses
   —<u>The Young Scientist Book of Medicine</u> (Usborne)
   —<u>Bacteria and Viruses</u> by LeMaster (Childrens Press)

4. Meningitis
   —Medical dictionary
   —Family medical book

5. Scarlet fever
   —Medical dictionary
   —Family medical book

6. Measles
   —Medical dictionary
   —Family medical book

7. Immunizations
   —<u>Inspector Bodyguard Patrols the Land of U</u>, "How Your Body Fights Chickenpox," by Vicki Cobb
   —<u>Basic Care Bulletin</u>, Medical Training Institute of America
   —<u>The Young Scientist Book of Medicine</u> (Usborne)
   —<u>Bacteria and Viruses</u> by LeMaster (Childrens Press)

8. Purpose of and United States relationship to territories (both past and present)

9. Your state's history and resources
   —Encyclopedia
   —<u>American the Beautiful—(State Name)</u> (Childrens Press)

10. Eyes and eyesight
    —<u>The Young Scientist Book of the Human Body</u> (Usborne)
    —<u>Input and Output</u> (Provision Media)

11. Immune system

Page 119

Shores
Week 1

12. A biography on Fanny Crosby
—Fanny Crosby: Writer of 8,000 Songs
—The Blind Poet book and tape set by Doris Moose

Gather These Items:

1. Agar
—Combine
   1 boullion cube
   2 envelopes of Knox gelatin
   1 c. boiling water
   Pour into twelve sterilized dishes
—Explorabook by John Cassidy (The Exploratorium)
—Local hospital or lab
2. Cellophane tape
3. Cow's eye
—Slaughter house
4. Bible concordance
5. Video, "Immunizations: A Gift, An Obligation"
—Contact public health department, pediatrician, or local hospital to arrange viewing
6. Laura Ingalls Wilder Songbook by E. Garson

Suggested Field Trips:

1. Watch trains turn around in a railroad hump yard.
2. Visit a railroad museum. Ride an old-fashioned steam engine.

Notes:

Page 120

Shores
Week 1

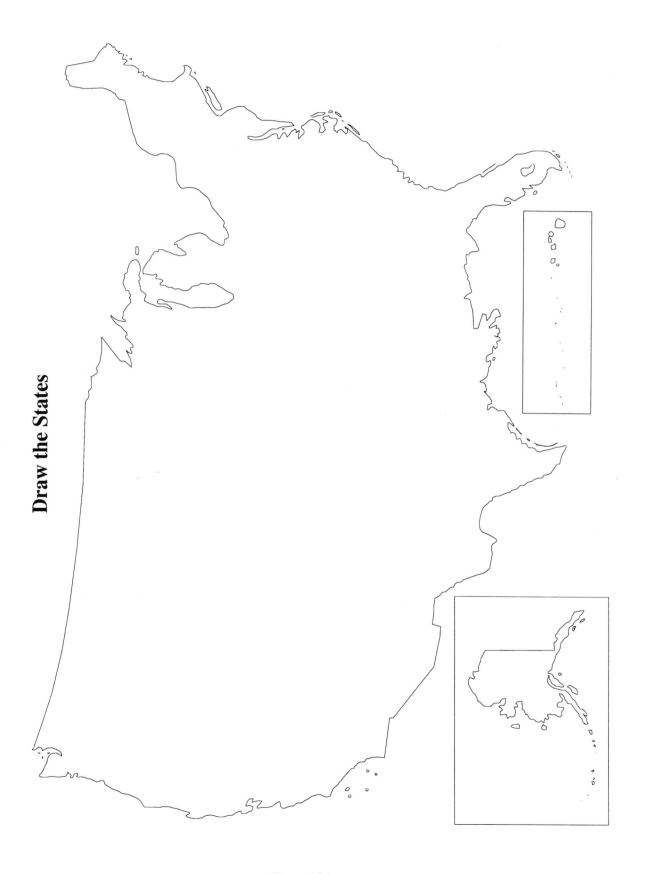

Draw the States

Shores
Week 1

Read Chapters 1 and 2.

Reading Comprehension:

Chapter 1
1. Who had scarlet fever? Who was caring for the ill?
2. What had happened to Mary as the result of her illness?
3. What had been Mary's reaction to her misfortune?
4. What type of communication had Mary and Laura forever lost (page 2)?
5. Why did Pa not like the country? What did he want to do? Why had the family not followed Pa's desires?
6. Who came to the Ingalls' house and what did she want?
7. What did they think about riding on a train?
8. What enabled them to pay their debts before moving on? What might a family with lesser character have done?

Chapter 2
9. What was Jack's reaction to moving? Where had Jack previously traveled with the family?
10. Why had Laura recently neglected Jack? Did she feel that he had understood?
11. Where did Jack sleep and why? What did Laura do that night before bedtime?
12. What was Pa's discovery the next morning?
13. What did Laura regret (page 13)?
14. What did Laura imagine Jack doing at the Happy Hunting Grounds?
15. What did Laura now know (page 14)?

Activities:

History	1.	Memorize and mark on your United States map Section 3.a. from General Activities.
History	2.	Study the purposes of United States territories, past and present.
Science	3.	Some sources think Mary may have developed meningitis from the scarlet fever. Research the cause, signs, symptoms, and effect of both meningitis and scarlet fever. What prevents these diseases from being as frequently catastrophic as they were in Laura's day? *(There are several causes of meningitis. It can be either bacterial or viral. Presently there is an immunization against one type of meningitis. That immunization is called the HIB. This probably would not have helped Mary. Antibiotics and steroids are used to treat bacterial meningitis. Be sure to include a brief study of cerebral spinal fluid. Scarlet fever is treated with antibiotics.)*
Science	4.	Explain to your child that immunizations cause the person to have protection against a particular disease. They cause the body's lymphocytes, or white blood cells, to distinguish the disease organism from the body and to neutralize or eliminate it upon site. Either the dead bacteria, dead virus, safely rendered virus, or toxin produced by the bacteria is injected into the person to cause an immunoresponse. Being immunized is like having the ability to read "Danger—bridge out"; it's

Shores
Week 1

like having a warning and protection from disaster. Being unimmunized is like not knowing how to read and finding a cliff instead of a bridge.

Science 5. Research how antibiotics are generally produced and obtained from bacteria, yeasts, or molds. (*Antibiotic compounds are antagonistic to bacteria, especially bad bacteria. Penicillin, the first widely used antibiotic, was accidentally discovered in 1929 when bacteria in a laboratory dish were killed by mold spores floating in the air. Later, they discovered penicillin was ineffective against many types of diseases, especially those caused by viruses. Other antibiotics have since been developed that cause destruction of different bacteria.*)

Science 6. Begin growing bacteria in an agar dish. See General Activities 1.a. and b.

Bible 7. Laura was very weary from caring for the ill and the house. The author, later in her life, suggested reading Matthew 11:28-30 and Romans 8:31-39 when weary. Read these scriptures. Set a schedule to memorize the passage from Romans by the end of this unit.

Writing 8. Write about your relationship with an animal and your permanent separation by death or change in location.

State Geography 9. Draw a map of your state. Label with agricultural, mineral, forest products, and industries.

Literature 10. Fanny Crosby (1820-1915) was alive during the same time period as Mary. Because they were both blind they faced some of the same challenges. Read a biography of the blind poet Fanny Crosby. Finish by the end of Week Three.

General 11. Remember this week to schedule and make time for General Activities.

DAY 2

Read Chapters 3 and 4.

Reading Comprehension:

Chapter 3
1. What had they done preparing for their departure?
2. How did Laura compare traveling in a wagon to traveling on a train (page 16)?
3. Why did Mary delight in the fact that she could tell that Laura was fidgeting? What senses, other than sight, did she use?
4. Why did Laura move to the other side of Carrie (page 18)?
5. Who heard the train first?
6. How did Mary "see" the seat (page 20)?
7. For what future event in Laura's life did the job of being Mary's eyes prepare her? (*By describing the world around her through necessity to Mary, Laura became equipped to write descriptive books.*)

Page 123

Shores
Week 1

Chapter 4

8. Who helped get the luggage to the motel?
9. What fueled the train (page 29)?
10. How did the train turn around?
11. What was Laura's opinion of Pa (page 31)?
12. How did the town sound to the Ingalls?
13. Why did they dread going to the dining room?
14. Why were the dishes covered with screen?
15. Who cut Mary's meat?
16. What did the waitress assume about the Ingalls? Why do most families come in the spring?
17. What did they do while they waited for Pa?

Activities:

Memorize	1.	Memorize and mark on your United States map Section 3.b. from General Activities.
State Geography	2.	Draw a map of your state. Label with landmarks and geographical features. Write about the land, the elements, and the Indians whom the first explorers of your state's region probably encountered.
Science	3.	Study about types of viruses. Divide a piece of paper into three equal vertical sections. Label each section with the following headings: Bacteria, Both Bacteria and Viruses, and Viruses. List as many diseases as possible under each category.
Health/Art	4.	Research how germs get into the body and how infections spread. Use this information to make a health poster.
Science	5.	Study about measles and rubella. (Measles is another disease that can cause blindness.)
Writing	6.	Look around. Pretend that you are being Mary's eyes. Write two paragraphs describing what you see.
Science	7.	What event on page 24 proves that their society did not apply the knowledge of the germ theory?
Living	8.	Mimic how they washed their hands (page 32).
Field Trip	9.	Visit a railroad station with a hump yard and watch the trains turn around.
Field Trip	10.	Visit a train museum. Ride an antique steam engine.
Vocabulary	11.	What are satchels (page 29)?
Bible	12.	People can be physically blind as Mary was, or spiritually blind. Look up blind (spiritually) in a Bible concordance. Discuss the causes and effects of spiritual blindness. (John 12:40; II Corinthians 4:4; I John 2:11.)
Health	13.	View video: "Immunizations: A Gift, An Obligation." This gives an understandable overview of many diseases that, due to immunizations, are uncommon today. It is very much pro-immunizations.

Page 124

Shores
Week 1

DAY 3

Read Chapters 5 and 6.

Reading Comprehension:

Chapter 5
1. What did they eat for lunch (page 39)?
2. Were the Ingalls environmentally conscious?
3. Who was Lena? What did she offer to have Laura help her with?
4. Why did Hi and family owe the railroad money?
5. What woke Laura?
6. Why did Lena not undress?

Chapter 6
7. What did Laura and Lena think about being married young?
8. What did the young bride's mother think about the marriage?
9. When would be the next time Lena would have such a carefree afternoon (page 55)? What had they done?

Activities:

History | 1. | Memorize and mark on your United States map Section 3.c. from General Activities.

State History | 2. | Write about the first white men to come to your state. (Missionaries, trappers, explorers.)

Science | 3. | Study about the eye. What different parts of the eye are needed to see? What can impair vision or cause blindness?

Science | 4. | Dissect a cow's eye. Identify each part of the eye.

Language | 5. | Explain the common saying "You look as if butter would melt in your mouths" (page 51).

Bible | 6. | What commands did God give to man in Genesis 1:28-30? How have the Ingalls obeyed this command?

Music | 7. | Sing from Laura Ingalls Wilder Songbook, page 110.

Page 125

Shores
Week 1

DAY 4

Read Chapters 7 and 8.

Reading Comprehension:

Chapter 7
1. In the second paragraph on page 58, how was Laura able to tell how big the river gets?
2. Look at the last complete paragraph on page 58. What does the last sentence in this paragraph mean to you?
3. How was this prairie different from the others?
4. What scared the Ingalls?
5. What surprise awaited Ma at camp?

Chapter 8
6. What kept Laura from quickly fetching the water?
7. What did Pa sternly warn Laura about? *(Pa warned Laura to avoid the men.)* What was Carrie's response? What was Laura's inward response (page 76)?
8. Pa was pleased to see that everything was nicely arranged. What did he notice was missing?
9. Besides work, what did the girls do for enjoyment?
10. How did Mary know Laura had just put her bonnet on?

Activities:

History	1.	Memorize and mark on your United States map Section 3.d. from General Activities.
State History/ Writing	2.	Research what factors opened the area of your state to settlers (political, economic, railroad, homesteading, gold rush, etc.). Write one or two pages about this time in your state's history.
Art	3.	Using your favorite medium, illustrate the picture described on page 77.
Writing	4.	By dictation write the first complete paragraph on page 77. Correct by comparing to the book. Explain any mistakes.
Bible	5.	Pa warned Laura to avoid the men because of their rough language. What does the Bible say about perverse talk? (Proverbs 2:11-14; 4:24; 6:12; 8:13). How can perverse talk reveal the character of the man? Could Pa have been worried about more than the girls hearing rough talk? If so, what?
Science/Health	6.	Everyone in the Ingalls' family had been exposed to the same organism that caused blindness in Mary. Research what factors increase or decrease one's immune system.
Living	7.	Wear a blindfold; attempt to do simple tasks such as using the bathroom, washing your hands, or eating a meal.
Music	8.	Sing from <u>Laura Ingalls Wilder Songbook</u>, page 87.

Page 126

Shores
Week 2

Week Two Planning Guide

Gather Information on the Following:

(See suggested sources listed)

1. History of your state

2. Your state's constitution

3. The invention and history of the train

4. The history of railroads
   —Cornerstone of Freedom: The Story of the Golden Spike by Robert Greene

5. Motivational gifts
   —Institute in Basic Life Principles Advanced Seminar Textbook
   —Appendix of The Prairie Primer

6. Migration of birds

7. Tuberculosis

8. Chain of command, checks and balances of power in state and local government

Gather These Items:

1. A copy of your state's constitution
2. Duck meat
3. Pineapple Story, Institute in Basic Life Principles
4. Laura Ingalls Wilder Songbook by E. Garson

Suggested Field Trips:

1. Visit state historical sites or historical museums.
2. Take a duck hunting trip.

Notes:

Shores
Week 2

DAY 1

Read Chapters 9 and 10.

Reading Comprehension:

Chapter 9
1. What did the company do when someone was too old to work?
2. What should Laura do to keep the wind from drying out her hair?
3. What was the camp upset about? What were they going to do about it?
4. What do you think Pa did that night? What do you think happened to Jerry?

Chapter 10
5. What did Laura's mom tell her a lady should act like? Are the cultural expectations the same today?
6. How were Lena and Laura able to see one another? What did they do while they milked the cows?
7. Why were they leveling the tracks (page 101)?
8. What was the key to being a good boss?
9. How long do you think Pa and Laura watched the railroad being constructed?

Activities:

History	1.	Memorize and mark on your United States map Section 3.e. from General Activities.
State History/ Writing	2.	Research events that occurred in your state prior to statehood. Was it a territory? If so, discuss that period of history further. Who was the governing authority? Write one or two pages about this period of time.
Art	3.	Draw a picture of what the dump wagons looked like (page 103).
Living	4.	List the steps to building a railroad.
Character	5.	"Rome wasn't built in a day" is a common saying. Explain what this means to you. Read on page 105 the sentence where Pa made this comment. Are you working on any long-range projects?
History	6.	Read about the invention of trains.
Bible	7.	What traits does the Bible say make a good boss or leader? (Ephesians 4:9; Colossians 4:12; Mark 10:42-45.) *(God has given each person "motivational gifts." Read Romans 12:3-8. A Christian's personal gift is his "frame of reference" through which he speaks or acts as a Christian. All believers have one of the motivational gifts as listed in Romans 12:6-8.)* What are the seven motivational gifts listed? *(God gives the individual the desire to accomplish His will and the power to do it. For further information see Appendix A.)* According to Romans 12:6, what is the supernatural power that God gives the believer to accomplish His will? *(Failing to know his gift, the Christian may be influenced and persuaded to be and act like everyone else rather than uniquely contributing his*

Page 128

Shores
Week 2

part to the body of Christ with actions that are inwardly motivated.)
Which gift would enjoy orchestrating the construction of a railroad? What
motivational gift do you think your child exhibits? Which one does your
child believe he has?

Music   8.   Sing from <u>Laura Ingalls Wilder Songbook</u>, pages 34 and 119.

General   9.   Remember this week to schedule and make time for General Activities.

DAY 2

Read Chapters 11 and 12.

Reading Comprehension:

Chapter 11
1.   How was Pa's job different to Laura than any other he had worked?
2.   What happened as Laura watched from the shanty door?
3.   What did Pa bring to the house? What did Laura see in Pa's hip pocket?
4.   What happened on pay day? Explain the pay system.
5.   What did Big Jerry do? Why do you think he did it?
6.   What happened at the Stebbins' camp?
7.   Why did Laura like where they lived?
8.   When would Pa look for a homestead?

Chapter 12
9.   What had Pa mistakenly shot? How big was the wing span (page 124)? What did they do with it?
10.   Tell about the pelican. What did they use it for (page 125)?
11.   How were they collecting feathers? What would they do with the feathers?
12.   Where did Laura want to go? Why must they stay there?
13.   Why must Laura be a teacher?

Activities:

History   1.   Memorize and mark on your United States map Section 3.f. from General Activities.

Geography   2.   Find Iowa on the map.

Bible/Language   3.   Explain the common sayings "Better a live dog than a dead lion" (Read Ecclesiastes 9:4.) and "Discretion is the better part of valor (page 121)." Discuss.

History   4.   Prepare for a written report (Day 4) by reading about the history of railroads.

Page 129

Shores
Week 2

State History/ Writing	5.	Research what requirements were met to obtain statehood. What factors encouraged statehood? How and when was your state constitution drafted? Is there anything unique about it? Write one or two pages from your research.
Art/Science	6.	Identify and draw each bird mentioned on page 124.
Geography	7.	Find Montana on the map. Mark it with a picture of Uncle Henry.
Cooking	8.	Eat duck for dinner.
Bible	9.	Pa and Laura learned about relinquishing their own desires. Pa gave up his desire to continue west because of Ma. Laura purposed to become a school teacher, although this was not her heart's desire. Read I Corinthians 13:5; Ephesians 5:25-28; Matthew 5:37-40; James 3:14-18; Romans 12:10. What do these verses speak about to you? Today, Americans have developed self-reliance and self-will to the point of creating idols of them. Many people make plans for their life without ever seeking the heart of God. The Lord Jesus surrendered His will to Father God (Matthew 26:39, 41). One way to begin learning self-denial is through fasting. To further the study on yielding rights, read and discuss the Pineapple Story.
Field Trip	10.	Visit a state historical site, such as a battlefield, president's home, mission, fort, or trading post.

DAY 3

Read Chapters 13 and 14.

Reading Comprehension:

Chapter 13
1. Why would Laura not see Lena for a while?
2. Why could Pa not cut down trees for a house?
3. Why must they have coal?
4. Why did it look as if they must go East for the winter? What did Laura think about leaving?
5. What enabled them to stay the winter?
6. What was Mr. Boast's problem? his creative solution?
7. Why were there no laws and no officers, not even a county sheriff, to help Mr. Boast with his problem?
8. Where was Mr. Boast going?

Chapter 14
9. What are the advantages and disadvantages of hardwood floors?
10. What staples had the surveyors left?
11. How was Mary made comfortable first? What did Mary do to help the family?
12. How long did it take to get things settled in?
13. What was a grand dessert (page 143)?
14. Tell about Grace's trundle bed.

Page 130

Shores
Week 2

Activities:

History   1.   Memorize and mark on your United States map Section 3.g. from General Activities.

State History   2.   Research the history of your state from its induction into statehood until now. Finish by writing a report of what you learned.

State History/Art 3.   Draw your state's flag, bird, flower, and/or tree to make a cover for your state notebook. Why were these chosen and adopted? Does your state have a nickname? How did it come about?

Writing   4.   Write by dictation the paragraph on page 137 talking about Mr. Boast laughing. Correct by comparing to the original. Explain about the presence of a semicolon and its use. *(Each clause before and after the semicolon is a grammatically complete sentence, but the thoughts are related in a way that the writer does not want them separated.)*

Bible   5.   On what conditions were Laura's relatives leaving? Discuss Deuteronomy 32:35; Matthew 5:38-48; Romans 12:9-16; and Proverbs 21:22 in the context of their leaving.

Science   6.   Study about the migration of birds. Laura observed the birds alternate leaders. She felt it gave rest to the leader. What makes being in the front so difficult on the lead bird? *(The lead bird meets with all the force of air resistance. The leader must be strong enough to break this resistance; when he does this, he creates an "empty space" behind him of less resistance for the other birds. Try this principle by pulling your finger through standing water and feel the resistance.)*

Bible   7.   God gives laughter (Job 8:21; Psalm 126:2). Why do you think Pa and Mr. Boast were laughing? Read Proverbs 24:17-18. Do you think these verses could apply to this situation? Why or why not?

Music   8.   Sing from <u>Laura Ingalls Wilder Songbook</u>, page 40.

DAY 4

Read Chapters 15, 16, and 17.

Reading Comprehension:

Chapter 15
1.   Who helped Ma get breakfast?
2.   Who came by and got Pa? What did Pa do while he was gone?
3.   How did Laura assist Pa?
4.   Describe their evening.

Page 131

Shores
Week 2

Chapter 16
5.   What did Mary do to help the family?
6.   What did the Ingalls' women do after the housework was completed?
7.   What work did Pa do in the winter?
8.   What did Pa and Laura do during the storm? How did Pa make a checkerboard?

Chapter 17
9.   What did Carrie and Laura do for fun?
10. What did they see?
11. Were they in good physical shape? How did being in good physical shape help?
12. What did they use to keep warm that night?

Activities:

History	1.	Memorize and mark on your United States map Section 3.h. from General Activities.
History/Writing	2.	Write your report on trains and railroads. Include the government's role, the effect on westward expansion, the golden spike, and the race across country.
Science	3.	Study about consumption (tuberculosis). Describe orally the method of transmission, factors that cause the disease to become active, symptoms, and past treatment. Include information about the sanitariums used for isolating purposes. What methods are presently used to screen for the presence of the bacteria in the body? *(Skin test.)* The presence of disease? *(Culture, x-ray.)* What is the treatment? *(Special antibiotics taken for extended periods of time.) (Because of AIDS and the recent immigration of people with very high rates of tuberculosis to the United States, there have been increasing numbers of recent outbreaks of this disease.)*
Character	4.	After your study about tuberculosis, did Pa perform a risky task going after the old man? Do you think Pa knew that tuberculosis was contagious? If Pa had known of the risk of contracting the disease, do you think he still would have performed the deed?
Dance	5.	Learn a simple polka and/or waltz.
Geography	6.	What was meant by the supposition in the first sentence on page 154? Would the climate be just as warm going west as it would going south? Is this true? *(No, it is not, as the Ingalls will discover in* The Long Winter. *Warmer weather occurs when the earth's tilt on its axis gives the southern regions greater exposure to the sun's radiation.)* Examine the latitude and longitude lines (degrees) on a map.
Art	7.	Laura's clothing was described on page 164. Illustrate each article of clothing; label and state the type of yarn used in making the article.
State History	8.	Draw a diagram depicting the chain of command and checks and balances of power in your state and local government.
Music	9.	Sing from Laura Ingalls Wilder Songbook, pages 84 and 126.

Page 132

Shores
Week 3

Week Three Planning Guide

Gather Information on the Following:

(See suggested sources listed)

1. Louis Braille
   —<u>Louis Braille, The Boy Who Invented Books for the Blind</u> by Margaret Davidson (Scholastic)

2. Preventing sexual abuse
   —<u>Private Zone</u> by Frances Dayee

3. Historical information about the first settlers in your city

Gather These Items:

1. Dried applesauce
2. Items to make recycled gifts
3. <u>Laura Ingalls Wilder Songbook</u> by E. Garson

Suggested Field Trips:

1. Visit your state's capitol.
2. Interview your representative to the state legislature (See Week 3, Day 2).
3. Visit a school for the blind.

Notes:

Shores
Week 3

DAY 1

Read Chapters 18, 19, and 20.

Reading Comprehension:

Chapter 18
1. Why do you think the wolves returned?
2. Do you think God had a hand in showing them the land to live on?

Chapter 19
3. What had the Ingalls girls recycled for Christmas?
4. What was for supper on Christmas Eve?

Chapter 20
5. Who were the visitors?
6. Why had the Boasts not waited until spring?

Activities:

History	1.	Memorize and mark on your United States map Section 3.i. from General Activities.
Writing	2.	Reread the highlights of the Ingalls' Christmases on page 178 and 179. Write a composition from remembrances of your past Christmases.
State History/ Writing	3.	Write about last week's historical field trip and the part it played in the history of your state.
Bible/Art	4.	Read Romans 12:13; I Timothy 3:2; Titus 1:8; and I Peter 4:9-10. Each speaks of being a good hostess. List each of the ways Mrs. Ingalls was a good hostess. Make a poster displaying an example of how to be a good host(ess). Caption your poster with one of the verses above.
Crafts	5.	Make some "recycled" gifts.
Music	6.	Sing from Laura Ingalls Wilder Songbook, page 142.
General	7.	Remember this week to schedule and make time for General Activities.

Shores
Week 3

DAY 2

Read Chapters 21 and 22.

Reading Comprehension:

Chapter 21
1. How were Mr. and Mrs. Boast good guests?
2. Show how the plates and silverware were set (page 189).
3. What was Grace told about children's behavior (page 191)?
4. What creative way did Ma solve the dilemma of no presents for the Boasts?
5. What secrets had Carrie and Mary kept?
6. Why did Ma put Grace's new coat away (page 194)?
7. How did Ma make good biscuits without sour milk?
8. What was Christmas dinner?
9. Explain why the common saying "Hunger is the best sauce" is true. *(Socrates used this saying in "Cicero" followed by Erasmus in 1466; and later Cervantes quoted it in "Don Quixote" and Shakesphere in "MacBeth.")*
10. What was Laura's attitude about growing up?

Chapter 22
11. What did Mrs. Boast do for the New Year?
12. What did Pa think about the winter (page 205)?
13. How many acres had Mr. Boast filed on?
14. What detained Pa from filing?
15. What did Mr. Boast use instead of coal?
16. When the chores were done, what did Carrie, Laura, and Mrs. Boast do?
17. What did Mrs. Boast give Laura? While Laura read, what did Carrie and Ma do? What was "wrong" with the story?
18. How were stormy afternoons spent (page 208)?
19. What would Mrs. Boast share with Ma?
20. What had Pa promised Ma before leaving Minnesota (page 209)?
21. What did Mrs. Boast show Ma how to make?
22. When was Laura the happiest (page 213)?

Activities:

History	1.	Memorize and mark on your United States map Section 3.j. from General Activities.
State History/ Writing	2.	Gather information by phone, personal visit, or by letter from your local state representative about himself, the motivation behind his desire to be a representative, and how he sees the state legislature working. Write a brief biographical sketch of this person.
Vocabulary	3.	What are wristlets (page 192)?
Writing	4.	What did Pa do with Grace that Laura remembered him doing with her?
Living	5.	Eat dried applesauce.
Writing	6.	Write a letter to a friend.

Page 135

Shores
Week 3

Bible 7. Ma gave her best handkerchief and the present she had made for Pa. Read I Timothy 6:17-19 and Hebrews 13:16. Apply these verses to the situation.

Music 8. Sing from <u>Laura Ingalls Wilder Songbook</u>, pages 18, 26, 36, 56, and 124.

DAY 3

Read Chapters 23 and 24.

Reading Comprehension:

Chapter 23
1. Who were the surprise visitors?
2. What was Ma thankful for regarding the time they all had scarlet fever? What did Ma praise in Mary?
3. What was the first thing that Ma did when company arrived?
4. What news regarding Mary did he bring?
5. What made Laura want to study hard?
6. What important homesteading news did the preachers bring? What month was it?
7. What was Pa going to do in the morning? When was the last time he had planned to file?
8. Who did the naming of the town of De Smet honor (page 223)?

Chapter 24
9. Who arrived while Ma was packing Pa's lunch?
10. Why did the Ingalls allow the strangers to stay? What do you think about the Ingalls charging for food and lodging? How much did he charge (page 227)?
11. Did Pa leave the very next day? Why do you think that he did not?
12. Applied to the story, what does the common saying "Might as well be hung for a sheep as a lamb" mean (page 231)?

Activities:

History 1. Memorize and mark on your United States map Section 3.k. from General Activities.

Geography 2. Locate Iowa on a map. How do you think Mary will get there?

History 3. Read a book about Louis Braille. Schedule to finish by the end of Week 4.

State History/ 4. Write one page about a favorite event in your state's history or draw a
Writing map that cites famous places in your state's history.

Bible 5. Reread the first paragraph on page 219. Discuss what you think happened. *(The Lord gives times of refreshing. Read Acts 3:19. Paul had refreshment from godly visitors. See I Corinthians 16:17-18. Refreshment comes*

Page 136

Shores
Week 3

from the Holy Spirit.) Discuss this person of the Godhead with your child(ren).

Vocabulary   6.   What is a greenhorn (page 225)?

Reasoning   7.   God prepares us for future events. What previous event in the Ingalls' lives prepared them to care for the many house guests they had? *(Their time in Burr Oak, Iowa, assisting in running a hotel.)*

Safety   8.   Compare the preacher's visit with the five strange men. What precautions did Ma take? What do you think she might have been worried about with the men and her girls? Discuss preventing sexual abuse with your child(ren).

Bible   9.   The Bible tells us to be as wise as serpents, but as peaceful as doves (Matthew 10:16). How did the Ingalls perform this principle?

DAY 4

Read Chapters 25 and 26.

Reading Comprehension:

Chapter 25
1. Why did Ma not allow others to stay in the house anymore?
2. Explain the common saying "Fat was on the fire" (page 236).
3. What did Laura think might happen if Pa did not get the claim?
4. Retell about Pa getting the claim.
5. Who helped Pa get the claim? How did Laura identify him in the story (page 236)?
6. Explain this common saying "There's nothing for certain, but death and taxes."

Chapter 26
7. How did Laura feel about working (page 240)?
8. Why did Ma think the supplies cost so much more?
9. What decreased the amount of money Ma was making?
10. What caused their business to stop (page 243)?
11. What did they enjoy about no longer having guests in their house?
12. To what would the money they saved go?
13. What made Pa sad?
14. Why were the girls arguing?

Activities:

History   1.   Memorize and mark on your United States map Section 3.1. from General Activities.

Reasoning   2.   Why does Laura's nickname suit her?

Shores
Week 3

Local History/
Writing

3. For the remainder of this unit, study the history of your city. Research who were the first settlers in your area. What brought them to the area? Write their story and include it in your notebook.

Literature

4. Works of fiction contain basic elements that form the structure of the story. They are:

a. **Setting**—the time and place the story occurs.

b. **Characters**—the people in the story.

c. **Conflict**—the forces in the story acting against each other. These forces could be an external struggle between one character and another, or against the elements of nature. Two opposing forces could be within one character, which creates an internal conflict.

d. **Crisis**—the point in the story when the conflict is at its height.

e. **Climax**—the point in the story where the outcome of the conflict is resolved.

Identify each of the above elements in Chapter 25.

Bible

5. The Ingalls worked hard for the money, but who provided it? (Genesis 22:14; Psalm 65:9-10; Matthew 6:26.) God has many names referring to His character. One of His Names is Jehovah Jireh—the Lord will provide.

Music

6. Sing from <u>Laura Ingalls Wilder Songbook</u>, page 112.

Character

7. What inspiration did you draw from Fanny Crosby life? Which was your favorite poem or song which she wrote? How could the Ingalls have drawn inspiration from this?

Shores
Week 4

Week Four Planning Guide

Gather Information on the Following:

(See suggested sources listed)

1. Different architectural styles and periods

2. History of your city

3. History of the oldest standing buildings in your city

4. Influential people in your city (past and present)

5. Cottonwood tree
   —<u>Trees</u> A Golden Guide (Golden Press)

Gather These Items:

1. Pictures of your city's downtown in different stages of development or in different periods of history
2. <u>Laura Ingalls Wilder Country</u> by William Anderson
3. <u>Laura Ingalls Wilder Songbook</u> by E. Garson

Suggested Field Trips:

1. Visit the historical society or museum of your city.
2. Visit the oldest standing buildings in your city.

Notes:

Page 139

Shores
Week 4

DAY 1

Read Chapters 27 and 28.

Reading Comprehension:

Chapter 27
1. To where did the Ingalls move? How did Laura feel in town versus on the prairie?
2. What did Laura awake to one cold morning? How did this happen?
3. What was fortunate about the blizzard occurring at night (page 252)?
4. On page 253, what did Pa say about waiting for things to suit us? Discuss.
5. What did Laura not like about town? What did Carrie like about it?
6. What did Laura's mother want her to do with the next-door girls? What was their reaction?
7. What was Laura's attitude about being a teacher (page 256)?
8. What event encouraged Pa to move to the claim quickly?

Chapter 28
9. Why was each of the Ingalls happy to be moving (page 259)?
10. Who is Almanzo? Where does he live in relation to Laura? What impressed Laura about him?

Activities:

History	1.	Memorize and mark on your United States map Section 3.m. from General Activities.
Science/Language	2.	Compare the sounds of the country to that of the city. Make two columns to list them.
Living/Reasoning	3.	Pa took time to dig a cellar. What was the importance of a cellar?
Vocabulary	4.	What is a slough (page 264)? Slough is a homograph. From the dictionary what are the two meanings of slough? Which dictionary respelling fits the word usage in the story?
Local History	5.	What are the oldest buildings in your town? For what purpose were they built? Are they used for the same purpose today? Take pictures of these buildings. Label each with their past and present uses, and include them in your local history notebook.
History	6.	Look at pictures of architectural styles from different periods and regions. Study the history of architecture in the United States. What styles have influenced American architects? What styles are found in your city?
Music	7.	Sing from <u>Laura Ingalls Wilder Songbook</u>, pages 12 and 114.
General	8.	Remember this week to schedule and make time to conclude General Activities.

Page 140

Shores
Week 4

DAY 2

Read Chapters 29 and 30.

Reading Comprehension:

Chapter 29
1. What work did Pa accomplish in one day?
2. What playfulness did Laura exhibit (page 271)?
3. What happened to Grace? What was their fear?

Chapter 30
4. How did Laura find Grace? Where was she?
5. What had caused the unusual formation with violets?
6. Explain the common saying "A short horse is soon curried" (page 284).
7. Putting up what two things made this house seem like home?
8. What period of America's history was gone? In what period did they now live (page 285)?

Activities:

History	1.	Memorize and mark on your United States map Section 3.n. from General Activities.
Reasoning	2.	How deep was their well? Which well was deeper, the one in Indian Territory or this one? What does it mean when you hit water?
History	3.	Research the Timber Culture Act. Why did the government enact this?
Science/Art	4.	Research cottonwood trees. Identify and find one in your area. Draw a picture of one. Use construction paper to cut out leaves the same size and shape as a cottonwood. Place cutout leaves under your picture and using the side of a crayon, color lightly over your picture.
Local History	5.	Research and write about the history of your city. What factors have caused major increases or decreases in the population? Try to find old pictures of your city. Include the origin of your city's name.
Bible	6.	Read Matthew 18:10-14. Remember how Laura put all her effort into finding Grace and the joy she had in finding her? How much more does God rejoice when one of his children returns to Him!
Music	7.	Sing from <u>Laura Ingalls Wilder Songbook</u>, page 21.

Page 141

Shores
Week 4

DAY 3

Read Chapters 31 and 32. This Finishes the Book. Also read <u>Laura Ingalls Wilder Country</u>, Chapter 5, "Silver Lake and the Dakota Prairie."

Reading Comprehension:

Chapter 31
1. How did Laura help her Pa?
2. Why did Pa like living near the Big Slough?
3. What did Ma not like about it?
4. What did Pa do about the mosquitoes?

Chapter 32
5. After Pa had taken care of the mosquito problem, what did He do?
6. In which book did the Ingalls previously need to fight mosquitoes? What were they able to do this time to prevent mosquitoes from entering their house?

Activities:

History	1.	Memorize and mark on your United States map Section 3.o. from General Activities.
Local History/ Writing	2.	What people, past and present, have played an important role in your city? Write one page each on an influential person of today and of yesterday.
Character	3.	In a couple of paragraphs describe the character, Laura. Include her age, sex, relationship to the other characters, and her personality. Review motivational gifts and decide which one may have been hers. What positive character qualities do you see Laura developing?
Music	4.	Sing from <u>Laura Ingalls Wilder Songbook</u>, page 122.

Page 142

Shores
Week 4

DAY 4

Activities:

History	1.	Memorize and mark on your United States map Section 3.p. from General Activities.
Writing	2.	Write a book report about Louis Braille. As a format for your report, use the elements of fiction studied in Week 3, Day 4, Activity 4.
Local History/ Writing	3.	Write one or two pages about a unique occurrence in your city or points of interest to visit.
Social Studies	4.	Write a scripture using braille. This can be done using a stylus to form the raised letters or by writing dots for letters. If you have access, use a braille typewriter.
Bible	5.	Recite Romans 8:31-39.

Finish Any Undone Activities!

Long Winter

The Long Winter

The winter of 1880-1881 paralyzed large sections of the American Midwest with unrelenting bitter cold. This tested the survival prowess and character of the homesteaders. The Long Winter is only the Ingalls' story. As Laura recounts, her family was better off than many.

General Activities to Do throughout This Unit:

1. To occupy themselves during the cold winter months, the Ingalls women did handwork. Begin a craft project like Laura or Mary would have done as they sat around the fire. Do a needlework project of knitting, crocheting, embroidering, or tatting. Or observe someone who does some needlework, and note the finished project. Boys who choose not to do needlework or mending may whittle, do carpentry projects, or make latch-hook rugs (Almanzo made rugs for their home).

2 Memorize Psalm 34 or Psalm 37. Write or type verses on index cards. As your child memorizes them, place the cards in a file box for later quizzing.

3. The Long Winter is about the Ingalls' struggle to survive a very hard winter shut off from outside supplies and help. Discuss with your child the ways your family could be cut off from outside help. *(Blizzards, earthquakes, hurricanes, tornadoes, etc.)* Research and discuss with your child the people and agencies today organized to help in crises. *(Red Cross, search and rescue teams, the National Guard.)*

4. Discuss with your child what precautions you have taken to provide for your family in case of an emergency.

5. Perhaps you have not taken the necessary precautions. Research what items are needed; as a project, prepare an emergency basket for your home or car. You can obtain information about emergency preparedness from your local Red Cross Chapter or write:

   Public Awareness
   USDA, FSIS, ILA
   Room 1165 South Building
   Washington, D.C. 20250

   Have your basket completed by the end of this unit.

6. Show your child(ren) where in your home the cutoff valve is located for your gas and water. Explain why these may need to be turned off in the case of an emergency.

7. Complete a study about the weather. The Weather Report by Mike Graf is recommended.

8. Read a biography of Samuel Morse.

9. Begin a daily exercise program using aerobic, strengthening, and flexibility exercises. Put a star on the calendar each day this goal is met.

Long Winter
Week 1

Week One Planning Guide

Gather Information on the Following:

(See suggested sources listed)

1. Emergency preparedness and survival kits
   —Available through the American Red Cross
   —<u>Survival Skills</u> (Usborne)

2. Muskrats

3. Homesteading in the United States in the 1800's
   —Encyclopedia

4. Earth's water cycle and forms of precipitation
   —<u>Raindrops and Rainbows</u> by Rose Wyler, *for younger students*
   —<u>The Weather Report</u> by Mike Graf, *more in-depth*

5. Indians of South Dakota (Sioux and Blackfoot)
   —<u>Horsemen of the Western Plains</u> by Sonya Blecker
   —<u>Tepee Stories</u> by Marguerite Dolch Edward
   —Educational Coloring Book: <u>Plains Indians</u>

6. The Battle of Wounded Knee Creek

7. Medicinal use for ginger

8. Samuel F. B. Morse
   —<u>Samuel F. B. Morse</u> by John Tiner (The Sower Series)
   —<u>Samuel Morse and the Telegraph</u> by Wilma Hays
   —<u>Samuel F. B. Morse</u> by Jean Lee Latham, *for younger students*

9. Rotation of the earth on its axis and the effect this has on sunrise, sunset, and climate

10. Chicken's digestive system

Gather These Items:

1. Items to make ginger water
   —<u>The Little House Cookbook</u> by Barbara M. Walker
2. <u>Laura Ingalls Wilder Songbook</u> by E. Garson

Suggested Field Trips:

Page 146

Long Winter
Week 1

DAY 1

Read Chapters 1 and 2.

Reading Comprehension:

Chapter 1
1. What did Laura do to help?
2. What was Ma's opinion of Laura helping in the fields?
3. What did Mary do to help?
4. What positive character quality did Laura exhibit in this chapter?
5. Was it easy helping Pa?
6. How did Pa know it would be a bad winter?
7. Discuss what Pa said was the difference between animals and humans (page 13).

Chapter 2
8. What did the girls do wrong?
9. Whose fault was it?
10. Who did they meet?

Activities:

Writing/History/
Speech

1. Research and write a two-page report about the Homestead Act of 1862. Complete it by the end of the week. Or present an oral report at the end of the week. Dress in period clothing.

Cooking

2. Make ginger water (see The Little House Cookbook, page 185). What would a similar drink be today?

Living

3. What are some medicinal uses of ginger?

Language

4. On page 8, there is a sentence that describes the difficulty of the work. How is this description different from, if it were simply said, "The work was hard"? *(Descriptive language aids our imagination and imagery building.)* Have you ever worked, played, or exercised so hard that your arms or legs trembled?

Health

5. Pa and Laura worked hard in the fields and they walked most everywhere. They received plenty of exercise living life. There are three types of exercise needed for a healthy life:

    a. **Aerobic**—increases the heart rate significantly (strengthens cardiovascular system, decreases cholesterol, increases endurance, and increases elimination of toxins).

        i. **Weight bearing exercises**—necessary for depositing calcium in the bones. Examples: running, walking, skating, jumping rope.

        ii. **Non-weight bearing exercises**—examples: swimming, bicycling, hoeing.

Page 147

Long Winter
Week 1

    b. **Strengthening**—increases the muscle power. Examples: weight lifting, pull-ups, sit-ups, push-ups, gymnastics, hoeing, shoveling.

    c. **Flexibility**—increases the length of muscles, increases joint mobility, and increases moveability. Examples: stretching, toe touching, ballet, gymnastics.

Make a plan to daily alternate the three types of exercises.

Science/Vocabulary 6. Read about muskrats. Look up "nocturnal" in the dictionary. What animals in your area are nocturnal?

Safety 7. What would happen to a person, if they were very hot and quickly drank very cold water? *(When it is very hot outside, your body works very hard to keep its temperature at 98.6 degrees F. The hypothalamus, a specialized section of the brain, is the command zone for regulating your temperature. First your body sweats. When doing this, it loses electrolytes and water. Second, your respiration [rate of breathing] will increase. This increases water loss and the loss of carbon dioxide. If the carbon dioxide level gets too low trying to cool the body, one may faint. A particularly sensitive receptor site to the temperature of the environment surrounds the mouth. When ice cold water hits these receptor sites, a conflicting message is sent to the hypothalamus and the body may attempt to prepare itself for cold stress. This quick change may cause a headache or stomach ache. Some wives' tales say that drinking very cold water on a hot day has caused death from stroke. Whether true or not, when your body is under stress from heat and exertion, it is safest to drink liquid close to your body's temperature. Your body loses electrolytes through sweating. If after sweating you lick your skin, you will taste salt. These electrolytes are sodium, potassium, and phosphates. The sodium in the bloodstream causes the bloodstream to maintain its water content. With excessive sweating and no replacement of the electrolytes, weakness, tiredness, thirstiness, and dizziness may be noticed. Plain water does not contain these electrolytes. When the electrolytes are returned, the bloodstream volume or plasma balance is returned to normal. Therefore, when your body is stressed by excessive, prolonged heat, it is best to drink Gatorade or a similar drink that contains electrolytes.)*

Bible/Character 8. How do these verses apply to the story and to your life? Proverbs 10:5; 12:11; 20:11?

Bible 9. Discuss Proverbs 4:26 and 6:6-8 in the context of the second chapter.

History 10. As was mentioned in <u>On the Shores of Silver Lake</u>, the telegraph and the railroad followed the frontier. The inventor of the telegraph was Samuel Morse. Read about this important man of history. Plan to complete his biography by the end of this unit.

General 11. Remember this week to schedule and make time for General Activities.

Long Winter
Week 1

DAY 2

Read Chapters 3, 4, and 5.

Reading Comprehension:

Chapter 3
1. Why was Pa worried?
2. What did Ma surprise Pa with?
3. Why did not Laura like to sew? Did she do it anyway? Did she complain?

Chapter 4
4. How could Pa find his way to the stable?
5. Why did they need to be careful with water? What did Laura do to conserve water (page 38)?
6. What did they do all day?

Chapter 5
7. What happened to the cows?
8. What did Pa find?
9. What help did the haystacks provide?

Activities:

Science	1.	Look up "equinoctial" in the dictionary. Study the rotation of the earth on its axis and the effect this has on sunrise, sunset, and climate.
Science/Economics	2.	What does your family do to conserve water? Why does your family try to conserve water?
Science	3.	Learn about the water cycle. Study forms of precipitation.
Music	4.	Sing from <u>Laura Ingalls Wilder Songbook</u>, pages 15 and 50.

DAY 3

Read Chapters 6, 7, and 8.

Reading Comprehension:

Chapter 6
1. What is an Indian summer?
2. Why did Pa think that it would be a bad winter?

Chapter 7
3. What did the Indian have to say? What did the Indian have to gain by warning the settlers? Why do you think he did this?
4. Why was town a better place to spend the winter?
5. Why did Laura want to fly away?

Page 149

Long Winter
Week 1

Chapter 8
6. To where in town did they move?
7. What had Judge Carroll given for the rent due?
8. What did Laura think about people (page 70)?
9. Why did they fill the straw ticks with hay?
10. Where did Pa want to go and why did he not go there?

Activities:

| Bible | 1. | Discuss Genesis 4:9 and Romans 2:13-15 regarding the Indian. |

| History/Writing | 2. | What tribes of Indians lived where Laura's family lived? Read about the Battle of Wounded Knee Creek. Do a report on this last Indian battle. |

| Science | 3. | What is the difference between hay and straw? *(Straw is the stem of grains with the grain removed. It is low in nutrient value, because it is mainly cellulose, non-digestible plant fiber. Hay includes the stem, leaves, and immature seeds. It has a higher protein and nutrient value.)* |

| Language/Science | 4. | What does the common saying "Money is scarcer than hens' teeth" mean? Do hens have teeth? How do chickens eat their food? |

DAY 4

Read Chapters 9 and 10.

Reading Comprehension:

Chapter 9
1. Why were the girls sad before school?
2. What Psalms did Laura know?
3. What did Laura like about Cap?
4. Did Cap get home safely after the storm?
5. Describe how badly the snow affected them (page 94).

Chapter 10
6. What was Almanzo good at?
7. On page 99, discuss Almanzo's justification.
8. What were Almanzo and Royal worried about?
9. What was Almanzo's reason for not wanting to sell the wheat? Was this a wise decision?

Activities:

| Art/ Vocabulary | 1. | Look up "whiffle" in the dictionary. Draw a picture of a tree with whiffle characteristics. |

Page 150

Long Winter
Week 2

Week Two Planning Guide

Gather Information on the Following:

(See suggested sources listed)

1. Dietary intake of fat and its effect on the body
   —

2. Sunrise and sunset times on both the shortest and longest day of the year (locally and in South Dakota)
   —Consult your newspaper's solunar table
   —

3. Wind chill factor
   —<u>The Weather Report</u> by Mike Graf
   —

4. Crude oil, kerosene, coal
   —<u>Coal</u> by Betsy Harvey Kraft
   —<u>Oil and Gas from Fossils to Fuel</u> by Hershel and Joan Nixon
   —<u>Energy and Fuels</u> (Troll)
   —

5. Properties of solutions and mixtures
   —Encyclopedia
   —

6. The eye, cornea and snow-blindedness
   —<u>You and Your Body: Eyes</u> (Troll)
   —<u>The Body Book</u> by Jonathan Miller
   —<u>The Human Body</u> (Usborne)
   —

7. Ultraviolet light
   —

8. Effect of light deprivation
   —

Gather These Items:

1. <u>Laura Ingalls Wilder Songbook</u> by E. Garson

Suggested Field Trip:

1. If you live in a warm climate, plan a field trip to tour some place with a large walk-in freezer, such as an ice cream parlor or a restaurant, to experience all around "cold."

Notes:

Page 151

Long Winter
Week 2

DAY 1

Read Chapters 11 and 12.

Reading Comprehension:

Chapter 11
1. Who came back with Pa?
2. What did the girls remember about him?

Chapter 12
3. How did Laura help Mary?
4. What did Mary enjoy (page 117)?

Activities:

Music	1.	Sing the song on page 108-109, if you know it.
Geography	2.	Find South Dakota on a map of the United States. Discuss latitude and longitude lines on a map. On what latitude line is South Dakota?
Critical Thinking/ Science	3.	At what times does the sun rise and set where you live in January and July? From the previous study of "equinoctial," do you think these times will be the same or different from South Dakota? If different, what will the difference be? Research the sunrise and sunset times in South Dakota.
Economics	4.	How much money did Mr. Edward's leave (page 114), and what is its equivalent in today's terms?
Music	5.	Sing from <u>Laura Ingalls Wilder Songbook</u>, page 148.
General	6.	Remember this week to schedule and make time for General Activities.

DAY 2

Read Chapters 13, 14, and 15.

Reading Comprehension:

Chapter 13
1. What did the Ingalls do for church? Would you like doing that?
2. How cold was it (pages 129-130)?

Page 152

Long Winter
Week 2

Chapter 14
3. What did Laura wish she could do?
4. What do you think was the wisest idea for survival, if caught in a blizzard?
5. Why did Mrs. Boast not come to visit?

Chapter 15
6. What did they do to conserve coal? kerosene (page 140)? Why should they conserve?
7. What did the girls do to occupy their time during the blizzard?
8. What did Ma do to help keep the cold out?

Activities:

Field trip
1. If you live in a warm climate, visit a restaurant or grocery store with a large walk-in freezer to experience all around "cold."

Science/Math
2. What is the "wind chill factor?" Research how to calculate the "wind chill factor."

Bible
3. In light of Chapter 13, discuss Psalm 119:16, 52.

Bible
4. Have a family night like Laura's family did. The children's memory index cards may be used as prompting for the drills.

Writing
5. Write a composition about when you had to remain indoors a long time because of the weather. How did you feel about this?

Science
6. Research the effect of light deprivation on people. Discuss ways to combat the depression it causes during the winter months.

Environment
7. What fuels do we use? How can we conserve them? Give several reasons for conserving fuel.

Science
8. Where does kerosene come from? Study the process of distillation. What other products can be obtained from crude oil? What are their boiling points? Which is extracted first? *(Kerosene is one product extracted from crude oil. Crude oil consists of many different molecules intermingled in a solution. These differing molecules can be separated through the process of distillation, which relies on the scientific law that different substances have different boiling points. As one substance within the crude oil boils and turns to steam, the steam is siphoned off. At the next boiling point, another solution is extracted, and so on.)*

Science
9. A mixture is a combination of substances that forms without chemical reactions. A solution is a special kind of mixture in which a substance is spread evenly throughout another substance. The physical properties of substances can be used to separate mixtures. Separation may occur through filtering, evaporation, or settling. Make different mixtures and solutions. Have child(ren) identify what is a mixture and what is a solution. Discuss ways to separate the mixtures. (e.g.. spaghetti in water, tea with sugar, salt and water, different coins, vinegar with oil.)

Science
10. Research where crude oil comes from. *(Energy cannot be created or destroyed; therefore, oil is a product of another chemical reaction. One "old earth" theory is that over eon of time layers upon layers of dead plant and animal material have been squeezed under great amounts of*

Page 153

Long Winter
Week 2

pressure and heated under the earth's surface to produce underground reservoirs of crude oil. Coal, on the other hand, is decomposed plant life that has undergone pressure in the absence of oxygen.)

Music   11.   Sing from <u>Laura Ingalls Wilder Songbook</u>, page 150.

Read Chapters 16 and 17.

Reading Comprehension:

Chapter 16
1. Where did Pa go and why (page 151)? What took Pa so long (pages 154-155)?
2. What did Ma and the girls do that night?
3. What did Laura want? Was it practical?
4. Who left to go to Preston and why?

Chapter 17
5. What was the family out of? Which supplies were low?
6. What did they do to encourage each other?
7. What was Almanzo doing and why?

Activities:

Living   1.   After dark, shut off the electricity to your home, light a kerosene lantern, sit around and write letters, sing, or read.

Health/Science   2.   Read information about human dietary intake of fat and its effect on the body. Why were butter and fat meat drippings an important part of the Ingalls' diet? Discuss why we limit these now. Discuss the link between fat intake and cancer, obesity, and heart disease.

Art   3.   Decorate windows using stencils and artificial spray snow.

Long Winter
Week 2

DAY 4

Read Chapter 18.

Reading Comprehension:

Chapter 18
1. How do you "blacken the stove" (page 171)? What was the purpose of this? *(This made the stoves look new and prevented rusting.)*
2. What did Laura give for Christmas? What special treat did they have for Christmas? What did planning ahead make available for them on Christmas (page 183)?
3. What were both Ma and Pa good at (page 186)?
4. What did Pa invent?

Activities:

Health/Speech   1.   Research and give an oral report about snow-blindedness and how to prevent it. Be sure to include information about the cornea and ultraviolet light. *(Snow-blindedness is the temporary loss of sight due to injury to the outer cells of the cornea. It is caused by ultraviolet rays of the sun reinforced by those reflected by the snow.)*

Character/Bible   2.   On page 175, Laura had honest insight that sometimes she did not want to be good. Have you ever felt like that? Paul spoke of this in Romans 7:14-25. What does the Bible say you should do in those times? Read Romans Chapters 6, 7, and 8.

Writing/Art   3.   Write a descriptive paragraph or draw or paint a picture of something you would like to invent.

Long Winter
Week 3

Week Three Planning Guide

Gather Information on the Following:

(See suggested sources listed)

1. Frostbite
   —Inspector Bodyguard Patrols the Land of U by Vicki Cobb
   —

2. The difference nutritionally between unenriched white and unprocessed whole wheat flour
   —Basic Care Bulletin, Medical Training Institute of America
   —Encyclopedia
   —

3. Infiltration of New Age religion into school
   —The Right Choice—Homeschooling "The Moral Crisis in Public Education" by Christopher Klicka
   —

4. Livingstone's Africa
   —the text is online @ http://ulserver.speech.cs.cmu.edu/gutenberg/etext97/mtrav10.txt
   —

Gather These Items:

1. McGuffey's Fifth Reader or The Independent Reader
2. Don't Count Your Chicks by Ingri and Edgar Parin d'Aulaire
3. Materials for making a button lamp
   —See page 197 of The Long Winter
4. Laura Ingalls Wilder Songbook by E. Garson

Suggested Field Trips:

1. Visit a wheat farm or a mill to see unprocessed whole wheat.

Suggested Video:

1. "Stanley and Livingstone" released in 1939, starring Spencer Tracy

Long Winter
Week 3

DAY 1

Read Chapters 19 and 20.

Reading Comprehension:

Chapter 19
1. What good character attribute did Laura show in this chapter?
2. What did Ma use to grind the wheat?
3. What did Ma think to use instead of kerosene for light (page 192)?

Chapter 20
4. What does the common saying "count your chickens before they are hatched" mean?
5. Tell what happened on the antelope hunt.
6. How did Almanzo get his horse back? What did Almanzo see as his mistake?

Activities:

Living/Cooking   1.   Visit a wheat farm or mill to see unprocessed whole wheat. Contact someone you know who is interested in health food; sometimes they have their own mill and access to unprocessed wheat. Mill your own wheat and bake homemade bread.

Science/Nutrition   2.   What is the difference between whole wheat flour and refined white flour?

Living   3.   On page 193, what is Pa's statement regarding modern conveniences? List some conveniences or luxuries we've become dependent on.

Nutrition   4.   It is recommended to eat between six and eleven servings of bread daily. Put a star on a chart each time this is achieved. Remember a bowl of cereal may contain two to three servings.

Reading   5.   Have student read <u>Don't Count Your Chicks</u> aloud to younger children.

Art   6.   Make a button lamp using materials listed on page 197.

General   7.   Remember this week to schedule and make time for General Activities.

Page 157

Long Winter
Week 3

DAY 2

Read Chapters 21 and 22.

Reading Comprehension:

Chapter 21
1. How do you think the town of De Smet received word that the train would not run until spring?
2. What character qualities did Pa see for making it in the West (page 223)?
3. Tell the story of the train superintendent.
4. What was Laura old enough for now (page 223)?
5. What did they do to lift their spirits?

Chapter 22
6. What did the girls do for fun?
7. What unique way did Pa make to feed the horses? How did patience and perseverance fit his actions?
8. Why was the house warmer?
9. What did Pa find that he could not do?
10. Who was Paul Revere?

Activities:

Reading	1.	Read selections from <u>McGuffey's Fifth Reader</u>.
Bible	2.	Look up Proverbs 24:10 and Psalm 116:17. How do these verses relate to Chapter 21 and to your life?
Critical Thinking	3.	How was Laura's <u>Reader</u> different from yours?
Practical Living/ Bible	4.	<u>McGuffey's Readers</u> were used in the public schools of Laura's time. God was mentioned honorably in those books. Is God mentioned in the school textbooks of today? Discuss with your child(ren) the infiltration of humanism and New Age religion into school subjects. Relate these verses to the absence of God in our once godly schools: II Chronicles 7:14; Matthew 12:43-45; and Ephesians 3:19.
History	5.	Pa started reading about Dr. Livingstone. Watch "Stanley and Livingstone" and/or read excerpts from his book. The Ingalls' condition in <u>The Long Winter</u> is opposite of Dr. Livingstone's in Africa. This is a literary devise called jux ta position.
Bible	6.	Use your Bible concordance to find the mention of Tubal Cain. What did Tubal Cain do?
Music	7.	Sing from <u>Laura Ingalls Wilder Songbook,</u> page 140.

Page 158

Long Winter
Week 3

DAY 3

Read Chapters 23, 24, and 25.

Reading Comprehension:

Chapter 23
1. What did Ma say about complaining?
2. What does God say about complaining?
3. Why was killing Ellen and the heifer calf a last resort?
4. How did Pa get food?
5. Would Almanzo have let the Ingalls starve?

Chapter 24
6. How were the weather and the lack of food affecting them?

Chapter 25
7. What was Almanzo thinking about doing?
8. Which of Almanzo's parents' sayings is better (page 258)?
9. Based on earlier events in the book, what are the dangers that Almanzo will face on his mission?

Activities:

Bible	1.	Apply these verses to the story and to your life: Philippians 2:14-15; Psalm 111:5 (NAS).
Writing	2.	With your best handwriting, copy some verses about complaining. (See Numbers 11:1.)
Memory	3.	Memorize a favorite poem from <u>McGuffey's Fifth Reader</u> or <u>The Independent Reader</u>.
Bible	4.	Apply Proverbs 29:7 to Chapter 25.
Language	5.	What image of a blizzard does the word "scouring" give?

Page 159

Long Winter
Week 3

DAY 4

Read Chapters 26 and 27.

Reading Comprehension:

Chapter 26
1. Describe the work Pa had to do to get hay to the house so they would not freeze to death.
2. What special joke did Pa and Grace share (page 261)?
3. What did Pa plan to do for entertainment (page 261)?

Chapter 27
4. When was Almanzo not glad that he was free and independent? What do you think you might miss about not living at home?
5. What did Almanzo like about mornings?
6. Why did Almanzo like Cap (page 268)?
7. Was Anderson happy to see the boys?
8. How long had it been since he had seen someone?
9. What was the most convincing argument for him to sell the wheat?
10. From where did Almanzo get the courage to face the elements?

Activities:

Health/Writing   1. Write a report on frostbite. What is our body's response to cold? What is frostbite? What are the symptoms? What are the complications of frostbite? How do we treat it? What happens if frostbite occurs? *(Frostbite is injury to tissues due to exposure to the cold. When the body becomes cold, the body attempts to keep warm by shunting the blood from the cold extremities. The cold and prolonged lack of blood can cause damage. Usually the first areas of the body to freeze are the nose, ears, fingers, and toes. The flesh feels cold to the touch, and frozen parts become pale and feel numb. There may be some prickly or itching sensation, but they may feel no warning pain. In mild cases proper treatment of frostbite may restore normal circulation of the blood. In more serious cases the area may become painfully red and swollen with blisters. Severe frostbite can cause the tissue to die and gangrene can occur. Frostbite **should never** be treated by rubbing the affected area with snow. The frozen parts should be gradually and gently rewarmed. Cool or lukewarm water may be used to rewarm the frozen body parts. If water isn't available, then place it next to a warm body part. **Do not massage, use hot water bottles, or other heating devices.** This may further damage the tissue.)*

Safety   2. Did Almanzo correctly treat his frostbite? What should he have done instead? When exposed to the cold, how can we help prevent frostbite?

Character   3. Anderson spent a long time alone. Spend a few hours or an entire day in voluntary isolation. How did you feel during this time? What is the longest amount of time you have not seen another person?

Bible   4. Apply this verse to the story and to your life: John 15:13. This is a good memory verse.

Page 160

Long Winter
Week 4

Week Four Planning Guide

Gather Information on the Following:

(See suggested sources listed)

1. A list of the effects of different vitamin deficiencies
   —

2. Wind experiments
   —The Weather Report by Mike Graf
   —

Gather These Items:

1. Laura Ingalls Wilder Songbook by E. Garson

Suggested Field Trips:

Notes:

Long Winter
Week 4

Read Chapters 28 and 29.

Reading Comprehension:

Chapter 28
1. What did Pa get angry with (page 288)?
2. What made Pa mind the weather more than usual? What was Laura's solution?
3. Had they prayed for Almanzo and Cap? What made it okay in their eyes to pray for him (page 292)?

Chapter 29
4. Who did the town's people look to for wisdom?
5. What was Pa's argument?
6. What did Almanzo notice about Pa (page 308)?

Activities:

Bible	1	Discuss these verses considering these chapters: Proverbs 1:19; 15:27; Amos 5:9; and Matthew 5:9; 4:4. (This last verse is taken out of context, but it's a good one to share with your child.)
Nutrition	2.	Research the nutritional differences between whole wheat flour and non-enriched white flour. What vitamins does the white flour lack? The Ingalls used whole wheat flour. What additional vitamins did they receive by eating whole wheat instead of white? *(Whole wheat contains more trace minerals such as zinc and iron. The germ of the wheat also contains fat, a source of energy, B vitamins, and fiber.)* By eating only bread, what nutrients did the Ingalls lack? *(Vitamins A and C, protein, and half their calcium requirement.)* What effect do these deficiencies have on the human body?
Bible	3.	How was God's provision better than Laura's desire for white bread? How is God's will better than our will for us? See Psalm 61:2.
Bible	4.	God provided for the Ingalls. Look at the following verses: Philippians 4:11, 13, 19; Psalm 146:7; Psalm 37:25; Matthew 6:8-13.
Music	5.	Sing from <u>Laura Ingalls Wilder Songbook</u>, pages 43, 136, and 139.
General	6.	Remember this week to schedule and make time to conclude General Activities.

Long Winter
Week 4

DAY 2

Read Chapters 30 and 31.

Reading Comprehension:

Chapter 30
1. What put a warmth inside Laura?
2. What is Chinook and what differences did it bring?

Chapter 31
3. What was on the train? Where did Pa get the food to bring home?

Activities:

Bible   1. Apply Proverbs 17:22 and 16:24 to the story.

Bible   2. Pa called Ma "Nebuchadnezzar" when she suggested eating greens. Read the story of Nebuchadnezzar in the Bible (Daniel 5:17-24). Who was he? Why did he eat grass?

Science   3. Study wind. Research the fact that wind is caused by temperature differences and the rotation of the earth.

Bible   4. The last of the wheat was used the day the freight train came to town. Recall stories from the Bible when God's provision lasted only as long as needed. *(The Israelites and manna, the widow woman and the oil, etc.)*

Page 163

Long Winter
Week 4

DAY 3

Read Chapters 32 and 33. This Finishes the Book.

Reading Comprehension:

Chapter 32
1. What arrived on today's train?

Chapter 33
2. What did they do to the raisins before use (page 328)?
3. What do we do with raisins before use?
4. What did they do with the dishes (page 333)?
5. Besides the food and the company, what else did they enjoy? Why was it so special?

Activities:

Writing   1. Write a two-page report on Samuel Morse. Include in this report the effect the telegraph had on western expansion.

Vocabulary   2. What is saleratus (page 328)?

Music   3. Sing from <u>Laura Ingalls Wilder Songbook</u>, page 52.

DAY 4

Read <u>Laura Ingalls Wilder Country</u>, Chapter 6, "The Long, Hard Winter."

Finish Any Undone Activities!

Town

Little Town on the Prairie

In Little Town on the Prairie, Laura diligently prepares for her school exhibition in DeSmet. Her contribution to the exhibition includes a recitation of U.S. History from the text, The Model History: A Brief Account of the American People by Edward Taylor. Her actual text is in the Detroit Public Library; copies of this text may be available in larger, older libraries.

Group Activities to Do in This Book:

1. Plan a school exhibition to be held at the conclusion of your study of Little Town. Children can give recitations of favorite poems of the period, historical documents and addresses. Artwork can be displayed. Plan skits or historical reenactments. Dress in period clothing, and use The Little House Cookbook by Barbara M. Walker to make refreshments. Invite relatives and friends.

2. Plan a family spelling bee for Week 3, Day 3.

General Activities to Do throughout the Book:

1. The events in Little Town occurred in 1882. To coincide with the story, our study in the Primer will include American history from the writing of the Constitution to 1882. Below are brief "historical reviews" for memorization. Use these reviews as part of the recitations in your school exhibition. Have your child write or type each memorized section on a 3 x 5 card and keep it in their file box.

Historical Reviews:

a. All hearts turned to General George Washington to be the first President of the United States. He was inaugurated in 1789. He had a national debt from the Revolutionary War. To provide funds, taxes were levied on imported goods and liquor. His foreign policy consisted of keeping the U.S. free from European alliances.

b. Second was John Adams (1797-1801). Adams had secured the adoption of the Declaration of Independence, nominated George Washington for President, and had the reputation of having the clearest head and firmest heart of any man in Congress. During his administration the relationship with France became seriously strained.

c. Third was Thomas Jefferson (1801-1809), who wrote the Declaration of Independence, established religious freedom and the right to own private property. With the Louisiana Purchase, he obtained from Napoleon all the land between the Mississippi and the Rocky Mountains. He was unostentatious and soon the public debt was diminished, the treasury replenished, and army and navy reduced.

Town

d. Fourth was James Madison (1809-1817). During this term was the War of 1812, the invasion, the defeat, the burning of the Capitol and the White House in Washington. There were brave sea battles fought by sailors on American's few ships against the British, the most powerful navy in the world. We had shown the impossibility of any foreign ruler gaining a permanent foothold on our territory.

e. Fifth was James Monroe (1817-1825), who dared to tell the older, stronger nations never again to invade the New World. The famous Monroe Doctrine declared that any attempt by a European nation to gain dominion would be considered by the U.S. as an unfriendly act.

f. During the term of the sixth president, John Quincy Adams (1825-1829), also known as the "old man eloquent", the country entered a period of prosperity. The Erie Canal opened and the first railroad in the United States was completed. The first wagon wheels rolled into Kansas.

g. Seventh was Andrew Jackson (1829-1837), who went down from Tennessee and fought the Spanish, took Florida, then the honest United States paid Spain for it. He withdrew the money from the Bank of United States and deposited it into local banks. This made money easier to borrow.

h. The eighth president was Martin Van Buren (1837-1841), who faced the country's financial collapse from the Jackson administrations' policies. Confidence was destroyed and trade stood still. Businesses, states and the nation could not pay their debts.

i.   Ninth and tenth were Harrison and Tyler's administrations (1841-1845). The magnetic telegraph was invented. The first line was built with money given by Congress. Michigan became a state in 1837.

j. Eleventh was James Polk, (1845-1849). He was Commander-in-Chief during the Mexican War. Gold was discovered in California. Iowa became a state.

k.   Twelfth and thirteenth were the Taylor and Filmore administrations (1849-1853). Slavery became the great debate during their term. The Compromise of 1850 was made.

l. Fourteenth was the Pierce administration (1853-1857). Slavery continued to be the focus during this term. The Kansas-Nebraska Bill dealt with slavery. It was the cause of warfare on the border.

m. While the fifteenth President, James Buchanan (1857-1861), was in office slavery remained the focus of the nation. The Supreme Court made the Dred Scott Decision. The Congress passed the Fugitive Slave Law and John Brown seized the United States Arsenal at Harper's Ferry. Brown proclaimed freedom to all the slaves in the vicinity. Kansas became a state in 1861.

n. Lincoln was elected the sixteenth President in 1861. The South seceded and Civil War was fought. He wrote the Gettysburg Address and the Emancipation Proclamation. Lincoln was assassinated soon after the end of the Civil War in 1865.

o. The seventeenth president, Andrew Johnson (1865-1869), capably took command after Lincoln's assassination. He peacefully disbanded the army. This proved to Europe that we were the most stable government in the world. The seceded States were readmitted, the thirteenth and fourteenth amendments were ratified. But Congress attempted to impeach him. Laura Ingalls was born during his term.

p. The eighteenth president, Hiram Ulysses Grant (1869-1877), was a veteran commander in both the Mexican and Civil Wars. During his term the Pacific Railroad was finished, making travel between New York and San Francisco possible in less than a week. It carried pioneers and developed new sources of industry. This enabled the United States to become open to the silks, teas, and spices of Asia. War with the Sioux Indians occurred, including the battle at Little Bighorn with General George Armstrong Custer.

q. During the nineteenth administration (1877-1881), Hayes withdrew U.S. troops from the South. Congress made gold the standard for currency.

r.   The last year, 1881, the twentieth president, James Garfield was shot on July 2; he died September 19. Vice-President Chester Arthur became President. Letter postage rates were decreased from three cents to two cents an ounce.

2. Make a presidential time line using newsprint, butcher block, or computer paper. Start with George Washington and end with Chester Arthur. Write each president's name in the middle of the paper and measure the time served using a determined scale, such as 2-3 inches equaling one year. The upper part of the paper can be devoted to important U.S. events such as the War of 1812, the progressive development of the nation's flags, the gold rush, the completion of the transcontinental railroad, and the Civil War. The lower section of the time line can contain history specific to each president such as Thomas Jefferson building Monticello or Lincoln's log cabin. Your child may want to include their own portrait of each president under their time line. Work on this daily along with the memorization or as a review at the end of your study. Plan to complete it by the end of your studies in the Primer.

Town

3. Read your newspaper's daily editorial page and look for quotes from famous presidents you are studying. Thomas Jefferson is frequently quoted. Include these quotes on any reports your child does on the presidents. Or get a book of quotes from famous people.

4. Read biographies of Thomas Jefferson, Andrew Jackson, Clara Barton and Abraham Lincoln. To slow the pace, this reading can be alternated with the regular Daily Activity schedule. After doing one week's Activities, alternate the next week with biography reading and catching up on Activities and memorization.

5. Daily listen to Little Bear Wheeler's devotionals about the Civil War.

6. View PBS home video series "Civil War, Episode 1-9" at a rate of one or two per week. (This may be extended into the next book.) Film series by Ken Burns, produced by Florentine Films, and WETA TV.

   a. "The Cause 1861"
   b. "A Very Bloody Affair 1862"
   c. "Forever Free 1862"
   d. "Simply Murder 1863"
   e. "The Universe of Battle 1863"
   f. "Valley of the Shadow of Death 1864"
   g. "Most Hallowed Ground 1864"
   h. "War is All Hell 1865"
   i. "The Better Angels of Our Nature"

7. While watching the above video series, work on time line or do handcrafts together.

8. Research the location of your favorite president's home or one near your location. Plan a visit to a former president's home or his library. This is a great end-of-unit activity.

9. Laura, the author, felt Romans 12 was necessary to meditate upon in order to live successfully with others. Memorize this chapter by the end of the book.

Town
Week 1

Week One Planning Guide

Gather Information on the Following:

(See suggested sources listed)

1. George Washington
   —<u>George Washington</u> by Ingri and Edgar Parin d'Aulaire
   —<u>Great Americans and Their Noble Deeds</u> by Milton Hadley
   —<u>George Washington</u> (Holiday House), *a picture book for younger siblings*
   —Encyclopedia

2. Sheep sorrels (an herb)
   —<u>Weeds</u> A Golden Guide (Golden Press)
   —Refer to an herb book under Rumex acetosella or sour dock

3. John Adams

4. Thomas Jefferson
   —<u>Tom Jefferson</u> by Monsell/Wagner (Childhood of Famous American Series)
   —<u>Young Thomas Jefferson</u> (Troll)
   —<u>Thomas Jefferson and the American Ideal</u> by Russell Shorto *more in-depth*
   —<u>A Picture Book of Thomas Jefferson</u> by David A. Adler (Holiday House), *for younger siblings*

5. James Madison

6. James Monroe

7. The care of chickens
   —<u>Backyard Chickens</u>

8. Louisiana Purchase

9. Health and societal factors that occur from alcohol abuse
   —Local MADD chapter

Gather These Items:

1. Make lemonade
   —<u>The Little House Cookbook</u> by Barbara M. Walker
2. <u>We The People</u> by Peter Spier
3. Civil War Cassette tapes by Little Bear Wheeler
4. "Justin Morgan Had a Horse" video
5. <u>Don't Count Your Chicks</u> by Ingri and Edgar Parin d'Aulaire
6. Photocopies of the "Louisiana Purchase" map, if more than one child is using the <u>Primer</u>.

Town
Week 1

Suggested Field Trips:

1. Arrange a trip to a dairy. Arrange to bottle feed a calf.

Notes:

Town
Week 1
For Use with Day 3

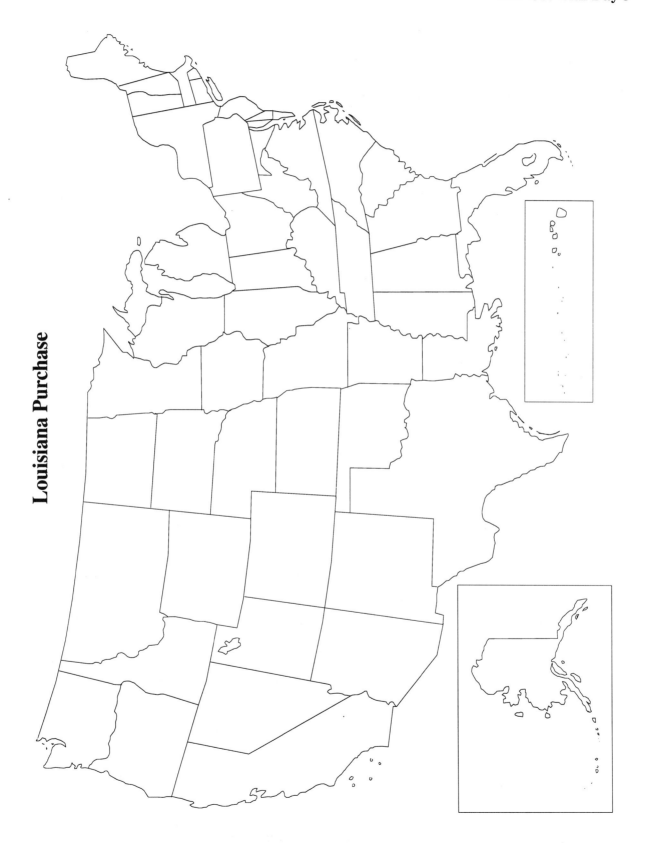

Louisiana Purchase

Town
Week 1

DAY 1

Read Chapters 1, 2, and 3.

Reading Comprehension:

Chapter 1
1. What did Laura think about having a job in town?

Chapter 2
2. With what and how was the baby calf fed? Why didn't they allow the calf to nurse?
3. What was a delight to both Carrie and Grace?
4. Why did Laura not play in the freshly plowed ground (page 9,10)? What do you wish that you could do, but are unable because of your age?
5. On a sunny day what did Grace discover? Have you ever done this?

Chapter 3
6. What was the Ingalls' problem?
7. How could a cat help?
8. What happened to Pa while he was sleeping?
9. On page 23, what character qualities did Pa show?
10. Why did Pa pay for an unweaned kitten?

Activities:

Field Trip	1.	Visit a dairy. Bottle feed a calf.
Writing	2.	Write a one page report on what happened when you or Laura bottle fed the calf.
History	3.	Memorize George Washington's historical review (a).
History	4.	Read We the People. Research George Washington.
Bible	5.	Was Springtime a time for visiting? See Ecclesiastes 3:1-8.
Bible	6.	What revelation of God had Mary experienced? How had this changed her life (page 13)? Read Psalms 31:19, Nahum 1:7.
Bible	7.	What are three reasons the Bible gives for suffering in II Corinthians 1:3-11? *(Three reasons for suffering: II Corinthians 1:3 ". . . so that we can comfort those in any trouble with the comfort we ourselves have received from God." II Corinthians 1:9 ". . . we might not rely on ourselves but on God." II Corinthians 1:11 ". . . then many will give thanks on our behalf for the gracious favor granted us in answer to the prayers of many." NIV)*
Science	8.	What are sheep sorrels? If possible taste one or find one in an herb identification book.
Economics	9.	Have you ever tried to give a kitten away? What do you think is the difference? *(Supply and demand.)*

Page 172

Town
Week 1

General   10.   Remember this week to schedule and make time for General Activities.

DAY 2

Read Chapters 4 and 5.

Reading Comprehension:

Chapter 4
1. What is a cockerel? What is a pullet?
2. What was Mrs. Boast doing for the Ingalls?
3. What would they do to the hens that were too old to lay?
4. What did they put on their lettuce for salad dressing? Was this healthier than what we put on today?
5. Tell the amazing surprise story.

Chapter 5
6. What was Laura's first day of work like?
7. How had life at home prepared her for this job?
8. How was this family different from Laura's?
9. What compliment did Mrs. White give her?

Activities:

Living   1.   Research the care of chickens.

History   2.   Memorize John Adam's historical review (b).

History/Writing   3.   Write a one page report on either George Washington or John Adams.

History   4.   Begin reading a biography about Thomas Jefferson. Finish by the end of the week.

Bible   5.   Apply Acts 20:35 and Galatians 6:7-10 to Chapter 4 of the book.

Reading   6.   Have student read <u>Don't Count Your Chicks</u> aloud to younger children.

Town
Week 1

DAY 3

Read Chapters 6 and 7.

Reading Comprehension:

Chapter 6
1. What did Laura do with her money?
2. Because of homesteading, where did the wives, boys, and girls live during the summer?
3. What did the husbands do and why (page 49,50)?
4. Why was the Ingalls family better off than most (page 50)?
5. How did they keep the bugs out of their homes?
6. What did Pa think about saloons? What did Ma think?

Chapter 7
7. What surprise did Laura and Pa have?
8. What was Carrie's job? What was Grace's job?
9. That evening what did Laura find out that Pa and Ma were thinking? How did that make Laura feel?
10. What would Laura's $9.00 go towards purchasing?

Activities:

Writing	1.	Write one page on the care and protection of chickens.
History	2.	Memorize Thomas Jefferson's historical review (c).
Vocabulary	3.	Look up ostentatious in the dictionary. What is **un**ostentatious?
Social Studies	4.	What is a dry county? Are there any in your state? How does your state restrict liquor sales or serving?
Bible	5.	What does the Bible say about drinking? Read Ecclesiastes 10:17; Proverbs 20:1; Ephesians 5:18; Proverbs 21:17, 23:20,21, and 23:29-35.
Health/Art	6.	Make a health and safety poster utilizing the information of Proverbs 23:29-35.
Health	7.	What are some societal and health problems that occur from excess of liquor? *(Be sure to include loss of life from drunk drivers, loss of income from poor work habits, increase in family problems, liver problems, death.)* Write or call MADD for information.
Art	8.	Draw a picture of the design of the chicken coop.
History/Geography	9.	Study about the Louisiana Purchase. Color the area obtained by the Louisiana Purchase green on the United States map provided.

Page 174

Town
Week 1

DAY 4

Read Chapter 8.

Reading Comprehension:

Chapter 8
1. What were the Ingalls awakened by?
2. How did Carrie button her dress?
3. How far did they walk into town? How far have you walked?
4. Why did Pa and the girls leave the house soberly?
5. What important United States document did both Laura and Carrie know by heart?
6. What did Pa sing after the recitation?
7. Who wrote the Declaration of Independence?
8. Why did they read it on this day?
9. Who won the buggy race?
10. What handicap did the horses have to overcome?
11. Did Almanzo whip his horses?
12. Who was applying for the job of school teacher?
13. What special treat did they have this day?

Activities:

History	1.	Memorize James Madison's historical review (d).
History	2.	Write a two page report on Thomas Jefferson.
Writing	3.	Write how your family celebrates the Fourth of July.
Living	4.	Watch the video "Justin Morgan Had a Horse."
Bible	5.	What did Laura think gave you the right to be free (page 77)? Apply the following verses: II Corinthians 3:17; Galatians 5:13; Galatians 5:1; I Timothy 1:17.
Bible	6.	Apply Proverbs 12:10 to Almanzo's character.
PE	7.	Plan an errand to walk two miles round trip.
Cooking	8.	Make homemade lemonade (not frozen!).

Page 175

Town
Week 2

Week Two Planning Guide

Gather Information on the Following:

(See suggested sources listed)

1. John Quincy Adams

2. Andrew Jackson
   —Frontier Patriot (Troll)
   —Andrew Jackson and the New Populism by William Gutman *more in-depth*

3. Martin Van Buren

4. James Polk

5. The War of 1812
   —Andrew Jackson and the New Populism by William Gutman *more in-depth*
   —Encyclopedia

6. Spanish needle grass
   —Weeds A Golden Guide (Golden Press)

Gather These Items:

1. Pieces of cashmere and cambric fabric
2. Blackbird pie
   —The Little House Cookbook by Barbara M. Walker

Suggested Field Trip:

1. Plan a trip to a backyard chicken coop or a poultry farm. As an alternative, if zoning, finances, and time permit, raise hatchlings and start your own backyard chicken coop.

Notes:

Town
Week 2

DAY 1

Read Chapter 9.

Reading Comprehension:

Chapter 9
1. What funny grass did Laura and Mary get into?
2. What did Pa do to get rid of it?
3. What was Ma's key for thankfulness (page 90)?
4. What were corsets? Why were they used?
5. Besides for eating, why did they grow oats and corn?
6. What happened to the oat and corn crop?
7. What did they do to salvage some of the corn?
8. What unusual dish did they eat for supper?
9. What sacrifice did Pa make to send Mary to college?
10. What does "We must cut our coat to fit the cloth" mean?

Activities:

History	1.	Memorize James Monroe's historical review (e).
History	2.	Memorize John Quincy Adams' historical review (f).
History	3.	Begin reading Andrew Jackson's biography and finish by the end of the week.
History/Writing	4.	Read about the War of 1812 and write a report on its causes and outcome.
Vocabulary	5.	Look up "cashmere" and "cambric" in the dictionary. Visit a fabric and yarn store or a better department store and feel these fabrics.
Science	6.	Research Spanish Needle grass. *This herb screws its seeds into the ground with changes in the humidity.*
Cooking	7.	Make either blackbird or chicken pie for dinner.
Bible	8.	Apply James 1:2-4 to this chapter.
General	9.	Remember this week to schedule and make time for General Activities.

Town
Week 2

DAY 2

Read Chapter 10.

Reading Comprehension:

Chapter 10
1. How was Mary's leaving a "sweet and sour moment?"
2. What did Laura choose to do to keep everyone occupied while Ma and Pa were gone?
3. What did Laura think was harder than she expected (page 116)?
4. What did they do on Sunday?
5. How did they know Ma and Pa were coming?
6. What is an autograph album?

Activities:

History   1.   Memorize Andrew Jackson's historical review (g).

Bible   2.   Apply Mark 2:27 to Laura.

Writing   3.   Write a one page report on either John Adams or James Monroe.

DAY 3

Read Chapters 11 and 12.

Reading Comprehension:

Chapter 11
1. Who at school made Laura feel comfortable?
2. Who did Laura make feel comfortable?
3. Who was Laura unhappy to see?
4. What did Nellie do?
5. What did Ma say about criticizing her teacher?
6. How did Pa bring peace?

Chapter 12
7. What did the girls do before and after school? on Saturdays?
8. How did the Ingalls prepare for winter? How did the town prepare?
9. What should Mary be able to do soon?
10. Why was living in town better for Carrie?
11. What was wrong with Carrie?

Page 178

Town
Week 2

Activities:

History	1.	Memorize Martin Van Buren's historical review (h).
Writing	2.	Write a one page report about the time Laura was attempting to surprise her mother with a clean house and what happened, or a time when you were attempting to help and things went wrong.
Bible	3.	Apply Romans 13:1,2 to Laura's attitude toward Miss Wilder.
Bible	4.	Apply Matthew 23:12 to Nellie.
Art/Living Writing	5.	Make or buy an autograph album. Have friends or siblings do the same. Memorize or review a favorite poem or saying to write in one another's book. Compose a short friendship poem to write in another's book. Bring autograph books to a gathering, such as the school exhibition, and sign each other's books.

DAY 4

Read Chapters 13 and 14.

Reading Comprehension:

Chapter 13
1. Who was at the head of the class?
2. What did Laura do during recess?
3. Did they ever try to include Nellie?
4. What did Almanzo buy with his profit from the wheat crop? Was this good money management?
5. What did Laura want?
6. What did they use for a drinking fountain? How did this show they did not either know about or apply the germ theory?

Chapter 14
7. Discuss what happened in Chapter 14. What should Laura have done? What would you have done?
8. Was Miss Wilder seeking good council about her problems with the classroom?

Activities:

History	1.	Memorize the Harrison/Tyler historical review (i).
Writing	2.	Write a two-page report on Andrew Jackson.
Bible	3.	Apply Romans 13:1-2 to Chapter 13 of <u>Little Town</u>. Apply II Timothy 2:16,17; James 3:13; II Timothy 2:23 to Laura's comment to Nellie. By trying to include Nellie, what principles of manner or Biblical principles were the students using?

Page 179

Town
Week 3

Week Three Planning Guide

Gather Information on the Following:

(See suggested sources listed)

1. Abraham Lincoln
   —<u>Abraham Lincoln</u> by Ingri and Edgar Parin d'Aulaire
   —<u>Abe Lincoln: Log Cabin to White House</u> by North (Landmark Book)
   —<u>Lincoln: A Photobiography</u> by Russell Freedman
   —<u>Abraham Lincoln</u> by Collins (The Sower Series)
   —<u>Great Americans and Their Noble Deeds</u> by Milton Hadley
   —<u>A Picture Book of Abraham Lincoln</u> (Holiday House) *for younger siblings*
   —

2. John Brown
   —<u>Now is Your Time: The African/American Struggle for Freedom</u> by Walter Dean Myers
   —Encyclopedia
   —

3. The Dred Scott Decision
   —<u>Now is Your Time: The African/American Struggle for Freedom</u> by Walter Dean Myers
   —Encyclopedia
   —

4. The Compromise of 1850
   —Encyclopedia
   —

5. Supreme Court of the United States (function, how appointed, their authority to reverse decisions)
   —

6. Mexican War
   —

7. Mexico and its culture
   —

8. Simple electrical experiments and properties of electricity
   —<u>TOPS Learning Systems: Electricity</u> by Ron Marson
   —<u>Electricity</u> (A Troll Book)
   —<u>Young Scientist: Electricity</u> (An Usborne Book)
   —<u>Eye Witness Science Electricity</u> by Steve Parker
   —

9. Reasons for bathing
   —

Gather These Items:

1. See the telegraph experiment on the next page
2. Items to make a Mexican dinner
3. <u>The American Dictionary of the English Language</u> (the 1828 edition by Noah Webster)

Page 180

Town
Week 3

Suggested Field Trip:

1. Visit a school for the blind and see how they help blind people adapt to living. Or arrange to watch an occupational therapist aid their clients in living with their physical disability.

Notes:

Town
Week 3

Make a Simple Telegraph Using an Electromagnet

Coded messages can be sent through an electric circuit using an electromagnet.

Gather These Items:

- insulated copper wire (enamel-coated copper wire is available at Radio Shack)
- 2 large iron nails
- scrap wood pieces
- dry cell battery
- thin tin metal strips
- smaller nails or screws for anchors

Procedure A: Making the Electromagnet

1. Make a stand from wood scraps as illustrated in Figure 1. Secure two large nails to it one inch apart from each other.

2. Tightly wrap insulated wire 30 times around the two iron nails as shown in Figure 2.

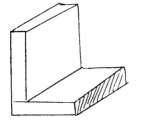

(Figure 1)

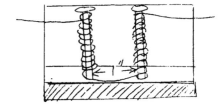

(Figure 2)

3. Attach the two ends of wire to each of the terminals of the dry cell. As electricity flows through the wire around the nails, it produces a magnetic field which will attract metal objects. Try various objects such as iron shavings, paper clips, etc., to test the magnetism.

Procedure B: Making the Telegraph

1. Disconnect the electromagnet from the dry cell.

2. Make the telegraph transmitter by attaching a T-shaped tin strip to the wood stand above the electromagnet. The strip should be above the nail heads but not touching. See Figure 3. (Note: If you cannot obtain tin metal strips, you can use the lid of a tin soup can cut to shape with metal cutters.)

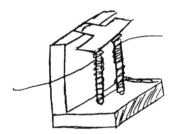

(Figure 3)

3. Make the telegraph switch by securing one end of a tin strip to another scrap wood piece. Secure another screw or nail underneath, but not attached to, the other loose end of the strip. Leave enough height on the screws or nails to wrap wire around them.

4. Connect the switch, transmitter and dry cell together in series with insulated wire as shown in Figure 4. (Note: You will need to scrape the insulation off the ends of the wire with a knife to make the connections conduct the current.)

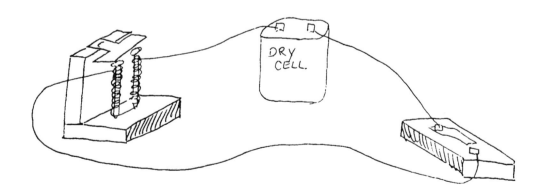

(Figure 4)

Observations:

1. What happens to the T-shaped metal strip when you close the switch?
2. What happens when you release the switch?

Town
Week 3

Tap out messages using Morse Code: A dot (•) is a short sound, a dash (-) is a longer sound.

Morse Code

A	•-		T	-
B	-•••		U	••-
C	-•-•		V	•••-
D	-••		W	•—
E	•		X	-••-
F	••-•		Y	-•—
G	—•		Z	—••
H	••••			
I	••			
J	•—		1	•——
K	-•-		2	••——
L	•-••		3	•••—
M	—		4	••••-
N	-•		5	•••••
O	—		6	-••••
P	•——•		7	—•••
Q	—•-		8	—••
R	•-•		9	——•
S	•••		10	——

Page 184

Town
Week 3

DAY 1

Read Chapter 15.

Reading Comprehension:

Chapter 15
1. What does Nellie's gossip about Miss Wilder reveal about her character (page 172)?
2. What had Laura's unforgiveness caused?
3. Instead of their lessons, what did the boys learn in the morning?
4. How did Kitty protect herself from dogs?
5. What did the school board do during their visit?
6. How does the poem written in Laura's autograph book characterize the chapter?

Activities:

History	1.	Memorize James Polk's historical review (j).
History/Cooking	2.	Research the Mexican-American War. What was the outcome? Prepare a Mexican dinner and present an oral report to guests.
Social Studies	3.	Study about Mexico, our southern neighbor, and its culture.
History	4.	Begin reading a biography on Abraham Lincoln. Finish by the end of the week.
Bible	5.	What does the Bible have to say about gossip? See Proverbs 6:16,19; 11:13,19; 16:28; 25:23; 26:20; and Galatians 5:19.
Art	6.	Make a warning poster about gossip.
General	7.	Remember this week to schedule and make time for General Activities.

DAY 2

Read Chapters 16 and 17.

Reading Comprehension:

Chapter 16
1. Who is their teacher? Why do you think they have a new one?
2. Who was Cap trying to give candy to? Why?
3. What are name cards?
4. How did Mary finally get the candy from Cap?
5. What is a bobolink (page 192)?
6. What did Ida say about name cards?
7. How was Laura feeling about name cards? How has she shown this sin before in previous books?

Page 185

Town
Week 3

8. Did Nellie's cards come from the East? What did this show about Nellie's character?
9. How did Pa surprise Laura?
10. What was the War of 1812?
11. Why was Laura running late to school?
12. How did she get to school quickly?
13. What did Almanzo say about his name?
14. How did Almanzo get his name?
15. How had Almanzo lived up to the name that was given him?

Chapter 17
18. What did Ma think of bangs?
19. Why were both Ma and Pa not enthusiastic about church? Did their attitude effect their children's? Why did they not change churches?
20. How did Laura curl her hair (page 204)?
21. What did the girls think of the social?
22. What did Laura think of the preacher?

Activities:

History	1.	Memorize the Taylor/Fillmore historical review (k).
History/Bible	2.	Read about the Compromise of 1850. What does the Bible say about compromise? *Our God is not a God of compromise. (See Psalm 5:4; Luke 16:13.)*
Character	3.	Review the definition of "vanity" from the 1828 Webster Dictionary. See the previous paper on vanity written during the study of <u>On the Banks of Plum Creek</u>. Edit and build upon your ideas. How can name cards be an expression of vanity? How can they be used to help a social gathering rather than hurt?
Political Science	4.	Compare the debate and issue of slavery to today's abortion issue.
Business	5.	Why are name cards used today?
Personal	6.	Tell how your name was chosen? What does your name mean or who were you named after?
Bible	7.	Apply these verses to Laura's attitude toward her pastor: Romans 10:14,15; I Thessalonians 5:12,13; Hebrews 13:17; I Timothy 5:17,18.

Town
Week 3

DAY 3

Read Chapters 18 and 19.

Reading Comprehension:

Chapter 18
1. What was Laura wanting to be different?
2. What did the whole town want?
3. What meeting was arranged?
4. What did they do? Who won?

Chapter 19
5. What did they do for entertainment?
6. What new building was finished?
7. How often did they have church?
8. What did Pa require of Laura and Carrie when they returned from church?
9. How were the winter days kept full (page 226)?
10. What were grown people not to do (page 228)?
11. What impressed Laura about the food?
12. How much was Laura studying?
13. What was the Literary Society doing this week?
14. How did Pa make a cradle for Grace's doll?

Activities:

History	1.	Memorize the Pierce historical review (l).
History	2.	Read about John Brown. Give an oral report about him.
Health	3.	Research reasons for bathing. (Include in your oral report social and health reasons, such as decreasing the bacterial count, removing parasitic eggs such as pin worms, and the frequency one needs to bathe.)
Bible	4.	Require your child(ren) to repeat the text of the message from your church service.
Career	5.	Visit a school for the blind and see how they help blind people adapt to living. If this isn't available, then arrange to watch an occupational therapist aid their clients in living with their physical disability.
Bible	6.	When Laura thought that she could take it no more, God supplied the entertainment. Apply I Corinthians 10:13.
Spelling	7.	Have a family spelling bee.
Vocabulary	8.	At the spelling bee, "mimosaceous" and "xanthophyll" were spelled. What do these words mean?

Page 187

Town
Week 3

DAY 4

Read Chapters 20 and 21.

Reading Comprehension:

Chapter 20
1. Tell what happened at the party.
2. What two games did they play?
3. What did the girls offer to do?
4. What impressed Laura the most about the party?

Chapter 21
5. What did the older boys and girls play during recess?
6. What worried the girls?
7. What did Nellie say when it was over?
8. Whose opinion did Cap worry about? Why?
9. Describe the night's entertainment at the literary.
10. Which one was Pa? What worried them?
11. What excuse did Laura give for not studying?
12. What did Laura know that she must not do anymore? Who besides herself would it affect?

Activities:

History	1.	Memorize James Buchanan's historical review (m).
History	2.	Read about the Dred Scott Decision. Do an oral report about Dred Scott.
Political/Bible	3.	God's standards do not change. Man's standards may. How was the Dred Scott decision reversed? Older students may study about the history of the Supreme Court reversing previous decisions. Study about the Supreme Court justices and how they are chosen. What effect can the retirement or death of a justice have?
Cooking/Science	4.	Eat white cake with orange slices. Why does the orange taste more sour than usual?
Play	5.	Play drop-the-handkerchief. (*It's similar to duck, duck, goose, except that a handkerchief is dropped.*) Or play blind-man's bluff. (*Blindfold one person, spin them around then have them find and identify a person by touch.*)
Science	6.	Do electrical experiments. Study about the electric telegraph. (See telegraph experiment handout.)
Drama	7.	Plan a "literary" and invite friends.
Character/ Vocabulary	8.	Look up "indulgence" in the 1828 Webster Dictionary. What is self-indulgence? How was Laura self-indulgent? Name a time that you were self-indulgent.
Bible	9.	Apply these verses to self-indulgence: Proverbs 21:17 and 25:28.

Page 188

Town
Week 4

Week Four Planning Guide

Gather Information on the Following:

(See suggested sources listed)

1. Andrew Johnson
    —

2. Sentence diagraming
    —

3. The Battle of Little Big Horn
    —

4. The Civil War
    —<u>Facts the Historians Leave Out: A Confederate Primer</u> by Tilley *more in-depth*
    —<u>Story of the Confederate States</u> by Derry *more in-depth*
    —<u>Confederate Trilogy for Young Readers</u> by Williamson
    —<u>Fight for Freedom</u> (Scholastic)
    —

5. Clara Barton
    —<u>Clara Barton: Founder of the American Red Cross</u> by Augusta Stevenson (Childhood of Famous Americans)
    —<u>Great Americans and Their Noble Deeds</u> by Milton Hadley
    —

6. —How to write a term paper
    —

Gather These Items:

1. <u>Laura Ingalls Wilder Country</u> by William Anderson
2. <u>Thunder at Gettysburg</u> by Patricia Lee Gavah

Suggested Field Trips:

Notes:

Town
Week 4

DAY 1

Read Chapters 22 and 23.

Reading Comprehension:

Chapter 22
1. Who first spotted the blizzard?
2. On page 266, Ma said, "You may be well prepared to teach school and still not be a schoolteacher, but if you are not prepared, it's certain you won't be." What does this mean? Apply this to something that you aspire to do or something that you have accomplished because you were prepared.
3. What did Laura hope for (page 266)?

Chapter 23
4. What did Laura put up with in order to be in style?
5. What did Laura think of while she did the dishes?
6. What was the order of the people sitting in the church?
7. What did Laura think of the revival?
8. What is a revival?
9. What were Ma and Pa talking about when Laura walked in?
10. Why do you think Almanzo asked to see her home?

Activities:

History	1.	Memorize the Abraham Lincoln historical review (n).
Writing	2.	Write a two-page report on Abe Lincoln.
Sociology	3.	How do the people in your church arrange themselves? Draw a picture depicting the different groupings.
Living	4.	Attend a revival.
History	5.	Read a biography of Clara Barton. Finish by the end of the week.
History	6.	Read Thunder at Gettysburg by Patricia Lee Gavah.
Writing	7.	Older students need to write a term paper with a bibliography. Allow time for the student to research and write a paper on the Civil War.
General	8.	Remember this week to schedule and make time to conclude General Activities.

Town
Week 4

DAY 2

Read Chapter 24.

Reading Comprehension:

Chapter 24
1. How many nice dresses does Laura have?
2. How did Laura and Ida do on their recitation?
3. Was it short or long?
4. How did Laura feel while she said her part?
5. Who escorted her home?
6. What did Almanzo ask Laura to do?
7. What was her mother's hesitation?

Activities:

History	1.	Memorize the Andrew Johnson historical review (o).
Writing	2.	Read about and write a one page report on Andrew Johnson. Include why there was an attempt to impeach him.
Social Studies	3.	What is the definition and the process of impeachment?

DAY 3

Read Chapter 25. This Finishes the Book.

Reading Comprehension:

1. What did the visitor to Laura's house do?
2. What did Laura's first teaching job mean to her family? To her?

Activities:

History	1.	Memorize the Ulysses Grant historical review (p).
History/Speech	2.	Study the Battle at Little Bighorn with General Custer. Give an oral report at dinner.
Vocabulary	3.	What is orthography? geography? grammar?
Language	4.	What is a diagramed sentence? Diagram the sentence that Laura diagramed using the method that you are familiar with.
Bible	5.	Apply the readiness spoken of in Matthew 24:36-44 and II Timothy 2:15 to Laura.

Page 191

Town
Week 4

DAY 4

Read Laura Ingalls Wilder Country, Chapter 7.

Activities:

| History | 1. | Memorize the Hayes and the Garfield/Arthur historical reviews (q and r). |

Finish Any Undone Activities!

Golden Years

These Happy Golden Years

<u>These Happy Golden Years</u> recounts further events of the Ingalls' lives in De Smet. Laura continues her contribution to the family by working as a teacher, which is quite a responsibility for a fifteen-year-old young woman. She faces an added challenge in this book with the awakening prospects of courtship. Laura traverses her teen years with the blossoming realization that she will not always contribute to her parent's household, but will someday have a household of her own.

The <u>Primer's</u> studies emphasize the courtship of Almanzo and Laura. Parents know their children best and should be sensitive to when an in-depth study of courtship principles should be undertaken. However, children observe at an early age what their culture's courting or dating patterns are. You can begin to instill healthy, godly ideas of courting now before unacceptable cultural norms take root. You do not want to wake up one day ready to discuss "dating" with your son or daughter to find that they have already established opinions that do not conform to your expectations. Are your children receiving their views of dating from the television airwaves? Instead, use the <u>Primer</u> to open discussion now and help alter incorrect views or to form and reinforce godly ones.

To some Laura's and Almanzo's courtship may seem an idealistic and impossible situation in today's society. To others their courtship may still stray from other principles they want to impart. In either case as discussions occur, clarify your expectations with your child.

Before beginning this book, it is important that you, the parent, reevaluate the position you hold about dating. How were your views formed? Christians tend to be enamored with the pleasantness of dating, and unfortunately, we've allowed worldly norms to infiltrate the church to the point where we have not seriously considered testing whether "dating" is the right method for choosing a companion. Have you ever questioned what is God's view of dating? of courting? What is His ideal? Does your view line up more with NBC, your next-door neighbor's, the church's, or God's Word? We are not to be conformed to the world. When we look to the prevailing culture for standards, we demonstratively conform to this ungodly age. However, when we look to God's standards, we find that truth and wisdom lead to life.

The following resources are given for parental use and will help further your study of godly courting principles.

Books:
—<u>Christian Family Living</u> by John Coblentz.

—<u>Dating with Integrity</u> by Holzmann.

—<u>The Sexual Seduction of American Culture—Romanced to Death</u> by Paul deParrie.

Speakers and Tapes:

—"The Advanced Homeschooling Workshop" by Gregg Harris.

—"Preparing for Romance" and "A Talk to Godly Teens About Sex and Romance" by Jonathan Lindvall.

—"Warning! Dating is No Game" by Little Bear Wheeler.

—"Biblical Courtship" by Douglas Wilson

Golden Years

Group Activity to Do in This Unit:

1.   Plan a taffy pulling party for Week 2, Day 3.

General Activity to Do throughout This Unit:

1.   Memorize Psalm 27.

2.   Read a biography of an 1800's American evangelist.

Week One Planning Guide

Gather Information on the Following:

1. An 1800's American evangelist. Some suggestions are Sojourner Truth, Jedidiah Smith, Peter Cartwright, D. L. Moody, Phoebe Palmer, Samuel Morris, Billy Sunday
    —Attack in the Rye Grass (Trailblazer Series) about Marcus Whitman
    —Quest for the Lost Prince (Trailblazer Series) about Samuel Morris
    —Abandoned on the Wild Frontier (Trailblazer Series) about Peter Cartwright
    —Kidnapped by River Rats (Trailblazer Series) about William and Catherine Booth and the Salvation Army
    —Mother of an Army by Charles Ludwig
    —Danger on the Flying Trapeze (Trailblazer Series) about Dwight Moody
    —Warrior's Challenge (Trailblazer Series) about David Zeisberger
    —D. L Moody by David Bennett
    —Walking the Road to Freedom, A Story About Sojourner Truth by Jeri Ferris
    —Charles Finney by Milly Howard (Bethany House)
    —D. L. Moody: God's Salesman (Moody Press)
    —Billy Sunday (Sower Series)
    —

Gather These Items:

1. Bible concordance
2. Laura Ingalls Wilder Songbook by E. Garson

Suggested Field Trips:

Notes:

Page 195

Golden Years
Week 1

DAY 1

Read Chapters 1 and 2.

Reading Comprehension:

Chapter 1
1. What character quality had Laura exhibited in the past that had prepared her to teach school (page 3)?
2. What did the Ingalls do with the dishwater? What do you do with it?
3. How far was it to Brewsters'? When did Laura expect to be able to return home?
4. What reception did Laura receive? What was Laura's response to the poor reception?
5. What needed to be done (page 9)? Why did Laura not do it?

Chapter 2
6. How was the blackboard made (page 13)?
7. What time did school start (page 14)? Why did it start so late?
8. How did she behave like a teacher?
9. Describe Laura's students.
10. What did Laura do for punishment?
11. What safety measure did the school need to take? From which direction would a blizzard come (page 20)?
12. Why did Laura not need a dustpan to clean the schoolhouse?

Activities:

Bible	1.	What was Pa's twofold advice (page 3)? What does the Bible say about watching your speech? (James 3:5-11; Psalm 39:1; Proverbs 21:23.) We are to have confidence, but our confidence is to be in the Lord (Proverbs 14:26; Philippians 3:4-8; I Peter 1:21.) Yet we are to pray for wisdom and believe and act as though we have received it (James 1:5-8).
Bible	2.	How did Laura feel on her first night in the Brewsters' home? Laura, the author, suggests reading Psalm 27 when lonely or fearful. Read this Psalm and imagine Laura reciting this to herself the first night at the Brewsters'. Set a schedule to commit Psalm 27 to memory by the end of this unit.
Writing	3.	Write about how you felt the first time that you were away from home. Write about what you did and what happened.
Writing	4.	By dictation, write the second paragraph on page 7. Correct your writing, using the book; discuss discrepancies and underline all the verbs. Discuss the image that each verb creates.
Bible	5.	Laura felt that she could hardly swallow the food, although it was tasty. Read and apply Proverbs 15:17 to her situation.
Literature	6.	Laura was given a godly heritage by her parents. In the 1830-1840's America underwent the Second Great Awakening. During this time men like Jedidiah Smith, also known as the Mountain Man, and Peter Cartwright spread the gospel in the West. There was a hunger for God

Page 196

Golden Years
Week 1

and the things of God. Evangelistic tent meetings were held. As an outgrowth of the revival of American spirits, Christians turned toward social issues. The first was slavery. Then after the War Between the States, they worked against poverty. Women's Christian Temperance and Salvation Army were formed. Pick an 1800 evangelist to read about the spiritual condition of the nation and the faithfulness of the men and women serving Him.

General   7.   Remember this week to schedule and make time for General Activities.

DAY 2

Read Chapters 3 and 4.

Reading Comprehension:

Chapter 3
1. Describe Mrs. Brewster's character.
2. What was Laura's hope for the weekend?
3. Friday afternoon, what surprise came? Why do you think that Almanzo came?

Chapter 4
4. What look did Laura notice on Almanzo's face as he looked at the Brewsters' house (page 31)?
5. What had Almanzo designed and made?
6. Who had Almanzo spoken to about picking up Laura?
7. What did Laura tell her parents about?
8. What did Laura think made the morning brighter (page 35)?

Activities:

Bible   1.   The Bible has much to say about a contentious wife. Read Proverbs 21:19; 25:24; 27:15; 12:4; and 14:1. What calamities befall the man that picks a woman with poor character?

Bible/Art   2.   Read Proverbs 14:1. Compare the role models that Laura observed in her mother and Mrs. Brewster in the light of this verse. How do you observe your mother building your home? Make a card exhorting her in this endeavor.

Writing   3.   Write a letter thanking your mom for using godly principles in her life, childrearing, and/or marriage.

Courting   4.   Before bringing Laura home, Almanzo asked Mr. Ingalls' permission to do so. **Courting should have parental involvement from the beginning.** Read the example from the scriptures in Genesis 24:2-4. Before approaching Mr. Ingalls, Almanzo may have written his father or asked counsel from his elder brother, Royal. He may have discussed not only Laura but such things as personal readiness, future goals, and the possible procedure toward these goals. Perhaps they prayed about the decision. If his parents expressed strong objections, he would not have

Golden Years
Week 1

gone on. Mild objections may have been worked out with clarification. Although we do not know with any certainty if Almanzo initiated this relationship based on parental counsel, we do know that it was begun with parental consent. If Almanzo had approached Laura first, she then should have asked him to discuss it with her father. Choosing a marriage partner is one of the most important decisions that one makes. Read these important scriptures regarding seeking counsel: Proverbs 1:5; 11:14; 12:15; 13:10; 15:22; 19:20.

(From <u>Christian Family Living</u> by John Coblentz, page 75ff. Copyrighted 1992 by Christian Light Publications, Inc. Used by permission.)

Bible 5. Did Laura come home and complain about the Brewsters? Why or why not? This was a trial. We need to pray for greater spiritual power to bring blessing out of every pressure and every trial. Suffering helps us grow. Tribulation is a tool to make us more patient. Read II Thessalonians 1:3-5. Strong Christians make their petitions only to God and watch for Him to answer.

Music 6. Sing from <u>Laura Ingalls Wilder Songbook</u>, page 144.

Read Chapters 5, 6, and 7.

Reading Comprehension:

Chapter 5
1. How did the students who did not know their lessons make it hard on Laura?
2. How was Laura's teaching experience causing her to have empathy toward Miss Wilder (page 51)?
3. How was Laura embarrassed?

Chapter 6
4. Whose advice did Laura seek in managing her students?
5. It is said that a woman sets the tone of the house. What tone did Mrs. Brewster set?
6. Why do you think that Almanzo was making the weekly trip to pick up Laura?
7. Why did Laura find it difficult to talk with Almanzo (page 55)?
8. Why did Laura feel guilty (page 55)? Which of Almanzo's reasons for making the long trip was Laura wondering about?
9. How was Laura coping with living at the Brewsters' house (page 56)?
10. Why could Martha and Laura not be friends?
11. Tell how Laura managed each of her problems at school.
12. What impressed Clarence about Laura?
13. Did Ma and Pa's advice work?
14. If Laura were not the teacher, what would she have thought about Clarence? Of whom did he remind her?

Page 198

Golden Years
Week 1

Chapter 7
15. What worried Ma and Pa?
16. What did Laura tell Almanzo? Why did she tell him that?
17. About what did Mrs. Brewster show concern (page 63)?
18. Describe Laura's "snow day" at home with the Brewsters. What happened that night? What did Mrs. Brewster want Mr. Brewster to do? Why would he not do it?
19. Why was Laura surprised to see Almanzo?
20. What character qualities was Almanzo exhibiting?

Activities:

Courting
1. What did Clarence say when Almanzo arrived? Did Laura consider Almanzo her beau? Laura had unknowingly given an impression that Almanzo was her beau. Outsiders closely watch boy/girl relationships. We are told to flee the very appearance of evil. Name some ways a boy/girl relationship (or perhaps an activity) could give the wrong appearance.

Bible
2. What does "Least said soonest mended" mean? How does Ma's saying fit the situation? Is this good advice? This common saying was developed by Cervantes (1547-1616) for his work, Don Quixote, Act 3, Scene 10. Find some scripture that gives the same advice. (Use Proverbs 11:12; 10:19; 13:3; 15:1; 17:27-28; 29:20.)

Bible
3. Pa quoted, "Wise as a serpent and gentle as a dove." From where did this quotation originate? *(The Bible.)* Use your concordance to find the scripture and read this quotation in its original context.

Language
4. Martha was trying to learn complex and compound sentence structures. A simple, complete sentence contains a subject and a predicate. A subject is the part of the sentence that is being talked about, usually a noun and its modifiers. A predicate is the part that tells something about the subject, usually a verb and its modifiers. A compound sentence is composed of two simple sentences joined by a conjunction (and, or, but), or a semicolon (;). A complex sentence is made up of one main simple sentence and at least one dependent clause. A dependent clause cannot stand as a sentence on its own. Dependent clauses usually have key words initially such as when, while, and whenever.

    a. **Simple sentence**—Laura milked the cow.

    b. **Compound sentence**—Laura milked the cow and Mary fed the chickens.

    c. **Complex sentence**—While Laura was milking the cow, Mary fed the chickens.

Writing
5. Write from dictation the third complete paragraph on page 56. What are two proper nouns in this paragraph? *(Tommy and Ruby.)* Correct any spelling or punctuation errors and point out the different types of sentences found in this paragraph. *(The first sentence is a compound sentence; the second is complex; the third is simple.)*

Page 199

Golden Years
Week 1

Bible

6. Clarence caught up with Martha and Charles in their studies. What provoked him to do this? Clarence lacked vision regarding his study. What does the Bible say about lack of vision? (Proverbs 29:18.) What is your vision?

Courting

7. Laura did not want Almanzo to mistakenly think she was interested in courting. In your initial conversations with your child about courting, emphasize that our highest motivation in anything we do is to please God. The first priority one must consider before courting is to seek God's direction for one's life. When we observe Laura at this point, she only envisions herself contributing to the support of her present family. She has not begun to seek God's direction for marriage. A second consideration should be that marriage is the only proper motivation for "dating." The purpose of dating is to find a marriage partner. So courting should occur with the same prayerful discernment that one would exhibit for marriage. The following is a list of three common ways in which the purpose of dating is violated:

a. Dating many partners. When a young man or a young woman dates many partners for "the fun of the moment," expressly not wanting to become serious with any one person yet, he or she is establishing a defective bonding pattern that may erode the foundation of their future marital faithfulness. The person's end becomes "the hunt" rather than endurance in a relationship.

b. Dating one person repeatedly, simply as friends. This denies reality and will inevitably bring hurt.

c. Dating too early. To begin dating before one would want to be married puts unwholesome pressures on the couple. When young men and young women wait to begin dating until they are ready for marriage, they have the freedom to steer their relationship toward marriage.

(From <u>Christian Family Living</u> by John Coblentz, pages 60-61. Copyrighted 1992 by Christian Light Publications, Inc. Used by permission.)

DAY 4

Read Chapters 8, 9, and 10.

Reading Comprehension:

Chapter 8
1. Why must Almanzo return home tonight?
2. What did Almanzo do when he stopped the horses (page 71)? Why did he do this?
3. Why must Laura not go to sleep in the cold?
4. How did Ma know that Laura did not have frostbite?
5. Why did Almanzo come to get Laura? What character qualities did this show?
6. Why had Laura not thought much about Almanzo (page 77)?

Page 200

Chapter 9

7. Who visited the classroom? Why did he visit?
8. What spoke poorly of Laura's discipline?
9. What did the superintendent have to say?
10. What were they out of?

Chapter 10

11. Why did Laura think that she could not quit her teaching job (page 82)?
12. Tell about Laura's last ride to the Brewsters'. Tell about Laura's last day at school.
13. How did her students surprise her?
14. How did she encourage them?
15. How did Laura feel about it being the end of the sleigh rides home?

Activities:

Courting

1. Discuss the six character qualities that should be present in one's life before courting occurs:

    a. **A growing relationship with Christ.** We are to be "married" to the Lord first—devoted to Him. Read Colossians 3:1-5; Proverbs 1:7; 9:10; Psalm 53:1-3. Who would want to marry any less than a person with wisdom and understanding?

    b. **Moral purity.** Read Proverbs 31:10-11. The young person who feeds his mind on immoral imaginations, impure stories or pictures, or who enjoys immoral practices is not prepared for the trustworthiness required in dating and marriage.

    c. **Submission to authority.** Read Titus 3:1-8. The rebellious son or daughter is particularly vulnerable to immoral temptations. Read II Timothy 3:1-7 with emphasis on verses two and six. Frequently, two disobedient young people will be attracted by their common complaints and negatives rather than by their common goals or commitments.

    d. **A Biblical concept of love.** Biblically, love is associated with sacrificial commitment. It is proved in the willingness to give of one's time, abilities, and resources for the well-being, care, and support of another. It requires wise and serious thought, as well as giving, despite the intensity of feeling. While love between a man and a woman has its strong feelings, they come and go. An enduring love does not operate primarily by feelings, but by a commitment that is both sacrificial and selfless.

    e. **Biblical values.** In childhood we live with a view to the immediate. In adulthood we learn to live with a view to the future. In Christ we are taught to live with a view to eternity. Homes are built on values.

Golden Years
Week 1

    f. **A sense of responsibility.** Young people who are contemplating dating need to know that working and saving precede buying, that work precedes relaxation, that mistakes call for restitution, that problems require solutions, and that privileges call for trustworthiness.

(From <u>Christian Family Living</u> by John Coblentz, pages 64-70. Copyrighted 1992 by Christian Light Publications, Inc. Used by permission.)

Art

2. Illustrate and label each of these principles of readiness found in either Almanzo's or Laura's life. The following are some suggestions:

    a. Tell how Almanzo displayed Biblical love. Draw a picture of Almanzo arriving to pick up Laura (pages 68-69).

    b. Illustrate how Laura showed submission to authority.

    c. Almanzo said that he had to return to take care of stock. Which principle did this demonstrate?

Continue this project throughout the unit as more examples are discovered.

Bible

3. Laura, the author, meditated on II Timothy 3 when things went from bad to worse. Read this chapter with special emphasis on verses 10-16. Imagine how these verses might have been special for Laura during this time.

Writing

4. Rewrite yesterday's dictation (Activity #5), making every sentence into a simple sentence. To do this you will end with more than three sentences. Compare the readability of the new paragraph to the original.

Golden Years
Week 2

Week Two Planning Guide

Gather Information on the Following:

(See suggested sources listed)

1. Logging industry
   —To Be a Logger by Lois Lenski
   —

2. History of the women's right to vote
   —

3. Anti-family legislation
   — "Citizen" by Focus on the Family
   — "Washington Watch" by Family Research Council
   —

Gather These Items:

1. Fresh farm eggs
2. Store bought eggs
3. Items to make taffy
4. The American Dictionary of the English Language (the 1828 edition by Noah Webster)
5. Laura Ingalls Wilder Songbook by E. Garson

Suggested Field Trips:

1. Arrange to see an organ and all the features listed on page 158 in These Happy Golden Years.
2. Visit a horse farm or stables and arrange to watch someone break a colt.

Notes:

Golden Years
Week 2
For Use with Day 3

To the Virgins, To Make Much of Time

Gather ye Rose-buds while ye may,

Old Time is still a flying:

And this same flower that smiles today,

To morrow will be dying.

The glorious Lamp of Heaven, the Sun,

The higher he's a getting;

The sooner will his Race be run,

And nearer he's to Setting.

The Age is best, which is the first,

When Youth and Blood are Warmer;

But being spent, the worse, and worst

Times, still succeed the former.

Then be coy, use your time;

And while ye may, go marry:

For having lost but once your prime,

You may for ever tarry.

- - - Robert Herrick

(1591-1674)

Golden Years
Week 2

Read Chapters 11, 12, and 13.

Reading Comprehension:

Chapter 11
1. When did Laura wish that Mary would come visit?
2. Why did Laura's friends not come visit?
3. Why did Almanzo think Laura might have changed her mind? Was this a good reason for her to have changed her mind?
4. Why was everyone so happy (page 94)?

Chapter 12
5. When Laura discovered about the composition, what did she do? Could she have offered an excuse instead of staying in for recess?
6. What do you especially like about Laura's composition? What do you think about ambition?
7. What did Pa praise Laura for (page 99)?
8. What was Laura's reason for earning money?
9. What was to be Laura's new job? How had she been prepared for this?

Chapter 13
10. Who came to visit? What was he like? What had he done for a living?
11. How were Ma and Uncle Tom alike?
12. Why did Laura feel sorry for her sisters (page 104)?
13. Why did the soldiers burn the stockade?
14. What similar experience had happened in the Ingalls' family?
15. Why was Almanzo quiet?
16. What did they enjoy doing together?

Activities:

Geography	1.	Find the state of Wisconsin on the map entitled "Laura and Her Friends' Travels" (from "Prairie") and label it with a drawing of "Uncle Tom."
Vocabulary	2.	What are gulches (page 106), bastions (page 107), and switch (page 112)? Write which dictionary definition fits the context.
Social Studies	3.	Research the logging industry.
Courting	4.	When in a group, the courting couple is encouraged to be accountable for their actions, while still allowing them to get to know each other. How did Almanzo arrange to get to know Laura in a group setting? Discuss with your child group occasions or activities that a young couple could enjoy while getting to know one another.
Writing	5.	Interview your mom and dad about how they met. Then write one or two paragraphs about your findings in a journalistic manner. Include what they initially thought of each other. What encouraged them to get to know each other better? *(This is the first of many such interview/reports assigned. Other topics will include how parents courted, what*

Page 205

Golden Years
Week 2

character qualities attracted them to each other, how they became engaged, etc. You may wish to read ahead so that the interviewing will remain pertinent to the topic at hand. Your child may also want to keep each report together in a special Family History notebook or binding.)

Writing   6.   Almanzo's quietness stemmed from jealousy. Look up "jealous" and "jealousy" in the <u>American Dictionary of the English Language</u> (the 1828 edition by Noah Webster) and review their definitions. Using the dictionary, write a couple paragraphs on jealousy. This is a similar project to that of Laura's composition about ambition.

Bible   7.   Laura was successful in school and teaching. In Joshua 1:8 the Lord tells us what we must do to be successful. The Lord tells us, if we put Him first all the other things will be added unto us. (Matthew 6:33.) Remember, it was the Lord that gave Laura strength to teach school for Mary's sake, although it was not her heart's desire. What did the Lord "add unto her?" *(Answers may vary. She remained the head of her class. Almanzo was interested in her as a woman of godly character.)*

General   8.   Remember this week to schedule and make time for General Activities.

DAY 2

Read Chapters 14 and 15.

Reading Comprehension:

Chapter 14
1.   What was Laura's new job?
2.   What previous events in Laura's life had prepared her for this? When had Laura learned to twist hay?
3.   Why did the teamster go quickly through the slough?
4.   How did they get hay? Was this in the teamster's job description?
5.   What had happened to their nearest neighbor?
6.   Why did Mrs. McKee see the Homestead Act as anti-family? What did she see as a solution to the problem (page 119)?
7.   What was Laura's week like? What did the women do on Saturday? What was Sunday like while Mr. McKee was at home?
8.   How long did Laura stay with Mrs. McKee? Why did she return home?
9.   What did Mrs. McKee say about an old bachelor? Did Laura want to marry? Why or why not?
10.   Who would they find to replace Laura?

Chapter 15
11.   How did they collect eggs?
12.   Was Kitty still a good hunter? Had she had kittens?
13.   Was Kitty friendly to Mary? Why or why not?
14.   Why was Mary not afraid to travel alone?
15.   What gifts had Mary brought?
16.   Had it been worth their sacrifice to send Mary to college?
17.   How did Mary learn to read Braille quicker than the other girls?

Page 206

18. What made Ma's smile tremble (page 127)?
19. Describe how Mary wrote.
20. What did Laura say about Mary putting her cold feet on her?

Activities:

Art
1. Illustrate what the teamster and his passengers looked like after they crossed the slough. Encourage the student to show perspective in his picture. If necessary, look at other artwork to show how an artist portrays perspective.

History/Speech
2. Research the history of the Nineteenth Amendment, Women's Right to Vote, for presentation as an oral report. Use visual aids. If your daughter is doing this report, she may want to dress as a suffragette.

Politics
3. Mrs. McKee felt that giving women the right to vote would end anti-family policies. This has not proved to be true. Discuss with your parents some anti-family legislation. *(Some ideas for discussion: draft of women into the military, abortion, anti-homeschooling laws, child care tax credits to accredited agencies, taxing married couples at a higher rate than two single people.)*

Language
4. Practice your letter-writing skills by composing a formal, persuasive letter to the appropriate legislator who has authored or introduced a bill that is anti-family. Keep your argument to a particular point and be sure to state your position clearly. Support your point with relevant, well-thought-out data. You may need to contact the pro-family or pro-life lobbyist in your state to research the current bills pending legislation. If you type, you will want to use your best typing skills to polish this assignment.

Science
5. Crack open chicken eggs from chickens that are free to forage. Compare them to a store-bought egg. What is the difference in the thickness of the shell, the yellowness of the yoke, etc.? What do you think makes the difference? Discuss your hypothesis with your parent. How could your hypothesis be proved or disproved? Write out your hypothesis and your procedure for proof.

Bible
6. Mary thanked her mother for encouraging her Bible memory work. Remember Joshua 1:8. What does Proverbs 23:24-25 say about the mother of a wise child? Read Proverbs 31. What verse speaks of her children's attitude toward her? What shall happen to a woman who fears the Lord?

Bible
7. On page 118, what is Ma's saying regarding having enough? How does Ecclesiastes 5:10-11 say something similar to this saying?

Golden Years
Week 2

DAY 3

Read Chapters 16 and 17.
Reading Comprehension:

Chapter 16
1. Before going to work, what were Laura and Mary's days like?
2. What were the teenagers busy doing in the summer?
3. Whom did they see in town? Why did Laura not recognize him?
4. Who was interested in Almanzo?
5. What did Pa say about wanting to earn money (page 134)?
6. What did Mary offer to do if Laura went to work?
7. Why did Pa say there was a large turnover in town? Why was it hard to get to know people (page 135)?
8. Who planned to write a book? Who had originally planned to be a school teacher? Who ended up being the famous authoress?
9. How did Laura feel when talking about Almanzo?
10. Describe how Laura's days and evening were spent.
11. How did they celebrate the Fourth of July?
12. What was Laura thinking about Almanzo? Would she try to contact Almanzo to tell him that her thoughts about him were changing?
13. Why was Pa thin, tired, and restless?
14. What was Pa's bet with the United States?
15. Why did Pa and Laura do things they would have preferred not to have done?

Chapter 17
16. Who came to visit? Why did she seem like family?
17. What did they do at night?
18. What did Arthur and Alice use to keep them warm on their way home?
19. What were Almanzo and Cap doing? What did she remember about the hard winter?
20. Who came to the door? Why was Laura hesitant to go with Cap?
21. How did Laura show that she had confidence in Almanzo?
22. What did Almanzo do every Sunday after that?
23. How did Almanzo look out for Laura's safety (pages 145-146)?
24. What was Laura's special Christmas present? Who was it from?

Activities:

Writing
1. Rewrite Week 2, Day 1, Activity 5 or 6. Use a thesaurus to look up the verbs you used in each sentence, and substitute more descriptive ones for them. For example, instead of "walked," use "shuffled." Secondly, identify your simple sentences. Combine at least two of them to make a compound sentence. Thirdly, if you did not use a complex sentence, modify a simple sentence into a complex one. Rewrite your paper and compare it to the original.

Vocabulary
2. Look up "disparaged" (page 132).

Literature/
Reasoning
3. On page 135, Mary begins to quote a poem by Robert Herrick (1591-1674), "To the Virgins, To Make Much of Time." Read this poem in its entirety. How does this poem fit the moment and the conversation of the girls? What is symbolism in poetry? (*The poet uses symbolism to intensify*

Page 208

Golden Years
Week 2

the meaning of the poem. A symbolic word or image in poetry will mean the thing the word actually represents and also something more. This "something more" should be interpreted by the context of the poem. After reading this poem several times, you will get a feel for what the images symbolize.) What does the imagery of the rosebuds symbolize in the first stanza of the poem? *(Youth and virginity.)* What does the image of the Sun represent? *(The passage of time.)* What is the attitude conveyed in this poem concerning the relationship between youth and time? *(The sentiment is one of glorifying one's youth and living out one's desires because time will ultimately expire and with it all opportunities. This is a classic expression of carpe diem— "seize the day." "The age is best which is the first . . . the worst times still succeed the former.")*

Bible/Writing
4. What is the attitude God wants us to have about time? (See Ephesians 5:15-16; Psalm 90:12.) How does God want you to spend your youth? (I Kings 18:12; Psalm 71:5, 17; Ecclesiastes 12:1; Lamentations 3:27; II Timothy 2:22.) Contrast the two attitudes of how to spend one's youth from God's perspective and from futile man's point of view. Write a paper, first describing each attitude, then contrasting them, and finally, commenting on how you choose to live out your youth. It may be helpful to read the parable of the wise and foolish virgins in Matthew 25 to help with your comparison of the youth in the poem and a godly youth. *(Many writers of the seventeenth century such as Robert Herrick were concerned with the relationship between time and morality. Man's inability to maintain godly standards and to live a purposeful life was influenced by the ideas that the passage of time would eventually leave its stamp of futility on all his efforts. This attitude echoes the writer of Ecclesiastes who says, "Vanity, vanity, all is vanity" [Ecclesiastes 1:2].)*

History
5. In the encyclopedia read about Robert Herrick. Find out about his life and the times in which he lived.

Cooking
6. Make taffy. Invite friends over and have a taffy-pulling party.

DAY 4

Read Chapters 18 and 19.

Reading Comprehension:

Chapter 18
1. Why did they need to quickly move to the claim?
2. What did the school district want Laura to do?
3. What did Laura do during slow times and lunch (page 152)?
4. How did Laura feel about her life?
5. What did Pa suggest Laura do with her money?

Golden Years
Week 2

Chapter 19

6. What did Laura need? What did she do to get new clothes?
7. What were Pa and Ma doing (page 157)?
8. Why should they not call their place a claim shanty anymore?
9. How long was Laura's hair?
10. What did Carrie do after she was ready for church (page 161)?
11. Look on page 163 and explain both Ma's and Pa's sayings.
12. What did Carrie point out to Laura (page 164)?
13. What did Laura do when Almanzo put his arm around her (page 166)?
14. Why had Almanzo not been by to see Laura sooner (page 169)?
15. How far did they ride?

Activities:

Bible 1. Did Laura have time to study for the exam? She had to be prepared quickly. What does the Bible say about being prepared? Read II Timothy 2:15; 4:2; Matthew 25:1-13.

Math 2. How much was Laura's pay to be (page 149)? How much more would the pay be than when she stayed with the Brewsters and taught (page 99)? How much more than when she worked as a seamstress (page 130)?

Art 3. Draw what the inside of Perry Schoolhouse looked like. Use shading techniques.

Writing 4. Compare and contrast Laura's first teaching job with her second.

Bible 5. Reread aloud the song, "Happy, Happy Golden Years." What does it mean to you? The Bible speaks how quickly life goes by. Read Ecclesiastes 7:14.

Bible 6. Pa and Laura both looked longingly westward. Does Ecclesiastes 6:9 speak to this scene?

Living 7. How long was Pa's bet with the government? How long is your parents' home or car loan? How long is the typical home loan of today?

Vocabulary 8. Look up tremolo (page 158), forte (page 158), bustle (page 162), and polonaise (page 162).

Courting 9. **Courting must include healthy, open communication.** The long buggy rides gave Laura and Almanzo a time to talk and to get to know each other. What is the difference between admiration and love and infatuation? *(Infatuation is fed by the imagination, rather than real knowledge and understanding of a person.)* List some topics that a couple could discuss to stimulate good conversations. Would going to the movies be a healthy way to build a relationship, or would it increase infatuation? *(When situations encourage open conversations, a couple will learn how the other feels and thinks, and will get to know the other's character. Some topics for discussion may be one's childhood, how one feels about God and their spiritual walk, one's favorite books, hobbies, projects, sports, trips, etc. Outings should not be limited to time alone conversing. You learn more about a person by seeing them in a variety of circumstances and surroundings. A couple must be careful to plan outings that encourage a healthy exchange and not "give the devil an opportunity" to tempt them.*

Page 210

Golden Years
Week 2

Again, a couple will be safer in a group that will hold them accountable for their actions. On Laura's and Almanzo's ride, the untamed ponies occupied Almanzo's hands and required much of his concentration, but still allowed them to converse. The ponies served somewhat as "chaperons." Their ride was far safer, romantically speaking, than couples today going for a carefree drive in a car. Another important way to get to know the character of a courter is by working with them on projects. There is much work to be accomplished within a marriage. It is as important to work well as to play well together.)

Courting 10. Laura refused to allow Almanzo to touch her. What did she do to avoid Almanzo's arm around her? Her behavior is a sharp contrast to what is seen even in the most "harmless" G-rated movies of today. Engaging in physical intimacies in a courting relationship distorts discernment and can undermine the basis for respect and trust necessary for solid marriages. It is also wrong biblically. Read Ephesians 4:19; 5:1-4, 6; Colossians 3:5; Matthew 5:28; I Thessalonians 4:1-8; I Corinthians 6:12-20; Hebrews 10:26-27.

a. When dating, physical restraint is an expression of love and respect. Read Titus 2:6-8, 11-14.

b. Lack of restraint reveals a lack of character—selfishness. Read Proverbs 10:17; 25:28. Marriage partners who cannot control their self-gratifying impulses easily find themselves tempted to look beyond their marriage for stimulation.

c. Physical contact is progressive. One small act will lead to the next.

d. Lack of restraint undermines respect.

e. To arouse the sexual desires in another person when those desires cannot be righteously satisfied defrauds the other person. Passion cheats the couple of true joy and peace—a righteous walk with God; and if the couple chooses to end their relationship, it cheats their future partners.

f. Courtship is a process of decisions. Wise decisions require careful thought. Restraint is necessary because physical intimacies in courting destroys objectivity. This principle extends even beyond the matter of affectionate physical contact. A couple may be unrestrained in the amount of time or the frequency of time they spend together. Any lack of restraint keeps them from objectively looking at the situation.

(From Christian Family Living by John Coblentz, pages 79-84. Copyrighted 1992 by Christian Light Publications, Inc. Used by permission.)

What caused Almanzo and Laura to be restrained in the amount and frequency of time spent together? *(Their responsibilities regarding work.)*

Art 11. Make a warning poster regarding dating, using one of the above verses in Activity #10.

Music 12. Sing from Laura Ingalls Wilder Songbook, pages 38 and 70.

Page 211

Golden Years
Week 3

Week Three Planning Guide

Gather Information on the Following:

(See suggested sources listed)

1. Sound waves and the ear
   —Blood and Guts by Linda Allison
   —Sounds Interesting by Dr. David Darling
   —Experiments in Sound by Nelson F. Beeler
   —Input and Output (Provision Media)
   —The Young Scientist Book of the Human Body (Usborne)

2. How precious and semiprecious stones are cut, polished, and made into jewelry

Gather These Items:

1. The music for "America the Beautiful"
2. The American Dictionary of the English Language (the 1828 edition by Noah Webster)
3. Laura Ingalls Wilder Songbook by E. Garson

Suggested Field Trips:

1. Attend a choral production; listen for the different voice classifications/pitches.
2. Arrange a tour of a school music department. Have them introduce the five basic elements of music: dynamics, rhythm, melody, harmony, and tone color.
3. Begin singing lessons or join a choir.
4. Find a treadle sewing machine. Try sewing with it.

Notes:

Golden Years
Week 3

Read Chapter 20.

Reading Comprehension:

Chapter 20
1. "It never rains but it pours" is a common saying. What does this mean? Apply the situation to Ma's comment.
2. What did Almanzo think of the possibility of growing trees on the prairie (page 171)?
3. Why do you think Almanzo brought Nellie with them?
4. What character qualities did Nellie display?
5. Why did Laura suggest going by the Boasts'?
6. What did Laura do to show Nellie's true character?
7. How did Laura think that she compared to Nellie?
8. On page 177, what difference did it make that Almanzo did not have a cow?
9. What prompted Laura to tell Almanzo not to come for her if Nellie were to be there? What did she think about the consequences of that?
10. What did Mary's letter say? What did Ma think about it?
11. What did Almanzo think of Nellie?
12. What surprised Laura about Almanzo (page 181)?
13. On Sunday how did Almanzo surprise Laura?
14. Contrast the ride with Nellie to that with Ida.
15. What did Laura miss about being with her crowd of friends (page 183)?
16. Explain the meaning of the song Laura sang (page 184). Why would she not do what the song said?

Activities:

Bible/Writing   1. Nellie was flattering Almanzo. Find some of the flattering statements on pages 173 and 174. In the American Dictionary of the English Language (the 1828 edition by Noah Webster) read the entries for "flatter" and "flattery." What does the Bible say about flattery? Nellie talked a lot. What does the Bible say about talking too much? Use your concordance to find some verses on flattery and talking. From what you have learned, write a composition on flattery.

Bible/Art   2. The Bible tells men to be wary of women with beckoning eyes. Read the following verses: Proverbs 2:10,16-19; 5:3-21; 6:24-35; 7:1-27; 9:13-18; 22:14; 23:26-28. Use one of these verses to make a warning poster for a young man.

Courting   3. Laura and Almanzo's relationship had progressed beyond friendship to courting. Almanzo no longer announced that he would come by on the following Sunday. Yet he always came and Laura was always ready. Estimate the elapsed time since Almanzo first walked her home from the revival or brought her home from the Brewsters' to this present point in time.

Vocabulary   4. Look up "lamented" in the American Dictionary of the English Language (the 1828 edition by Noah Webster).

Page 213

Golden Years
Week 3

    Writing   5.   Interview your mother and father and talk about what they did to get to know each other during courtship. What character qualities attracted them to the other? Write one or two paragraphs on this topic. Add it to your Family History notebook.

    Literature   6.   What is the main idea in this chapter? Who are the characters? What is the conflict and how is it resolved?

    Music   7.   Sing from <u>Laura Ingalls Wilder Songbook</u>, page 106.

    General   8.   Remember this week to schedule and make time for General

DAY 2

Read Chapters 21 and 22.

Reading Comprehension:

Chapter 21
1. What did the Ingalls decide to do for the Fourth of July?
2. What did Pa say Almanzo would be good at?
3. What was Ma's feeling about Laura riding with Almanzo (page 186)?
4. What work did Carrie offer to do? Do you think that it is common for younger children to be expected to help less than the older children did when they were that age?
5. Why had Almanzo sold the colts?
6. Why did they want the top of the buggy up? Why could they not use the top?
7. Did Laura enjoy the thrill of taming horses?
8. What did Ma have the girls do when the storm was close by? Why did she have them do this?
9. What delighted Laura about the storm (page 197)?
10. What did Pa think about debt? What previous experience had Pa had with debt? (Remember <u>On the Banks of Plum Creek</u>.)
11. How did Barnum react differently when Laura drove him? The second time Laura drove what difference did she feel in the reins? Have you ever experienced this?
12. What did Almanzo want Laura to do with him Friday night?

Chapter 22
13. What was different about school this year?
14. Who was going to the Friday night sing?
15. Where was Nellie?
16. Who befriended the new girl? Why?
17. Why would Almanzo and Laura need to leave singing school a little early?
18. What happened when Almanzo and Laura left the singing lesson? Why had Barnum acted like he did?
19. Did Laura complain?

Page 214

Golden Years
Week 3

Activities:

Writing/Language   1.   Discuss with your parent yesterday's writing assignment. Identify the adjectives and adverbs you used. Add or replace the ones used with more descriptive adjectives and adverbs. Use a thesaurus if necessary. Identify all the simple, compound, and complex sentences. Make a compound sentence from two simple sentences. Identify your main idea in each paragraph. How does each sentence support the main idea?

Bible   2.   Read Proverbs 30:18-19. Describe how this applies to Almanzo.

Music   3.   A voice student studies and trains his/her voice to develop and improve four basic singing skills:

     a.   **Breath control.**

     b.   **Pitch range.**

     c.   **Smooth transitions throughout the range.**

     d.   **Good resonance.** Resonance strengthens and beautifies the tone and is accomplished by relaxing the throat muscles so that the throat opens to the greatest diameter. Voice students also are trained to read music notation.

If you know someone trained in singing, ask them to demonstrate these basic skills.

Science   4.   People produce sound when vibrating air passes through the vocal cords. The vocal cords are elastic. The pitch of the tones produced when the cords vibrate may vary depending on the degree of tension. Use a tuning fork to demonstrate the variances between high and low pitches. Use either a guitar or other stringed instrument to show how the tightness and the diameter of the strings cause different pitches. Since a man normally sings lower than a woman, form a hypothesis about whose vocal cords are longer, wider, and thicker.

Music   5.   Voices are classified according to their pitch range. They are classified as follows:

     a.   **Bass**—the lowest pitch range, usually sung by a man. The bass sings the bottom note of a four-note chord.

     b.   **Tenor**—the highest male pitch range. The tenor sings the third note from the top of a four-note chord.

     c.   **Alto**—the low female pitch range. An alto sings the second note from the top of a four-note chord.

     d.   **Soprano**—the highest pitch range, usually sung by a woman. The soprano sings the top note of a four-note chord.

Identify a four-note chord in the hymn "America the Beautiful." Point out or play on a piano the note that each voice sings.

Page 215

Golden Years
Week 3

Music   6. Identify the names and values of notes, holds, slurs, rests, bass, tenor, and treble clef.

Music   7. Play a musical scale on an instrument. Try to sing a scale.

Music   8. Sing from <u>Laura Ingalls Wilder Songbook</u>, page 100.

DAY 3

Read Chapters 23, 24, and 25.
Reading Comprehension:

Chapter 23
1. How was Laura able to get Barnum to walk?
2. How did Laura feel as Barnum walked through town?
3. Why did Almanzo take Laura to singing school? Was he concerned with her interests and talents or was he only willing to involve her in his interests?
4. Was Almanzo generally prompt?
5. How did Almanzo ask Laura to marry him?
6. What did Almanzo give Laura? What did he promise?
7. What did Laura say about little houses?
8. When did Laura allow Almanzo to give her a kiss?
9. Had Almanzo talked to Pa?
10. What was Laura too shy to say?

Chapter 24
11. How did Laura feel about being engaged?
12. How did Laura find out Ida was engaged?
13. What was Pa's news for Laura?
14. What did Carrie and Grace want Laura to do?
15. What would be the benefit of the Ingalls staying on the claim this winter (page 221)?
16. How would the girls go to school and back?
17. On his way to pick up the girls from school what did Pa do? Did Laura hear from Almanzo?

Chapter 25
18. Describe how Laura popped corn.
19. What did Grace get in trouble for (page 225)?
20. Compare this Christmas to Laura's previous Christmases.
21. What was the Christmas Eve surprise?
22. What did the girls think about each Christmas?

Activities:

Science/Art   1. In the encyclopedia look up the names of the stones in Laura's ring. Where do these stones come from? How are gems cut and polished? Draw what it looked like on Laura's hand.

Writing   2. Interview your parents to find out how your parents became engaged. Write a paragraph or two describing the event and add this to your ongoing Family History report.

Courting	3.	Children are to honor their father and mother as the Bible says. Before marriage, a daughter honors her parents by being subject to their advice and decisions. Permission to marry should be asked of her parents by the suitor. Engagement or betrothal is a serious commitment, and the engagement period should only be as long as needed to get ready for the wedding. Verbalize how Almanzo demonstrated these principles of engagement.
Writing	4.	Write out the steps involved in making popcorn.
Music	5.	Relate the five elements of music to the hymn "America the Beautiful":

    a. **Melody**—organization of notes into a recognizable unit. The top notes of the hymn are the melody. In a hymn the sopranos usually sing the melody.

    b. **Harmony**—two or more notes sounded simultaneously, adding depth and richness to the melody. Find in the hymn where two, three and four notes are played together creating harmony.

    c. **Rhythm**—the organization of sound and silence. This hymn contains several different note values—half notes, quarter notes, and eighth notes—that create the rhythm of the song.

    d. **Dynamics**—the loudness and softness in music indicated by such terms as forte (loud) and piano (soft).

    e. **Tone color**—the quality of sound produced—characteristic qualities that cause one instrument or voice to sound different from another.

Music	6.	Sing from <u>Laura Ingalls Wilder Songbook</u>, pages 60, 94, 98, and 130.

DAY 4

Read Chapters 26, 27, and 28.

Reading Comprehension:

Chapter 26
1. What did Laura and Almanzo do on Sundays during the winter?
2. How did Laura feel in the room full of strangers?
3. What was Ma's advice about the exam? What did Laura think of Ma's advice?
4. Did Ma open Laura's letter?
5. What enabled Laura to get a different, larger school?
6. On page 235 the last paragraph, Laura remembered Ma's saying. What was it? Apply it to this chapter.

Golden Years
Week 3

Chapter 27
7. How was this both an end and a beginning?
8. What did Laura's teacher confess?
9. On page 238, what does the common saying "For better or worse" allude to?

Chapter 28
10. Why did Laura keep her smiles unseen at school?
11. How was Laura's last year teaching?
12. Who did Laura stay with? How was it, staying with this family?
13. How did Pa know that Ma would like a sewing machine (page 242)?
14. What surprise awaited Mary?
15. What did Laura do with most of her money earned for the first month? What did Pa say?
16. How would Laura's getting married affect her relationship with Mary?

Activities:

Bible/Writing	1.	Laura's teacher admitted he did not allow Laura to graduate because he was prideful. In the <u>American Dictionary of the English Language</u> (the 1828 edition by Noah Webster), read the definition of pride. Use your concordance to find scriptures about pride. From these two sources write one page of your findings about this character flaw.
Living	2.	Laura's sheets were made from muslin. What is muslin? Compare muslin to the material your sheets are made from.
Art	3.	Draw a picture of Laura's dress.
Literature	4.	What does the common saying "To feel like a bird out of a cage" mean?
Vocabulary	5.	What is grippe (page 234)?
Music	6.	Identify by type (quarter, eighth, half, whole) and letter name the notes used in "America the Beautiful."
Science	7.	For the remainder of this unit, study about sound waves and the workings of the ear.

Page 218

Golden Years
Week 4

Week Four Planning Guide

Gather Information on the Following:

(See suggested sources listed)

1. Safety measures to take during a tornado
   —Tornado Alert by Franklyn Branley

2. Cause of tornadoes
   —Tornado Alert by Franklyn Branley

Gather These Items:

1. The McGee and Me, "Twister and Shout" video
2. Laura Ingalls Wilder Country by William Anderson
3. Laura Ingalls Wilder Songbook by E. Garson

Suggested Field Trips:

Notes:

Golden Years
Week 4

DAY 1

Read Chapters 29, 30, and 31.

Reading Comprehension:

Chapter 29
1. Why did Laura mention that her feathers were well sewn?
2. On page 254, to what did Laura compare the clouds? What image does this leave with you?
3. Tell about the damage from the cyclone.

Chapter 30
4. What made Laura want to laugh at church?
5. What would Mary miss about Laura?
6. What did Mary say about the passage of time?
7. What did Laura think about the future?
8. Why did Laura not want to wait until next June to marry?

Chapter 31
9. After Mary left, what did they do to cheer themselves?
10. What was Laura's innovative idea for sewing the sheets?
11. What had happened that caused Almanzo to give Laura a surprise visit on Tuesday?
12. What was Laura's hesitation about the wedding ceremony? What did Almanzo say to that?
13. What did Ma think about Laura being married in black?
14. Why could they not have any kind of wedding ceremony?
15. What was Pa's input and advice?

Activities:

Science	1.	On a hot day, why would it be more pleasant to ride than sit in the house?
Safety	2.	Watch the McGee and Me video, "Twist and Shout."
Safety	3.	What safety measures should be taken when there is a tornado? Discuss what precautions should be taken if you are indoors, outdoors, or in a vehicle.
Science	4.	What climatic factors cause tornadoes?
Bible	5.	Laura questioned if she could always obey her husband. Almanzo knew that Laura was not rebellious and was obedient and respectful to her parents. He knew that she was a hard worker and was a very giving person. Knowing all this, he could determine that she would likely be the same toward him. Read these verses on marriage, then decide what you think the scripture says about a woman's role in marriage. Ephesians 5:22-32; Titus 2:3-5; I Peter 3:1-6; I Samuel 25.
Living/Courting	6.	Look at your parents' wedding pictures with them.
Writing	7.	Write one page on what you speculate may have happened to Nellie over the remainder of her life.

Page 220

Golden Years
Week 4

General   8. Remember this week to schedule and make time to conclude General
                 Activities.

DAY 2

Read Chapters 32 and 33. This Finishes the Book.

Reading Comprehension:

Chapter 32
1. How did Carrie and Grace help prepare for the wedding?
2. Why were Almanzo and Laura to be married at ten o'clock?
3. What do you think of Almanzo breaking the sabbath?
4. What did Pa buy Laura for a wedding present?
5. What did Ma give Laura? Why did Ma also give Laura a tablecloth (page 275)?
6. Besides Fawn being Laura's favorite young cow, why was this a generous gift?
7. How did Laura spend her last night at home?

Chapter 33
8.   Tell about Laura's wedding.
9.   What had Ida given Laura?
10. Why did Ma's food taste like sawdust?
11. What did Grace say to make everyone laugh?
12. Why had Almanzo driven Prince and Lady? What does this show about him?
13. What did Laura think about her kitchen?
14. Why did Laura put the butter in the cellar?
15. Where was the little book from?
16. Why did Laura know that she did not need to be homesick?

Activities:

Writing   1. Write one page about what you think may have happened to Ida.

Music   2. Sing from <u>Laura Ingalls Wilder Songbook</u>, page 30.

Page 221

Golden Years
Week 4

DAY 3

Read Laura Ingalls Wilder Country, Chapter 8, "Laura, Almanzo, and Rose."

Activities:

Writing 1. Write one page on what you think happened to Cap Garland.

History 2. Discuss the spiritual condition of the United States during the 1800's. Use the evangelist biography and the Little House books as a source of information. How does it compare with today?

DAY 4

To discover what happened to Laura's friends, send a self-addressed stamped envelope to:
Cadron Creek Christian Curriculum
4329 Pinos Altos Rd
Silver City, NM 88061
or
e-mail: CadronCreek.com.

Chapter 9, "Friends, Relatives and Neighbors of the Little House Books and What Happened to Them," of The Story of the Ingalls by William Anderson contained this information in the 1982 edition, but the newer edition does not.

Were any of your speculations about these people close to reality?

Finish Any Undone Activities!

Farmer Boy

Farmer Boy

Farmer Boy generally follows Little House of the Prairie in the series listing; however, it is included here after These Happy Golden Years, because Laura probably heard many of Almanzo's stories during the long buggy rides they took while courting. Laura never visited the farm on which Almanzo lived; however, she vividly records it from the remembrances of her husband. The events in Farmer Boy take place in New York in 1866, a year that Almanzo grows from a young boy to a responsible youth. Interestingly, this was the year that Caroline Ingalls was pregnant with Laura.

It is hard not to contrast the differences between Almanzo's upbringing on an established farm with Laura's childhood on the rugged frontier. As you read, look for ways to contrast their experiences.

In Farmer Boy, Almanzo begins learning the rigors of running a successful farm. He is anxious to learn the care and training of the animals; and he helps in all the routine of planting, harvesting, and protecting the crops. In the process, he learns the value of work and self-reliance. Almanzo is also seen as one who is observant of the laws of nature. Therefore, the Primer focuses on the study of plants and states of matter.

Additional Reference Material:

Photosynthesis

Energy and matter cannot be created or destroyed. Only God can do this. Photosynthesis is the process by which plants take energy from the sun and produce food (sugars). During this process, excess oxygen is given off as a by-product (see Figure 1). Photosynthesis takes place only in green plants, algae, and some bacteria, because only these contain chlorophyll.

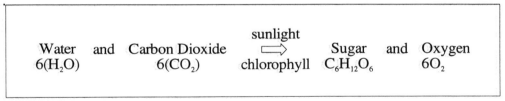

Figure 1

Chlorophyll is located within the cell in a disc-like structure called a chloroplast. Chloroplasts are not attached to the cell wall, but float in the cell's jellylike cytoplasm. In chloroplasts, light energy causes water drawn from the soil to split into atoms of hydrogen and oxygen. (Atoms are the basic building blocks of matter.) The hydrogen then combines with the carbon dioxide to make a simple sugar. The oxygen is released into the air for us to breathe. The simple sugar, together with nitrogen, sulfur, and phosphorus from the soil, make starch, fat, protein, and vitamins. Most of the gas exchange in plants occurs in small openings in the leaves called stomata.

A plant is a living organism; so when sunlight is present, it produces oxygen. Without sunlight, it does not produce oxygen; however, it consumes small amounts of this gas and gives off carbon dioxide.

Farmer Boy

General Activities to Do throughout This Unit:

1. If the season permits, have your child(ren) plan and graph a garden. If space is limited, investigate square-foot gardening. To begin, have them suggest which vegetables will sprout first. Watch and check whether their hypotheses proved true.

2. Work on a loom project. This can be as small as making potholders to as large as a blanket on a full-size loom. For an optional project, select a woodworking craft. Plan to complete the project by the end of this unit.

3. Study the three states of matter—solids, liquids, and gases. The suggested resource is <u>Solids, Liquids and Gases</u> (Milliken).

4. Set a schedule to memorize I Corinthians 13:1-8 by the end of this book.

5. Read a biography of Francis Scott Key.

Farmer Boy
Week 1

Week One Planning Guide

Gather Information on the Following:

(See suggested sources listed)

1. Wool
   —All About Wool by Claire Jobin

2. Sense of taste
   —Encyclopedia
   —Tasting (Troll)
   —Input and Output (Provision Media)
   —The Young Scientist Book of the Human Body (Usborne)

3. Three states of matter
   —Solids, Liquids, and Gases (Milliken)

4. Red cedar tree (picture and uses)

5. Biography of Francis Scott Key
   —Francis Scott Key (Sower Series)

Gather These Items:

1. Headcheese
2. Watermelon rind pickles
3. Items to make apples 'n' onions
   —The Little House Cookbook by Barbara M. Walker
4. Items to make birds' nest pudding
   —The Little House Cookbook by Barbara M. Walker
5. Items to make twist doughnuts
   —The Little House Cookbook by Barbara M. Walker
6. Items to make rye 'n' ingun bread
   —The Little House Cookbook by Barbara M. Walker
7. Stacked pancakes, described in Chapter 8
8. Samples of different types of wood
9. Small swatches of broadcloth, silk, merino, velvet
10. The American Dictionary of the English Language (the 1828 edition by Noah Webster)

Suggested Field Trip:

1. Visit a woodcrafter to look at different types of wood. What are the properties of each wood? What are the advantages? disadvantages? Also, note what tools a woodcrafter uses.

Page 225

Farmer Boy
Week 1

Read Chapters 1 and 2.

Reading Comprehension:

Chapter 1
1. At what age did Almanzo start school? At what age did you start school? What do you think accounts for the difference?
2. What were the teacher's lodgings?
3. What was the discipline for not knowing one's lesson?

Chapter 2
4. How was Almanzo's house different from Laura's? *(His was painted, larger, etc.)*
5. Why was Almanzo not allowed near the three-year-old horses (page 17)?
6. What did Almanzo wear for doing the chores in the barn?
7. What did Almanzo do daily for the animals?
8. What do calves like (page 19)?
9. What did Almanzo think was a sign of a good mouser (page 20)?
10. Who did Almanzo milk and why? Was Almanzo a good milker?
11. What pleased Almanzo (page 22)?
12. How did Almanzo perceive his father? What were the reasons that he gave for his perception (pages 22-23)?
13. Where did they get their water (page 23)?
14. Who could talk at the table?
15. Finish this saying, "Children must be _____ and _____ _____."
16. What had the Hardscrabble boys done last year?

Activities:

Social Studies/ Textiles	1.	Investigate the steps from wool production to sweater making. What are the benefits of wool over other clothing materials? *(Wool is waterproof and traps air to better insulate.)*
Art	2.	Draw Almanzo's clothes, including what color they were. Label materials used for construction (page 3).
Geography	3.	Find New York state on "Laura and Her Friends' Travels" map. Draw a farm on New York with a dot for Malone.
Literature	4.	Is this book fiction or nonfiction? Is it a biography or an autobiography? *(Biographical fiction.)* Do you think this book was written with Almanzo's permission?
Literature	5.	Discuss how the incident with the Hardscrabble boys adds interest to the story. Why are these characters even included in the book? *(Knowing about them adds to our sense of anticipation toward the outcome of that particular conflict; we are given the contrast in moral qualities to compare with those of the main character of the book.)*

**Farmer Boy
Week 1**

Literature	6.	On page 16, reread the second complete sentence. Have you ever lived where the winters delivered <u>that much</u> snow? Laura, the author, writes as if two feet of snow was nothing. This is a technique in literature known as an understatement. Hyperbole, the opposite of understatement, is an exaggerated description such as "I'm so hungry I could eat a horse." Laura understates the amount of snow in contrast to what it could be like; but to many readers that two-foot amount is still enormous. Rewrite the sentence on page 16 as a hyperbole—an exaggerated description.
Art	7.	Draw and illustrate the Wilder barn.
Living	8.	Eat headcheese and watermelon rind pickles.
Bible	9.	The Hardscrabble boys had beaten the previous teacher severely. Compare this with today's violence in public schools and the lack of justice in our judicial system. Why were the boys not tried and convicted of assault and battery? Apply Ecclesiastes 1:9; 3:15-16.
General	10.	Remember this week to schedule and make time for General Activities.

Read Chapters 3 and 4.

Reading Comprehension:

Chapter 3
1. How did Almanzo take care of his moccasins? Why was this necessary?
2. Why could not Almanzo have boots?
3. What does the term "bank the fire" mean?
4. How did each member of the family busy themselves after dinner?
5. Who provided the entertainment (page 33)?
6. What time was bedtime?
7. What did Father do in the middle of the night?
8. What time did Almanzo rise daily?
9. What was offered for breakfast?
10. Why did Almanzo not want to go to school?

Chapter 4
11. Why was Mr. Ritchie proud of Bill (page 41)?
12. What caused the children to cry and be unable to finish their lessons?
13. What surprise did Mr. Corse have?
14. What did Almanzo think about his father?

Page 227

Farmer Boy
Week 1

Activities:

Science	1.	What was the purpose of closing the dampers at night? *(Remember the properties of fire. Closing the dampers reduces the amount of oxygen; this reduces the rate of consumption of fuel.)*
Living	2.	Plan an "Almanzo family night." Eat popcorn and apples. Drink cider.
Science	3.	What unique things had Almanzo discovered about popcorn (page 34)? Do this experiment. Does it work? If so, why do you think it does? *(There is a lot of void space in the popped corn. The space, or the air present, is replaced by the milk molecules. The process must be done slowly to allow the air time to escape. Try this experiment with other liquids such as apple juice or water.)*
Vocabulary	4.	In a dictionary, look up these words: pannikin (page 31), hassock (page 33), and impudently (page 39).
Character/Writing	5.	What did Almanzo's father say about a man undertaking a job (page 40)? Write about how this statement can be applied to a problem or project in your life.
Bible	6.	Read Psalm 36:1-4. Apply it to the boys in these chapters. Read Proverbs 4:14-17. There really are evil people in this world.
Bible	7.	The teacher received counsel from Mr. Wilder. Apply these scriptures to Mr. Corse: Proverbs 1:5; 11:14; 13:10; 15:22; 19:20; and 24:6.
Art	8.	Make a poster utilizing one of the above scriptures encouraging a person to seek godly counsel.
Bible	9.	Read Exodus 20:12. This is a commandment with a promise. What is the promise? Almanzo honored his father and mother. He lived to be 92 years old. How does his length of life testify to God's faithfulness?

Read Chapters 5 and 6.

Reading Comprehension:

Chapter 5
1. From what type of wood was the calf yoke made? What qualities of this wood caused it to be chosen (page 50)?
2. When did Almanzo not go to school? When do you not have school?
3. What happened if Almanzo barely ate? if he ate too quickly?
4. What would happen if he did not clean the yokes properly (page 55)?
5. What surprise awaited Almanzo after lunch? How did he discover it?

Farmer Boy
Week 1

Chapter 6
6. Why was this a perfect day for cutting ice (page 65)?
7. Compare French Joe's and Lazy John's life-style to that of Almanzo's father.
8. Retell the joke about flipping a penny (pages 67-68).
9. What did Almanzo do to deserve a whipping? Why did he not get one?
10. What was Almanzo and Royal's job?

Activities:

Science/Art	1.	Research red cedar trees. What are some uses of its wood? Find one in your area and draw an identification picture, which includes the tree, its leaf, and seed or blossom.
Field Trip/Science	2.	Arrange a tour to a woodcraftman's shop. Look at the different types of wood and discuss uses, costs, and quality of finished products. Research other types of wood. How do they look? feel? What properties do they have? What advantages? disadvantages?
Bible	3.	What does Jesus say about yokes in Matthew 11:29-30? Prayerfully meditate on this verse. What is Jesus' yoke? What does he want you to learn from Him? What type of Master is He? If Almanzo and his father go the extra mile to get the right yoke for the oxen, how much more will Jesus do this for you!
Character	4.	Almanzo could not ask for a better example than the Lord Jesus Christ. Matthew 11:29 speaks about how Jesus is humble and gentle. Although you may know what "humble" and "gentle" mean, look them up in the dictionary, preferably in the <u>American Dictionary of the English Language</u> (the 1828 edition by Noah Webster). After reading these definitions, how was Almanzo's father trying to work these character qualities in him? How is Father God trying to work these qualities in you?
Science	5.	Almanzo relates the "dare" incident of touching the tongue to iron in the freezing weather. What would happen, if someone did this, and why? *(The moisture on the skin freezes and sticks to the iron. It is the same principle as touching ice cubes with moist hands. Most metals, such as iron, are excellent conductors. A conductor is a material that carries heat or cold.)*
Bible	6.	Apply Proverbs 15:21 to those that dare others to put their tongues on frozen iron.
Vocabulary	7.	What is a stanchion (page 64)?
Writing	8.	Write one or two pages about your favorite birthday or an unusual way a gift was given to you.
Science	9.	Why did they put sawdust over the ice? *(Sawdust is a poor conductor. Ice has to absorb heat to melt. The sawdust prevents the exchange of heat from the outside air, thus insulating the ice.)*
Cooking	10.	Make apples 'n' onions and birds' nest pudding. See <u>The Little House Cookbook</u>.

Page 229

Farmer Boy
Week 1

DAY 4

Read Chapters 7 and 8.

Reading Comprehension:

Chapter 7
1. What happened Saturday nights?
2. Why did Almanzo not like bath night? Did they wash their hair?
3. Who emptied the water and why (pages 82-83)?

Chapter 8
4. What was Sunday's lunch to be?
5. What were the hot bricks used for?
6. What did Almanzo remember his sisters as saying when he climbed into the sleigh?
7. How did Almanzo view his Mom in her finery? his sisters (page 91)?
8. What could Almanzo hardly bear to wait for? Is there anything that you feel that you cannot bear to wait for?
9. How long was church? What was required of Almanzo during the sermon?
10. What did they do one Sunday and why?

Activities:

Cooking	1.	Make twist doughnuts, rye 'n' ingun bread, apple pie with cheese and/or stacked pancakes. See <u>The Little House Cookbook</u>.
Science	2.	Begin to study the book <u>Solids, Liquids, and Gases</u> or a comparable text. Schedule to finish by the end of this unit.
Science	3.	On page 77, the frozen rainwater barrel is described. Why does water swell when it freezes? Why do other substances get smaller when cold? *(Generally, volume decreases when a substance changes from a liquid to a solid. This is because the molecules move more slowly in the solid state and are therefore closer together. Water, however, freezes into a crystalline structure that causes the molecules to attach in an outspread pattern, thus requiring more space than the liquid form. In the liquid state the water molecules have a strong attraction to each other; this is called cohesion.)*
Textiles	4.	Find pieces of broadcloth, silk, merino wool, and velvet in a fabric store. Mount swatches of each on a board and label.
Bible	5.	Almanzo remembered unkind words spoken by his sisters. Apply these verses to the girls' remarks: Proverbs 10:31-32; 12:18; 14:3; 15:1; 29:11; 11:22; and James 3:1-12.
Art	6.	Make a poster about harsh words; use one of the above verses.
Math	7.	How many miles per hour did their horses go on their way to church (page 88)? Compare this to the average speed your car travels to church.
Science	8.	Research the tongue and the sense of taste. Give an oral report with visual aids.

Page 230

Farmer Boy
Week 2

Week Two Planning Guide

Gather Information on the Following:

(See suggested sources listed)

1. Moosewood trees
   —

2. Lilacs, snowball bushes, violets, and buttercups (pictures)
   —Gardening catalog
   —

3. Wood Sorrels
   —<u>Weeds</u> A Golden Guide (Golden Press)
   —

4. Pollination, monoecious, dioecious, parts of a flower
   —<u>Studying Plants</u> (Milliken)
   —Encyclopedia
   —

5. Our national anthem "Star Spangled Banner"
   —Color the Patriotic Classics
   —

6. Stages and changes of the American flag
   —

Gather These Items:

1. Wood Sorrels
   —Grocery store or field
2. <u>Fourth of July</u> by Dalegish
3. Photocopies of "Maple Syrup" Sequencing Worksheet if more than one child is using the <u>Primer</u>
4. <u>Laura Ingalls Wilder Songbook</u> by E. Garson
5. A copy of the Declaration of Independence

Suggested Field Trips:

1. Observe a sheep being sheared or card and spin wool.
2. Visit a hospital physical therapy unit, and ask them to do a program on back care. Watch back care videos, if they have them available.

Notes:

Page 231

Farmer Boy
Week 2
For Use with Day 1

Sequencing Maple Syrup

Place the following events in the order in which they occurred.

_____ A.   The syrup was ready to sugar off.

_____ B.   Mother stored the gold-brown cakes on the top pantry shelves.

_____ C.   She poured the syrup into the big brass kettle on the cookstove.

_____ D.   Father dipped hot syrup into buckets.

_____ E.   Father bored a small hole and fitted a wooden spout into the tree.

_____ F.   Sap was rising in the trees.

_____ G.   Almanzo emptied sap into his big buckets.

_____ H.   They poured the sap into the great cauldron.

_____ I.   Father threw snow on the fire.

_____ J.   The sap boiled in the cauldron, they ate lunch, and they talked.

Page 232

Farmer Boy
Week 2

DAY 1

Read Chapters 9 and 10.

Reading Comprehension:

Chapter 9
1. What did Almanzo want to do instead of going to school?
2. What reasons did he give for needing to stay home?
3. What had Almanzo discovered about carrots?
4. How did Almanzo make the whip? Why was it not as good as a blacksnake whip?
5. For what did Almanzo need a whip?
6. Why must he always be gentle, quiet, and patient with the calves?
7. Who were the boys that came to visit? What did the boys do that afternoon?
8. What did Almanzo learn?

Chapter 10
9. How did Alice know Almanzo had been eating winterberries (page 113)?
10. What did they do with the last boiling of maple syrup (page 113)?
11. What job did Alice and Almanzo share?
12. What flavoring did Mother make for her cakes and candies?
13. What did the children race doing?
14. What extra was required of everyone during this time?
15. Why did they work extra long days?
16. Why did Father know that he would get a good price now?
17. How much money did they put in the bank?
18. How were the carpets cleaned (page 118)?
19. Describe their spring cleaning.
20. What flowers were blooming?

Activities:

Vocabulary	1.	What is an auger?
Science	2.	Find a picture of a moosewood tree.
Bible	3.	Almanzo's father was working patience into Almanzo by having him break calves. What does the Bible say about patience? Teach your child(ren) how to use a concordance. Some possible verses are Ecclesiastes 7:8; Romans 2:7; Romans 12:12; I Thessalonians 5:14; II Thessalonians 3:4; I Timothy 3:3; II Timothy 2:24; James 5:7-8.
Character/ Writing	4.	Look up the words "patience" or "patient" in the <u>American Dictionary of the English Language</u> (the 1828 edition by Noah Webster). After reading what the Bible and the dictionary say about patience, write a poem or a couple of paragraphs on patience.
Art	5.	On page 119, it lists the flowers that were blooming. Look these up, then paint a scene with these flowers.

Page 233

Farmer Boy
Week 2

Reasoning   6.   List the differences and the similarities between the maple sugaring episodes in Farmer Boy and Little House in the Big Woods. You may need to reread this in Chapters 7 and 8.

Science   7.   What was Father's weather rhyme (page 109)? Scientifically, why is it true? *(The warming and the cooling of the seasons occur because of the sun's heat and the earth's rotation on its axis. The short wave radiation from the sun [light] is turned into long range radiation [heat] as it bounces off the surface of the earth. As the earth's surface heats, the warmth radiates to the air above. The time it takes for the surface heat to radiate up creates a lag time between the most intense sun exposure and the hottest air temperature. Another reason for the lag time is that surface molecules are closer together and heat quicker, whereas air temperature changes slowly because the molecules are farther apart. An example of the lag time is seen daily. Noon is the time of the sun's greatest intensity. Yet, barring other climatic conditions, three or four o'clock in the afternoon is the hottest time of the day. Conversely, on the shortest day of the year, December 21, the earth receives the least amount of sun, but the coldest day of the year usually does not occur until January or February after the earth's stored radiant heat has diminished.)*

Sequencing   8.   Give child(ren) "Making Maple Syrup" Sequencing Worksheet. *(Answers: A.9; B.10; C.8; D.7; E.2; F.1; G.3; H.4; I.6; J.5.)*

General   9.   Remember this week to schedule and make time for General Activities.

DAY 2

Read Chapters 11 and 12.

Reading Comprehension:

Chapter 11
1. What had they done in the fall to prepare the garden (page 121)?
2. What did they do in the spring?
3. What does a good horseman always do (page 123)?
4. In what battle was Almanzo a soldier?
5. What made planting potatoes fun (page 126)?
6. What is hard about sowing grain?
7. Did Alice want to be a boy?
8. What boy's work did Alice like?
9. When did Almanzo know it was time to plant corn?
10. Describe the different methods used to plant each crop.

Chapter 12
11. What did Almanzo note about Mr. Brown as a horseman?
12. What could Almanzo do while grown-ups were talking (page 135)? What could he not do?
13. In what did Nick Brown pride himself?
14. What did he sell?
15. How and what did Nick Brown trade?
16. What did he give to the children?

Page 234

Farmer Boy
Week 2

17.   Other than tinware what did he leave them with?
18.   How was he a good guest?

Activities:

Science   1.   What is the purpose in spreading manure in the fall? *(Spreading it in the fall allows bacteria to breakdown the manure, which replenishes the soil with more nitrogen and other minerals. Nitrogen must be present for plants to make protein.)*

Science   2.   What is the purpose of harrowing the fields?

Science   3.   Draw a sequence picture depicting the life cycle of a potato (page 125).

Science   4.   Label the parts of a flower. Where do seeds come from? Include in your study monoecious plants (those in which one plant of the species is female and another is male) and dioecious (those in which the male and female parts are both found on the same plant).

Science   5.   Investigate the process of pollination in flowering. What are the different vehicles for pollination? *(Wind, birds, insects, and animals.)*

Bible   6.   Read Matthew 13:3-9. What can happen to the seed that is sown? In this parable, what does the seed represent? Meditate on this scripture to decide what can be done to make the seed grow.

DAY 3

Read Chapters 13 and 14.

Reading Comprehension:

Chapter 13
1.   Why did Almanzo listen intently to Father and the horse buyer (page 143)?
2.   How can one tell the age of a horse?
3.   What did Mother not like about having so much money in the house?
4.   Why did Almanzo need to milk the cows at the same time (page 147)?
5.   To whom did they show mercy?
6.   What happened in the middle of the night?
7.   What happened to the farmer near Malone?
8.   What did Mother believe about the dog?

Chapter 14
9.   When is sheep shearing time?
10.   Why is it done during warm weather?
11.   How were the sheep cleaned?
12.   What distracted Almanzo from his work (page 158)?
13.   When shearing sheep, of what does one need to be careful?
14.   At dinner what did Almanzo find out?
15.   How did Almanzo arrange not to finish last at the end of the day?

Page 235

Farmer Boy
Week 2

16. Explain "He laughs best, who laughs last." (This is an old proverb common in all languages quoted in the play "The Country House" written by Sir John Van Brugh in 1706.)
17. How did Father treat the hired help?
18. How were they paid?

Activities:

Bible
1. Apply to the story the following verses that deal with angels and God's protection, both past and present: Psalm 140:1-4; Hebrews 13:2; and apply Deuteronomy 7:17-21; Joshua 4:4-8.

Writing
2. God wants us to have reminders of His past protection. Write at least one page on a time that your family or you were Providentially protected.

Bible
3. God says it's good to be merry. Read Proverbs 15:15 and 17:22.

Bible
4. What does the Bible say about employers? (See Matthew 10:10.)

Field Trip
5. Watch or participate in a sheep shearing. How do modern methods of sheep shearing compare with the Wilder's method?

Health
6. Almanzo and his family were doing hard physical labor. It is important to use proper body mechanics in lifting heavy items. Learn the proper way to lift heavy items. Many children and adults develop chronic back problems when using improper lifting techniques.

Field Trip
7. Visit a hospital physical therapy unit and become instructed on proper back care maintenance.

DAY 4

Read Chapters 15 and 16.

Reading Comprehension:

Chapter 15
1. Why did only the small children go to school in the spring?
2. What ingredients were used to make soft soap? What ingredients are in soft soap today?
3. Where did they hoe? Where did they plow? Why?
4. Describe how uncomfortable Almanzo was when putting water on the plants. Why did he not complain (page 171)?

Chapter 16
5. What would Almanzo rather do than anything else (page 175)?
6. What was Almanzo dared to do (page 181)?
7. What did father say half a dollar was (page 182)? On page 184, what work did Father say went to make the half dollar? What did Almanzo think of the money after that?
8. What were Almanzo's options for the half dollar?
9. What did Father say won the revolution (page 188)? Who did he think made this country? Why?

Page 236

Farmer Boy
Week 2

Activities:

History	1.	Study what types of materials could have been used to dye the skeins of wool brown, red, and blue.
Art	2.	Draw a picture of the spacing of corn and pumpkins (page 165).
Science	3.	Why were the carrots thinned 2 inches apart? *(If the plants were too crowded, the competition for sunlight and nutrients would yield weaker plants.)*
Field trip	4.	Visit someone who cards, spins, and dyes wool. Watch the process.
Science	5.	Identify and draw a picture of wood sorrels. Gather it or buy some at the store and taste it.
Math	6.	How large is an acre? In a large field or parking lot, measure out an acre of land. Imagine hoeing that much land by hand.
Science	7.	What did the Wilders do to prevent the crops from damage by freezing? Why did their method work? *(In cold weather, putting water on crops can prevent freezing of the plant. How? As the water freezes, its molecules release heat. This heat is transferred to the plant. The frozen water also acts as an insulator against the more extreme cold outside. Once a plant gets cold enough to freeze, it dehydrates; but as the sun warms the plant and melts the frozen layer of ice, the plant reabsorbs the water before the sun scorches and kills it.)*
Math	8.	What percentage of the corn did they save (page 172)?
Bible	9.	The Wilders were diligent and had vision. What does the Bible say about this? Proverbs 10:4. The book said that all the important men stopped to shake hands with Father. Read Proverbs 22:29 and apply to the previous statement.
History/Reading	10.	Have your child read aloud <u>Fourth of July Story</u> to a younger child or at dinner time for the family.
Music	11.	Sing from <u>Laura Ingalls Wilder Songbook</u>, page 80.
Vocabulary	12.	What is a parasol? rampart? tariffs? free trade?
Music/History	13.	What song was sung on page 178? Research and give an oral report on this song.
History/Art	14.	What did the American flag look like in 1867? Draw a picture of it.
History	15.	Read aloud the Declaration of Independence in its entirety. Select portions to memorize.

Page 237

Farmer Boy
Week 3

Week Three Planning Guide

Gather Information on the Following:

(See suggested sources listed)

1. Fish

2. Pigs

3. Cholesterol and heart disease

4. Heart and vascular system
   —<u>The Human Body</u> by Jonathan Miller
   —<u>You and Your Body: Heart and Lungs</u> (Troll)
   —<u>The Young Scientist Book of the Human Body</u> (Usborne)

5. Dietary fat counter
   — "CPSI's Eating Smart Fat Guide"

6. Industrial uses for different roots, stems, leaves, seeds, and flowers

7. Purpose and methods of animal hybridization

8. Photosynthesis

9. Margarine
   —Encyclopedia

10. Treatment for burns

11. Directions for candle making

12. Nutrients (vitamins and minerals) found in fruits and vegetables, use of these nutrients, diseases caused by nutrient deficiencies

13. Guernseys, Jerseys, Devons, Durhams

14. Purpose and method of hybridization of animals

Gather These Items:

1. Items to make homemade ice cream (A hand crank ice cream maker would be preferable)
2. Items to make eggnog
   —<u>The Little House Cookbook</u> by Barbara M. Walker
3. Materials to make candles (Almanzo's family used tallow)
4. Beechnuts
5. <u>Too Many Chickens</u> by Mary Pride

Farmer Boy
Week 3

6. World Map
7. <u>Little House in the Ozarks</u> by Laura Ingalls Wilder
8. Stickers and poster board

Suggested Field Trips:

1. Visit an antique farm equipment show. Pay special attention to cradles and hay balers.
2. Have you and your children's cholesterol checked at a health fair or doctor's office.
3. Go to a county or state fair. Spend time looking at the livestock in particular.

Notes:

Farmer Boy
Week 3

DAY 1

Read Chapters 17 and 18.

Reading Comprehension:

Chapter 17
1. What was Almanzo trying to grow?
2. What did Eliza Jane see and do (page 194)?
3. What did they sometimes do on rainy days?
4. Why must they be quiet while fishing?
5. When do fish bite well?
6. Besides fishing, what summer fun did they do? What made it fun?

Chapter 18
7. What did Royal catch Almanzo doing? What did he do about it?
8. What did Almanzo do to make himself feel better?
9. How did they pick watermelons?
10. What do pigs do that horses and cows do not (page 211)?
11. Retell the story about the pig and the candy.
12. What happened the day before Ma and Pa were scheduled to return?
13. What did Eliza and Almanzo quarrel about?
14. What did Almanzo do and what was he worried about?
15. What surprise awaited Almanzo?
16. What did Eliza Jane and Almanzo discover about each other?

Activities:

Science	1.	Study the process of photosynthesis in green plants.
Science	2.	Grow a pumpkin using the milk-fed technique.
Science	3.	To grow a large pumpkin, why did Almanzo take off all the branches except one and all the flowers except one? *(All the nutrients and water will go toward one pumpkin-producing flower. This procedure will produce a large pumpkin.)*
Living/Reasoning	4.	Will the same procedure used in making a fine pumpkin work in families to produce successful, prosperous children? In other words, do children with few siblings, when given more parental attention, more money, or a greater share of the family inheritance, enjoy more success and prosperity? *(A child in a larger family may feel discouraged that someone from a smaller family may possess more advantages, such as having their own room. On the surface one may agree with this "pumpkin-patch" scenario. Yet a child in a large family greatly benefits from each of the other siblings. Large families contribute to unique character building experiences. Since God is the Provider and owns everything, He can give to His servants as their needs arise. If you have a large family, point out to your children that God is sovereign and can bless and prosper one from a large family. Joseph is a good example of this principle from the scriptures. Other examples from history are John and Charles Wesley, and Ludwig Van*

Page 240

Farmer Boy
Week 3

Beethoven. Also read Too Many Chickens *by Mary Pride to reinforce this idea.)*

Vocabulary 5. What are a bridle and a harness? What are their purposes?

Language 6. Reread the paragraph on page 196 describing the rain. Correlate each sentence with the appropriate physical sense that it uses in its description.

Writing 7. Write a one-page paper about what you like or do not like about rain. Include all your physical senses in your description.

Cooking 8. Make homemade ice cream. How many cups of sugar did your recipe call for? How many cups of sugar did the Wilder children use?

Living 9. Pick out watermelons and tell which one is ripe.

Science 10. Research pigs.

Science 11. Research fish. Include a diagram of its body, the senses it uses, its diet, and habitat. How could this information aid you in fishing?

Bible 12. Read I Corinthians 13, Proverbs 10:12 and 17:9. Apply these verses to Eliza Jane. What effect did her love have on Almanzo? Does I Corinthians 13 say that love is a feeling?

Bible 13. Remember to memorize I Corinthians 13:1-8 by the end of this book.

Writing 14. Recall a moment in which you developed a new appreciation for a sibling or parent.

Nutrition 15. Fruits and vegetables are the second layer of the food group pyramid. (Refer to the Additional Reference Material in "Big Woods.") Make a goal to eat the daily prescribed amount of servings for at least three days. To keep up with this goal make a calendar with large squares for each person. Have the student place a sticker in the square each time a fruit or vegetable is consumed.

General 16. Remember this week to schedule and make time for General Activities.

DAY 2

Read Chapters 19 and 20.

Reading Comprehension:

Chapter 19
1. What did the men and boys do to keep their heads cooler (page 229)?
2. What did Mother prepare for lunch for the men working in the fields?
3. What two things did Father think was beneficial to a man's productivity (page 231)?
4. How did they use all the bounty (page 233)?

Page 241

Farmer Boy
Week 3

5. How does one shock oats and wheat? Why must this be done?
6. Did they like the butter buyer? Why or why not?
7. Why did his mother go to town?

Chapter 20
8. What did they do with the best pumpkins? the others?
9. Why were they so careful with the apples (page 241)?
10. What did they do with the other apples?
11. How much is a hogshead of cider?
12. Why must he hurry to harvest?
13. How did they keep warm (page 245)?
14. How was Almanzo hurt?
15. How was Almanzo being selfish?

Activities:

Cooking	1.	Make eggnog.

Science 2. Study the heart and vascular system.

Health 3. Why should you limit your intake of such things as eggnog and ice cream? *(They are both high in cholesterol and fat, which are linked to heart disease. Cholesterol collects around the inside of the blood vessels, forming a hard plaque. This plaque causes the vessels to loose their elasticity and close the lumen of the vessel.)*

Science 4. To demonstrate cholesterol's effect on blood vessels, take a glass jar and pour warm bacon grease or lard into it to coat the inside. Allow it to cool and harden. The hardened grease builds up on the jar just as the plaque builds up on the blood vessel walls, eventually constricting them. To show the effect a smaller lumen has on the heart, take frosting and squeeze through a pinpoint hole and then one with a larger diameter. Which takes the most effort? Our body produces cholesterol from the fat we take in with our diet.

Nutrition 5. Discuss which foods are high in fat such as meat, eggs, whole milk, cheese, butter, oil, nuts, and peanut butter. Foods made from these things are high in fat. Examples are eggnog, cakes, cookies, pizza, doughnuts, french fries, etc. There is a relationship between sugar intake and higher cholesterol levels. Therefore, fatty, sugary foods are more dangerous. Almanzo ate foods very high in fat, yet he lived to be 92. Other factors are thus associated with heart disease. One is heredity. Two people can eat the same foods and yet have very different blood cholesterol levels. The other factor is exercise. Almanzo worked very vigorously. Exercise increases the amount of "good" cholesterol in your system.

Health 6. Have you and your children's cholesterol checked. Children's cholesterol should be compared with a percentile scale, and not compared to normal adult values. A child with a cholesterol level in the 90th percentile will grow to be an adult with a high cholesterol level unless diet and exercise change. A child or adult may be thin and still have elevated cholesterol levels. No child under two years old should have a dietary intake of fat less than 30%, because fat is necessary for proper brain development. Children older than two years old should have no more than 30% of their calories from fat.

Farmer Boy
Week 3

Math/Health	7.	Have your child write down everything eaten for two or three days. Calculate the average amount of calories from fat.
Bible/Health	8.	Read Job 12:11 (Amplified). Children need to acquire a taste for foods that are desirable for good health. It is better to develop a taste for "healthy" foods while young than to wait until bad eating habits have been established and in adulthood the tastes need to be changed.
Living	9.	Draw a picture of a cradle used for harvesting.
Bible	10.	Read Proverbs 31 and apply it to Almanzo's mother.
Science	11.	Plants are divided into roots, stems, leaves, flowers and seeds. Which parts of the harvested plants on the Wilder Farm were edible? For example, in a carrot the roots are edible, in corn the seeds are edible, and in spinach the leaves are edible.
Science	12.	Study about present-day industrial uses of roots, stems, leaves, seeds, and flowers. *(Roots: flavorings, dyes; stems: paper, quinine, linen; flowers: perfume; seeds: mustard, nutmeg, varnishes; leaves: tea, tobacco and flavorings such as peppermint, spearmint and sage.)*
Math/Living	13.	Almanzo and his family harvested their family's year supply of food. Estimate how many ears of corn (or other food like cereal) your family will eat in a year. Then keep a record of how many ears of corn (or boxes of cereal) your family eats in a month's time. At the end of the month, multiply the amount eaten by twelve to calculate your yearly total. How close was your estimation? Was the difference between your estimation and your actual calculation great? What would it have meant for Almanzo's family if their estimations had been wrong?
History/Business	14.	Almanzo's mother made butter. What is a modern-day substitute for butter? What made margarine marketable? *(Cost, then the* discovery of cholesterol.)
Health	15.	Because butter is an animal product, it has cholesterol. Recently there has been some evidence which hints that butter is less harmful than margarine. Remember that our body produces cholesterol with fat. Both butter and margarine have fat. The fat in margarine is artificially hydrogenated. Many people believe that our body does not process the hydrogenated fats as well as the natural ones. Others believe that butter may have enzymes that help our body properly use the fat. The following is how our family "makes" butter:

Blend:
2 sticks of softened butter
1/2 cup cold pressed safflower or canola oil
2 T. of fresh flax oil (contains beta-carotene and
    omega-3a)
1 t. lecithin (optional)

The above recipe has less cholesterol than butter, fewer unnaturally hydrogenated fats than margarine, the presence of enzymes, and the addition of nutrients that some studies have found beneficial for the immune system and heart. Perhaps one should reevaluate butter.

Page 243

Farmer Boy
Week 3

Character	16.	Look up "selfish" in the <u>American Dictionary of the English Language</u> (the 1828 edition by Noah Webster). Read and discuss. Apply Philippians 2:3-4.
Bible	17.	Why could Almanzo not bear to be so selfish anymore? Read Psalm 111:10. How did Almanzo fear the Lord?
Bible	18.	Almanzo said that they worked from candlelight to candlelight. What does Proverbs 10:5 say? Have you ever worked so diligently? Are there times in your life when you need to work diligently?
Living	19.	Read and discuss "The Man of the Place," page 65, from <u>Little House in the Ozarks</u>.
Health/First Aid	20.	Almanzo was burned. What are the care and treatment of a burn? *(Burns are an injury to the tissue from fire, steam, chemicals, electricity, lightning, or radiation. A first-degree burn involves a reddening of the skin. In a second-degree burn, the skin is blistered. A third-degree burn is the most serious type, involving damage to the deeper layers of skin. Occasionally the growth cells of the tissues in the burned area may be destroyed. For minor burns, apply cool water for up to 20 minutes. This simple technique can turn a second-degree burn into a first-degree burn. Do not apply butter or grease. First-degree burns over most of the body need to be seen by a physician. Death may result with even a first-degree burn that covers over two-thirds of the body. For major burns lay the victim down with the legs elevated and call 911. The head and chest should be kept lower than the rest of the body. In shock, the liquid part of the blood rushes to the burned area and there may not be enough left to maintain normal function of the heart, brain, and other vital organs. Blisters are not to be opened. Attempts should not be made to remove clothing from the burned area. If the victim is awake and can swallow, give fluids to quench his thirst. Try to keep as clean as possible to decrease the chance of infection until help arrives.)* What degree burn did Almanzo have? How did they treat it?

Page 244

Farmer Boy
Week 3

DAY 3

Read Chapter 21.

Reading Comprehension:

Chapter 21
1. What advice did his Father give him about betting (page 256)?
2. Why is a Morgan horse more practical than a Belgium horse (page 258)?
3. Why must they leave the fair at 3 p.m.?
4. What made a good ear of corn (page 267)?
5. What must the second place winner and those who did not win any prize do (page 269)? How did Almanzo know this?
6. Who won the blue ribbon for pumpkins?
7. How and why had Almanzo begun to lie?
8. What did he realize about his father's character?
9. How had the Wilder family done at the fair (page 274)?

Activities:

Living	1.	Find a picture of a Belgium horse.
Geography	2.	On a map trace the Belgium horse's coming to America (page 257).
Living/Science	3.	What purpose do Guernseys, Jerseys, Devons, and Durhams have on a farm? On a map find their place of origin.
Science	4.	Study the hybridization of animals.
Living	5.	What is the advantage of the Merino sheep over the Cotswold sheep? Why would anyone want a Cotswold (page 260)? Discuss quantity versus quality. When is it better to purchase quality? quantity?
Nutrition	6.	What nutrients are found in large quantities in fruits and vegetables? How are these nutrients used in the body? What effect would a lack of these nutrients have on one's body?

Page 245

Farmer Boy
Week 3

DAY 4

Read Chapters 22 and 23.

Reading Comprehension:

Chapter 22
1. How were beechnuts harvested?
2. What is lard? What was it used for?
3. What did they do with the cowhide (page 279)?
4. What were the cracklings used for (page 281)?
5. How were Joe and Lazy John paid?
6. Why did they wait until the bitter cold weather had come to stay until they did the butchering?
7. Describe how they made candles. How many must they make?

Chapter 23
8. Why did the girls rip their dresses out (page 286)?
9. Why was chore time earlier (page 288)?
10. Who came to visit? What type of guest was he? What was Almanzo to have?
11. What did the cobbler say about his seams (page 294)? Are the seams of your shoes waterproof?
12. Tell what the different parts of the corn were used for (page 292).
13. What effect did school have on each of the older children?
14. What did Royal want to be and why?

Activities:

Living	1.	Eat beechnuts.
Crafts	2.	Make candles.
Science	3.	What was poor man's fertilizer? (*Snow.*) Why did it work? (*The inside of a snowflake contains trapped air. The air contains nitrogen. Plowing the snow into the ground allows the nitrogen to be released into the soil. Without nitrogen, the plants cannot make protein.*)
Living	4.	What were the reasons Almanzo's family used tallow to make candles? (*Availability, workability.*)
Vocabulary	5.	Look up these words in the dictionary: lasts (page 292), awl (page 292, rasp (page 295), and deportment (page 296).
Speech/Language	6.	On page 288, read aloud how Almanzo felt. How was this paragraph better than saying "I felt lonely?"
Writing	7.	Write a paragraph to persuade a person whether one should drink from a cup or saucer.
Bible	8.	Apply I Thessalonians 5:12-13 to the cup and saucer discussion.

Page 246

Farmer Boy
Week 4

Week Four Planning Guide

Gather Information on the Following:

(See suggested sources listed)

1. The cow's digestive system
   —<u>The Amazing Milk Book</u> by Catherine Ross and Susan Wallace

2. Energy (sources, potential, kinetic, and conservation of energy)
   —Encyclopedia

3. History of public schools
   —<u>Going Home to School</u> by Llewellyn B. Davis
   —<u>The Right Choice—Homeschooling</u>, Chapter 3, "The Philosophical Crisis in Public Education" and Chapter 5, "The History of Homeschooling" by Christopher Klicka

4. History and present day use of apprenticeships

5. History of banks in the United States
   —Encyclopedia

6. Threshing machines (their inventor and effect on America)

7. Human digestive system

Gather These Items:

1. Robert Frost's poem, "The Road Not Taken"

Suggested Field Trips:

1. Thresh wheat, oats, or beans.
2. Watch hay being baled.
3. Visit a jewelry store to see precious stones, especially garnets. Also, ask to see the mechanisms inside a clock to watch the revolution of gears. Compare the difference between those that are run on mechanical versus electrical energy.

Notes:

Page 247

Farmer Boy
Week 4

Read Chapters 24 and 25.

Reading Comprehension:

Chapter 24
1. Why were they looking for wood?
2. Why did they choose oak for the bobsled?
3. Why was elm chosen for the tongue (page 302)?
4. Was it easy to find two trees alike?

Chapter 25
5. Why did Father not prefer the threshing machine (pages 307-308)? Why did Pa prefer using the threshing machine (page 227 in <u>Little House in the Big Woods</u>)?
6. What did Father say about saving time (page 308)?
7. Did Almanzo want to twiddle his thumbs?
8. What did raw wheat taste like?
9. How did Almanzo feel about his work (pages 310-311)?

Activities:

Vocabulary	1.	What is a cud (page 306), a flail (page 306), a peck (page 310)? What does "threshed" mean (page 310)? Which dictionary definition fits the usage in the book?
Science/Art/Writing	2.	Study a cow's digestive system. Draw and label the cow's digestive system. Write a paragraph describing its workings. Compare this digestive system to any others studied this year, including the human digestive system.
Living	3.	Thresh wheat, oats, or beans.
Science	4.	Study energy; include potential, kinetic, and the conservation of energy.
Science	5.	Why did Father wind the clock? What type of energy did the clock use to run on? *(Mechanical.)* Make a transfer of energy chain beginning with the energy from the clock all the way back to the sun. *(Clock running-> energy stored in the spring-> energy for force to wind the clock-> energy to move from eating plants and animals-> energy for plants to grow from photosynthesis-> energy for photosynthesis comes from the sun.)* Who created the sun?
Bible	6.	Almanzo was pleased with this work. Read Ecclesiastes 2:24-26 and 3:22. Apply this to Almanzo. Pray that it will be true of you also.
History/Writing	7.	Research threshing machines and the effect they had on America and American farm life. Include in this paper information about the inventor.
General	8.	Remember this week to schedule and make time to conclude General Activities.

Page 248

Farmer Boy
Week 4

DAY 2

Read Chapter 26.

Reading Comprehension:

Chapter 26
1. Who was coming for Christmas?
2. What did Almanzo use for cleaning the silver (page 313)? What is used presently?
3. What meat were they having for Christmas dinner (page 313)?
4. Who woke everyone? What time was it? Because they woke early, what were they able to do?
5. What did Almanzo get for Christmas?
6. What did Almanzo and Frank quarrel about?
7. Did Almanzo stand up to his friends who urged him to disobey (page 323)?
8. What do you think about Royal's reaction to the boys?
9. What did the boys play after dinner? Who won?

Activities:

Living   1.   Look at garnets in a jewelry store. Compare them to the other gems.

Bible   2.   Why is Christmas celebrated in your family? Who gave the world's perfect and precious gift? In the Old Testament the Jews were given appointed feasts to remind them of the great things God had done for them as a nation. Read Zechariah 7:5-6 (NIV). Consider this verse in light of your family's observance of Thanksgiving, Christmas, or Easter.

Bible   3.   Apply these verses to Frank and Almanzo's struggle: Proverbs 1:10, 15; 8:13; 14:16.

Writing   4.   Write about a memorable Christmas in your family.

Living   5.   Clean tarnished silver.

DAY 3

Read Chapter 27.

Reading Comprehension:

Chapter 27
1. On Almanzo's first day hauling wood, what two things did he do wrong?
2. What rule of the road did Almanzo follow?
3. What do you think about his father's passing him stuck in the snow?
4. What were the boys able to do?
5. For what future event did this trial help prepare him? *(Bringing back the wheat in* The Long Winter.*)*
6. Why did his father say that he must go to school (page 343)?
7. Why did Almanzo study hard at school?

Page 249

Farmer Boy
Week 4

Activities:

Writing   1.   Write a comparison/contrast paper on Almanzo and Laura. Knowing about both their upbringings, what character traits in Laura attracted Almanzo to her? What character traits in Almanzo did Laura find appealing?

Living   2.   If Almanzo were in public school today, could he stay home as frequently for the home learning experience? Why or why not? *(Truancy laws.)* Were his home learning experiences beneficial to him in the long run? Did Almanzo receive most of his education at home or in school?

History/Writing   3.   Research the history of public schools. Write a one to two-page report about it.

DAY 4

Read Chapters 28 and 29. This Finishes the Book. Also read <u>Laura Ingalls Wilder Country</u>, Chapter 13, "Almanzo and Malone."

Reading Comprehension:

Chapter 28
1. What did they wrap around the hay?
2. What rule did Almanzo break at the table?
3. What did Father say about learning (page 348)?
4. What do you think about Almanzo not going to school?
5. What did Almanzo find on the way to town?
6. How much money was in the wallet?
7. What could Father tell about the man who lost his wallet?
8. Who sold the hay? Why did Almanzo say $2.25 for a bale of hay (page 350)? How much did Almanzo receive for it?
9. Read the quotation in the first complete paragraph on page 352. Explain why this is true.
10. Why did Father give Almanzo the errand of returning the pocketbook (page 352)?
11. When Almanzo saw Mr. Thompson, why did he wait to speak (page 353)?
12. Was Mr. Thompson happy with Almanzo for returning the wallet?
13. What did Mr. Paddock do and why?
14. What advice did Father give Almanzo about spending money (page 361)?

Chapter 29
15. What did Mr. Paddock offer Father?
16. What did Almanzo see as the good points of being an apprentice? the bad points?
17. What did his father and mother see as the good and bad points?
18. What did his mother think about Royal becoming a storekeeper?
19. What did Almanzo want to do?
20. What did Almanzo want to buy? What was his father's response? Do you think Mr. Paddock's offer encouraged Father to give Almanzo the colt?
21. What would Almanzo be able to do instead of going to school?

Page 250

Farmer Boy
Week 4

Activities:

Vocabulary   1. Look up the meaning of: maul (page 344), withes (page 347), and liveryman (page 351).

Art   2. From the description given on pages 345 and 346 illustrate the hay press.

History/Oral   3. Study the history of apprenticeships. What were the reasons for becoming an apprentice? Name some apprentices that became famous. Are apprenticeships possible today? Could you become an apprentice in an occupation that you desire to do?

Living   4. Watch hay being baled today. Compare modern methods to the way it used to be baled.

History/Writing/   5. Study about the history of banks. Why and when have banks failed in
Economics   the past? What measures have been instituted to help prevent this? Write a report on the history of United States banking. What had been the most recent bank failure when Almanzo found the wallet? Was Mr. Thompson justified in his fear? What happened to the depositors' money when a bank failed?

Current Events   6. Study the most recent bank failures and the S & L bailout in 1991.

Math   7. What was the interest rate at Almanzo's bank (page 361)? What interest rate do you or your parents get on a savings account? Compare this to the interest rate in 1866. How much difference in interest in a year would it be for $200?

Living   8. Open a savings account at a bank.

Bible   9. What did Father say to the liveryman's compliment (page 351)? What does the statement mean? Apply this to Almanzo. Think of the biblical characters, who started out good but had bad endings.

Bible   10. Mr. Thompson falsely accused Almanzo. What does the Bible say about this? See Proverbs 18:13; 25:8; 29:20; II Timothy 3:2-3; Zechariah 7:10 (NIV).

Living/Reasoning   11. How did Mr. Case treat his customers? Why did he need to be so polite? Note the difference between a hired helper's service and that of an owner-run and operated business. Who generally knows more about the product and its location? Who is generally more willing to please?

Literature   12. Read Robert Frost's "The Road Not Taken." How could this apply to Almanzo? If Almanzo had taken the other road, do you think Laura and he would have met?

Character   13. What character qualities did Mr. Paddock see in Almanzo that prompted him to suggest Almanzo starting an apprenticeship?

Page 251

First Four

The First Four Years

These Happy Golden Years (1943) was the last book published while Laura was alive. After this she began writing The First Four Years, which recounts the many poignant events that marked the early years of her marriage to Almanzo Wilder. However, this time was punctuated by personal sorrow. In 1946 Carrie, the last of Laura's family, died. Then in 1949, after sixty-four years of marriage, Almanzo, too, was gone. For her to recall the early years considering these losses could have only compounded the strain of the subject she wrote of, for Laura referred to the first four years of their married life as "heartbreaking" in themselves.

Many criticize that The First Four Years is untailored and essentially "unfinished." It does lack the colorful character sketches notable in Laura's earlier books; similarly, themes and ideas lack the development found in her finished works. Despite the brevity, it is still Laura speaking to us; it is just as if an old friend sent a quick letter. It is good to hear from her just one more time.

Some studies in this book deal with roles in marriage, childbirth, and early childhood development. The general emphasis, however, is on how one deals with crisis in these situations. The parent must decide to what depth these subjects will be discussed, and in everything emphasize that God, whatever the difficulty, is a very present help in trouble.

Because the chapter divisions in this book generally contain more than twenty-five pages, the daily reading selections will be delineated by page numbers rather than by chapter.

General Activities to Do throughout This Unit:

1. Memorize Psalm 46, Proverbs 31, or Ecclesiastes 4:9-12.

2. Read a biography about Thomas Edison.

3. Recall lessons that Almanzo and Laura learned during their childhood and see how they are now walking in what they learned.

First Four
Week 1

Week One Planning Guide

Gather Information on the Following:

(See suggested sources listed)

1. Thomas A. Edison
   —Encyclopedia
   —Thomas Edison (Childhood of Famous American Series)
   —Thomas Alva Edison Easy Biographies (Troll)
   —The Thomas Edison Book of Easy and Incredible Experiments
   —Story of Thomas Alva Edison by Enid L. Meadowcroft

2. Facts of Life
   —The Wonderful Way That Babies Are Made by Larry Christenson

3. Nervous system (especially the spinal cord)

4. A video depicting the birth of an infant
   —If your local video store does not have a birth video, contact your local Lamaze teacher or a friend that video taped the birth of their child. (Preview it for appropriateness.)

5. Weather (particularly the formation of thunder clouds and hail)
   —Thunderstorm by Nathaniel Tripp

6. Graham flour
   —The Little House Cookbook by Barbara M. Walker

Gather These Items:

1. Little House in the Ozarks by Laura Ingalls Wilder
2. The American Dictionary of the English Language (the 1828 edition by Noah Webster)

Suggested Field Trips:

1. The home in the Ozarks where the "Little House" books were written:
   Laura Ingalls Wilder and Rose Wilder Lane Museum and Home
   Route 1, Box 24
   Mansfield, Missouri 65704
   Phone: (417) 924-3626

2. Where Laura lived in the Big Woods:
   Laura Ingalls Wilder Memorial Society
   Pepin, Wisconsin 54759

First Four
Week 1

3. Where Farmer Boy occurred:
   Almanzo and Laura Ingalls Wilder Association
   P. O. Box 283
   Malone, New York 12953
   Phone: (518) 483-1207

4. Little House on the Prairie Site
   P. O. Box 110
   Independence, Kansas 67301

5. Where Plum Creek events occurred:
   Laura Ingalls Wilder Museum Tourist Center
   Walnut Grove, Minnesota 56180
   Phone: (507) 859-2358

6. Time between books where Ingalls lived:
   Laura Ingalls Wilder Park and Museum
   Box 354
   Burr Oak, Iowa 52131
   Phone: (319) 735-5436

7. The town where Laura resided during her youth:
   Laura Ingalls Memorial Society, Inc.
   Box 344
   De Smet, South Dakota 57231
   Phone: (605) 854-3383

8. Home of Almanzo's parents:
   Laura Ingalls Wilder Site
   Methodist Church Museum
   Spring Valley, Minnesota 55975

Notes:

First Four
Week 1

DAY 1

Read the Introduction, Prologue and Chapter 1, Pages 1-21.

Reading Comprehension:

Chapter 1, Pages 1-21
1. On what did Laura write her manuscripts?
2. Other than the "Little House" series, what else did Laura write?
3. Tell about Rose.
4. How did the inhabitants of Dakota view the hot sunshine or the hard winds?
5. What is Laura's new name for Almanzo?
6. What was on Manly's mind when he unexpectedly came to see Laura? Why did he want to hasten the wedding?
7. Why did Laura not want to marry a farmer? What do you think about her reasons?
8. On page 4, explain the Irishman's saying.
9. How did Almanzo think he could make more money than the men in town?
10. What was Manly's compromise (page 5)?
11. What did Laura like about living on the farm instead of in the city?
12. What reasons did Manly give for marrying the next week?
13. On what conditions were Laura and Manly married (page 10)?
14. Describe their "honeymoon."
15. What had Manly given Laura as a wedding present (page 13)?
16. What chore did Laura dislike (page 16)? How was she spared from this?
17. What awaited Manly when he was done with the chores?
18. Who was coming to dinner the next day?
19. What is the difference between being a farmer's daughter and being a pioneer's daughter?
20. What went wrong with Laura's dinner without Ma's watchful eye? How did she feel about it?

Activities:

Vocabulary	1.	What is a contralto (page xx), a drop-leaf table (page 12), a pantry (page 12), and graham flour (page 13)? Show or demonstrate to aid comprehension of these words.
Art	2.	Draw Laura's kitchen as described on pages 11-13.
Bible	3.	God created woman to be a helpmate for man. Read Genesis 2:20-25. How did Laura want to help Manly (page 17)? Contrast this with Mrs. Brewster's unsupportive attitude toward her husband. Read Ecclesiastes 4:9-12. Consider these verses while reading the book.
Writing	4.	Interview your mom and dad about their honeymoon. Write one or two paragraphs and add it to your previously written Family History booklet.
Living	5.	What is marriage? Read the definition from The American Dictionary of the English Language (the 1828 edition by Noah Webster). Discuss marriage with your parent(s).
General	6.	Remember this week to schedule and make time for General Activities.

Page 256

First Four
Week 1

DAY 2

Read Chapter 1, Pages 21-44.

Reading Comprehension:

Chapter 1, Pages 21-44
1. What chore was especially hard for Laura? What did she do in the afternoon?
2. What did they do on Sundays?
3. How had Almanzo bought the plow? What was the benefit of this plow (page 23)?
4. What did Almanzo buy for Laura?
5. Instead of driving, what did Laura and Almanzo do for entertainment? What would they do frequently before breakfast?
6. Explain the second complete paragraph on page 27.
7. What did Laura wonder about (page 27)? What did she attempt to do about it?
8. In what way was Ole Larsen not a good neighbor? How did this affect Laura and Manly?
9. What did they decide to be a good investment for Laura's salary?
10. While Manly was in town, who were Laura's surprise visitors?
11. Why did Manly think that it would be a cold winter?
12. Why had Manly not spilt the milk in his efforts to reach the house (page 38)?
13. How did they know that the Larsens were all right (page 40)?
14. What had the damage been?
15. Since it was very cold, what would they do Sunday afternoons (page 42)?
16. Since Laura had moved to De Smet, with whom had they always spent the holiday?
17. What was given for Christmas? What did they decide to do for each other for Christmas?
18. To Laura, what was as good as visiting people (page 44)?

Activities:

Bible/Economics 1. What is a budget? Laura the author, felt that before planning a budget one should read Luke 19:1-27. Read this Bible chapter. Why do you think one should read this chapter before planning a budget?

Bible 2. Laura and Almanzo had borrowed money for the house and machinery. What does the Bible say about debt? Use your concordance to look up some verses about money and debt. *(Because God is our Provider, many believe that going into debt reveals one's ungratefulness with what the Lord has provided. It may also reflect a disbelief that the Lord knows what is best for us at any given time. If the money is not there at this time, it is because the Lord has a better time or way to fulfill this need. Others feel that when the value of an object is above what is owed, it makes the debt similar to an investment, and the acquisition of it justifies the means.)* Discuss with your child(ren) what your views are concerning debt.

Writing 3. Two episodes in this book are descriptively undeveloped compared to episodes in Laura's other books. These episodes are 1) when Laura helps Manly (page 24), and 2) when Laura trains her pony (page 25). Compare these events with the time Laura helped her father harvest hay in The Long Winter (Chapter 1) or when Laura rides ponies with her cousin in By the Shores of Silver Lake (Chapter 6). Use your imagination to further develop and then rewrite one of the above episodes.

Page 257

First Four
Week 1

Bible	4.	What did Almanzo think he needed to do to be neighborly (page 29)? How was the neighbor unneighborly? Read what the Bible says about neighbors. (See Proverbs 3:28; 11:12; 25:17; 27:14.)
Character	5.	Read and discuss "Good Neighbors" (page 229) in <u>Little House in the Ozarks</u>.
Living	6.	Laura found that working alone was very different from helping Ma. There is a very big difference between helping another and being the responsible overseer to ensure things are completed correctly. Discuss accountability with your child.
History/Science	7.	During the very bad blizzard, Laura would sing while she did her knitting. Thomas Edison had patented the phonograph in 1877. Read about Edison and his inventions. Also, do some of his experiments. Add drawings of Edison's more famous inventions to your timeline.
Character	8.	Almanzo decided a horse would be a good investment. What lesson in <u>Farmer Boy</u> did Almanzo learn from his father on how to use and make money?
Writing	9.	Interview your mom and dad about the first place they lived when they were first married. Describe it in one or two paragraphs and add your writing to the Family History booklet. Include photographs or illustration

DAY 3

Read Chapter 1, Pages 45-60.

Reading Comprehension:

Chapter 1, Pages 45-60
1. What was Laura helping Manly do when she began to feel sick (page 45)?
2. Explain the common saying "They that dance must pay the fiddler."
3. Why had Laura's house become more dingy?
4. How were the trees growing? What did Almanzo do to help?
5. What did Manly buy in town? How did he pay for it? What did Laura mind about the method of payment?
6. What happened to the wheat?
7. How did Laura pick the name Rose?
8. Why did Laura have to move?

Activities:

Health	1.	Use this time to discuss the facts of life with your child. A good book to read is <u>The Wonderful Way That Babies Are Made</u> by Larry Christenson.
Bible	2.	Manly wanted to make ice cream after the wheat crop had failed. Their guests declined the ice cream. How did their reaction relate to Proverbs 25:20

Page 258

First Four
Week 1

Science 3. What is hail? How are hailstones formed in the atmosphere? *(Hail is formed in upper atmospheric storm clouds when rising air currents lift water particles and cool them to the freezing point. The ice particles then fall from the cloud and are relifted by the rising air. This cycle continues, causing layers of ice to accumulate until the particles become heavy enough to fall to the ground. How cold is a storm cloud? The atmospheric temperature in a thundercloud drops 5.5 degrees Fahrenheit (F) for every 1000' increase in elevation. The upper parts of a thunderstorm are extremely cold, even when ground temperatures are very hot. For example, when the ground temperature is 100 degrees F, the temperature at the peak of a 20,000' storm cloud would be -110 degrees F (20,000) 1,000' x -5.5 degrees F = -110 degrees F).*

Math 4. How much did Laura and Manly owe (page 58)? What would eight percent interest be?

Writing 5. In a paragraph or two describe how you were named. What does your name mean? Add this to your Family History booklet.

Bible 6. "There is no great loss without some small gain" was a common saying used frequently by Ma. What small gain did Laura think of? What spiritual gain can be produced by tribulation? (Romans 5:3-4; James 1:2-4.)

Read Chapter 2, Pages 61-84.
Reading Comprehension:

Chapter 2, Pages 61-84
1. What must Laura do for Manly (pages 61-62)?
2. Was Almanzo trying to make the farm successful?
3. How did Laura spend time with Manly (page 65)?
4. How did they know it would be a warm winter?
5. What goose did Almanzo get (page 67)?
6. In the winter what did Shep and Laura do? Why had Manly made Laura a handsled (page 68)? What did Laura envision Shep doing?
7. Why did Almanzo fetch Ma? Mrs. Powers?
8. What did the doctor do when he arrived?
9. What help did Laura have after the baby was born?
10. How much had they paid for the doctor bill and help?
11. What did Laura say about a Rose in December (page 72)?
12. What did Manly buy for Christmas? How was it paid for?
13. What did Laura do on the first warm day? What did she learn about babies (page 75)?
14. What was hard for Mr. Boast to ask of Almanzo and Laura?
15. Why had the visitors lost their lives?
16. What had happened to Shep?
17. When Spring came, after the work had been done, what would Laura do?
18. Briefly describe their second year.
19. What loomed over the Wilder's (page 83)?

Page 259

First Four
Week 1

Activities:

Health   1.   Depending on the maturity and age of your child, show a video of a live human birth.

Health   2.   The doctor used anesthesia to help ease Laura's pain in childbirth. Today certain medications may be given to ease the pain. A mother is not put to sleep, however, except in some cesarean operations. If sleep is induced on the mother, the infant risks respiratory problems when it is born. One type of anesthesia used today in childbirth is the epidural. This is administered into the dura, the outermost and toughest of three membranes surrounding the spinal cord. Study about the spinal cord and its function in the body. At what part of the spinal column would the anesthesia need to be administered to decrease the discomfort from uterine contractions?

Bible   3.   The Bible has many references to the pain (discomfort) associated with childbirth. Use your concordance to look up a few of these scriptures to read.

Writing   4.   Interview your mother about the events surrounding your birth and birth itself. (For a different perspective, boys may want to interview their father.) Write one page about the event and add to your Family History booklet.

Living   5.   Discuss very general infant care (supporting the infant's head, feeding, burping, protecting from falls, positioning).

Bible   6.   Mr. Boast wanted to adopt Rose because he and his wife were unable to have children of their own. Had Laura and Almanzo not been able to care for Rose, they might have decided that adoption was in Rose's best interest. What are some things the Bible says about adoption? In the Book of Esther we read that Esther was raised by her uncle, Mordecai. Christians are adopted heirs of Jesus Christ (Romans 4:16-17; Galatians 3:7, 26-29; John 1:12-13; Ephesians 1:5.)

Science/Art   7.   Find a picture of a St. Bernard dog. Study the characteristics of a St. Bernard. Draw a picture of a St. Bernard dog.

Page 260

First Four
Week 2

Week Two Planning Guide

Gather Information on the Following:

(See suggested sources listed)

1. Gregor Mendel and his Law of Heredity
   —
2. Fire safety
   — "Fire in Your Home: Prevention and Survival"
   —Pamphlets from fire department or home insurance agency
   —

Gather These Items:

1. <u>Little House in the Ozarks</u> by Laura Ingalls Wilder

Suggested Field Trips:

Notes:

First Four
Week 2

Read Chapter 3, Pages 84-97.

Reading Comprehension:

Chapter 3, Pages 84-97

1. What had Manly brought home? How did he feel that it would save them money? Laura felt that they could not afford the stove, yet she said that it was Manly's business. What do you think about this attitude?
2. What was Laura doing that would help Almanzo feel warm in the cold (page 85)?
3. What illness struck the Wilders' home? How was Rose? Who cared for them?
4. What did the doctor say had caused Manly's paralysis?
5. How had Rose changed while she was gone?
6. What enabled them to be able to move back to the tree claim?
7. How bad was Almanzo's health (page 90)? How did Laura help?
8. When did they ride the ponies? Why then? What safety precautions did they take?
9. What new investment did they make?
10. What happened to the wheat field this year?
11. What is the 25th of August?

Activities:

Science
1. Laura contracted diphtheria. Why is this not a frequently acquired disease today? *(Most infants and children are immunized against it.)* What are the signs and symptoms of diphtheria? *(Diphtheria is caused by bacteria. Its first symptoms are a sore throat, fever, headache, and nausea. Patches of grayish or dirty-yellowish membrane form in the throat, and gradually grow into one membrane. This membrane, combined with the swelling of the throat, may interfere with swallowing or breathing. The diphtheria bacillus also produces a toxin that spreads throughout the body and may damage the heart and nervous system. Heart complications are usually more severe in adults. Diphtheria spreads in droplets of moisture from the mouth, nose, or throat of an infected person. It may also be spread by handkerchiefs, towels, eating utensils, or any object used by an infected person or sprayed by his coughing or sneezing. It may be spread by a healthy person that is a carrier of the disease or someone that is convalescing from diphtheria. An infected person can have bacilli in his throat for two to four weeks after he has recovered from the effects. The period between exposure and contracting the disease, or the incubation time, is generally between two and five days. Bed rest, antibiotics, and cleanliness are used to combat the infection. Oxygen can be given to relieve troubled breathing. An antitoxin is given to counteract the toxic reaction from the bacillus.)* Which of these treatments were used to help Laura and Almanzo recover? *(Laura described her care as crude.)*

Bible
2. Laura, the author, meditated on Psalm 91 when she was sick. Read this and tell why this is a comforting Psalm.

Art
3. Make a get well card using a particularly meaningful section of Psalm 91 as script inside. (If no one you know is ill, make the card and save it for when it's needed.)

		First Four Week 2

Living   4.   Laura's mother was there for her in times of need, even in her adulthood. Read from <u>Little House in the Ozarks</u>, the chapters on "Mother" and "Mother Passed Away."

General   5.   Remember this week to schedule and make time to conclude General Activities

DAY 2

Read Chapter 4, Pages 98-121.

Reading Comprehension:

Chapter 4, Pages 98-121

1. Laura reminded Almanzo of their three-year trial on the farm. Do you think that the farming had been a success?
2. Why did they buy the oxen?
3. What were Rose's toys?
4. From what was Laura going to protect her sheep? How had she planned to do it?
5. What made Laura's pregnancy pass easier this time? Who had brought them for her?
6. Retell about the high winds, herding the sheep, and fires.
7. Had the sheep proved profitable?
8. Why was lambing time busy?
9. What happened to the lambs that were not cared for by their mothers?
10. What were some things Rose did when Laura's back was turned?
11. What did Laura hate (page 119)? What did she decide she would not do (page 119)?
12. How much would Manly get for the wheat if he could sell it? How much did he have to pay for it?
13. What must pride not stand in the way of (page 121)?

Activities:

Living   1.   From <u>Little House in the Ozarks</u> read and discuss the chapter, "Whom Will You Marry?" on page 183.

Living   2.   Plant geraniums.

Math   3.   What was their profit from the sheep (page 115)?

Bible/Writing   4.   Using Proverbs 31, describe how Almanzo had found a good wife in Laura and how she was a benefit to him.

Writing   5.   In your Family History booklet write about a time when you or a family member were in a life-threatening situation and were spared.

Page 263

First Four
Week 2

DAY 3

Read Chapter 4, Pages 121-134.

Reading Comprehension:

Chapter 4, Pages 121-134

1. Why could Manly not "prove up" on his tree claim? What did he have to do?
2. What was cyclone weather? What had Laura become accustomed to doing?
3. What happened on August 5 (page 125)? Was the doctor helpful?
4. What did Laura want more than anything after the birth of her son? Why did Laura feel that it was necessary to care for her house again quickly?
5. How old was her son when he died?
6. What was the next crisis?
7. What was Laura worried about when the house caught on fire?
8. Where did they stay until a house was rebuilt?
9. How is a farmer an optimist (page 133)?
10. Laura thought she would always be a farmer. She quoted a common saying, "What is bred in the bone will come out in the flesh." What does this mean? (Sir Thomas Mallory wrote this line for "The Death of Arthur" in 1470.)

Activities:

Writing	1.	Have your mother and father recount some stories of your childhood mischief. Write these down to add to your Family History booklet.
Science	2.	Ma had lost her only son within a year of his birth. Laura's son died with spasms within a month of being born. It is rumored that Rose Wilder grew up and also had a son who died within his first year. These common experiences for the women in this family may reflect a hereditary problem. In 1865, the year that Mary was born, Mendel's Law of Heredity was written. Briefly review the different dominant and recessive genes.
Bible	3.	Laura never had any more children. Of the four children that the Ingalls had, the only grandchildren they had were Laura's. While Abraham had only one child, Isaac, a whole race of people began with the twelve tribes of Israel. When Rose died, the last descendant of Charles and Caroline Ingalls died. Read Genesis 17:20; 22:16-18; 26:4, 24; 28:3; 41:52; 48:4; Exodus 32:13; Psalm 105:24; 107:38; Isaiah 44:2; 29:5; 51:2; 66:9; Jeremiah 30:19; 33:22; Ezekiel 36:10-11; 37:26. Fertility is a blessing that God can give or remove at anytime. A December Rose was indeed rare.
Bible	4.	"Give us this day our daily bread" is a quotation from where? *(The Lord's prayer.)* How was this all that Laura and Manly had?
Bible	5.	Laura, the author, meditated on Psalm 46 when she faced a crisis. How could this Psalm minister strength to one undergoing a crisis?
Bible	6.	Read Psalm 145:14, Proverbs 24:16, and Romans 5:3-5. How do these scriptures give one strength to continue?

Science	7.	Read and discuss "Fire in Your Home: Prevention and Survival."
Literature	8.	How does the title, "A Year of Grace" fit this chapter? What does the <u>American Dictionary of the English Language</u> (the 1828 edition by Noah Webster) say about "grace?" What does the Bible say about "grace?" Use your concordance to do a word study on grace. Include the passage II Corinthians 4:7-18 and I Peter 5:6-10 in your study.
Writing	9.	Meditate on all that you have learned about grace. Write a one page composition or poem about grace.

DAY 4

Finish Reading <u>Laura Ingalls Wilder Country</u>.
Also Read <u>Little House in the Ozarks</u>, "Let's Visit Mrs. Wilder."

Activities:

Bible	1.	God does not call everyone to marriage. Mary questioned why Laura would want to leave their happy home. Mary was called to singleness. What does the Bible say about being single? (I Corinthians 7:32-40.)
Bible	2.	Read Ecclesiastes 12:11-14.

Appendix

Appendix

Motivational Gifts

Romans 12

Appendix

The Gift of Teaching

A. **Commandment:** To give him/herself to this motivational gift. NAS—to exercise the motivational gift of teaching.

Remember, each motivational gift energizes the whole life of the believer. The "teacher" motivational gift will have a great desire to live God's Word in his/her life, and to see others do so. (For an example of one with the "teacher" gift, see James.) Also, "teacher" motivational gifts are usually very strict on themselves, motivated by the expectation of "stricter judgment": "Let not many of you become teachers, my brethren, knowing that as such we shall incur a stricter judgment" (margin and KJV say, "greater condemnation"), James 3:1.

B.

	Characteristics	Illustrations (Luke)
1.	Need to validate truth	"That thou mightest know the certainty of these things, wherein thou hast been instructed" (Luke 1:4)
2.	By established systems	Relates to Old Testament and other Gospels (Luke 1:1-3)
3.	Gives credentials	Emphasizes qualifications
4.	Present truth in systematic sequence	"Set forth in order" (Luke 1:1-3)
5.	Delights in research	Longest Gospel Completeness (Acts 1:1)
6.	Importance and accuracy of reporting	Precise descriptions, for example, Luke 4:38 "great fever"
7.	Alertness to factual details	Luke's Gospel filled with details
8.	Silent until information heard, observed, discussed	No "verbal" statements of Luke recorded
9.	Need to exercise diligence and endurance	Faithful determination Remained with Paul in prison (2 Timothy 4:10-11)

Page 268

Appendix

C. Reaction to Discipline of Another Christian:

1. Wants all scripture to be applied correctly.
2. Wants factual details in chronological order.
3. Researches other ways of church discipline.

D. How the Gift of Teaching Can Be Misused:

1. Becoming proud of their knowledge.
2. Despising practical wisdom of uneducated people.
3. Communicating skepticism toward their teachers.
4. Criticizing sound teaching because of technical flows.
5. Depending on human reasoning rather than the Holy Spirit's teaching.
6. Giving information that lacks practical application.
7. Boring listeners with details of research.
8. Retreating into their own world of books.

Encouragement to "teacher" motivational gifts—Bless and set people free by the power of God's Word (John 8:31-32; John 17:17).

Appendix

The Gift of Prophecy

A. **Commandment:** "Let him use it in proportion to his faith" (NIV).

B.

	Characteristics	Illustrations (Peter)
1.	Need to express	Peter spoke (Acts 2:4; 3:12)
2.	Quick judgments	Spoke first (Matthew 14:28; 15:16)
3.	Spiritual perception	Ananias and Sapphira (Act 5:3-10)
4.	Rejects offenders	Reluctant to forgive (Matthew 18:21)
5.	Personal honesty	"I am sinful' (Luke 5:8)
6.	Impulsive; wholeherted	Matthew 14:28; John 13:6-10
7.	Painfully direct	Rebuked Jesus (Mark 8:31-33)
8.	Loyalty, commitment	Matthew 26:33; John 18:10
9.	Willingness to suffer	Acts 5:29-42
10.	Very persuasive	Conviction (Acts 2:14-47)

Page 270

Appendix

C. Reaction to Discipline of Another Christian:

1. Reacts to any attempt to cover over sin.
2. Emphasizes awfulness of sin.
3. Requires complete confession.
4. Senses when sinner not repentant.
5. Requires punishment to warn others.
6. Rejects sinner until there is true repentance.

D. How the Gift of Prophecy Can Be Misused:

1. Correcting people who are not their responsibility.
2. Jumping to conclusions about words, actions, and motives.
3. Reinforcing a condemning spirit.
4. Judging and exposing an offender rather than restoring the offender.
5. Cutting off a person who has failed.
6. Dwelling on the negative rather than the positive.
7. Lacking caution and tactfulness in expressing opinions.
8. Demanding a positive response to a harsh rebuke.
9. Condemning themselves when they fail.
10. Accusing others of deception, if they do not fully reveal faults.

Appendix

The Gift of Serving

A. **Commandment:** "He whose gift is practical service, let him give himself to serving" (Amplified). "(If our gift) is serving others, let us concentrate on our service" (J. B. Phillips).

B.

	Characteristics	Illustrations (Timothy)
1.	Sees practical needs	Desires to meet needs (Philippians 2:20)
2.	Joy to free others	Served Paul (Philippians 2:22)
3.	Disregards health and comfort	Physical ailments (I Timothy 5:23)
4.	Difficulty in saying "no"	I Timothy 4:9, 21
5.	Enjoys providing physical needs	II Timothy 4:13
6.	Needs appreciation Desires clear instructions	I and II Timothy
7.	Desires to be with others	Working with others (Acts 16:2; 17:14-15; 18:5; 19:22)
8.	Enjoys short-range projects Frustrated with long-range	I Timothy 4:16 II Timothy 2:3
9.	Feels inadequate and unqualified	I Timothy 4:14; II Timothy 3:10-14; II Timotny 1:5

Page 272

Appendix

C. Reaction to Discipline of Another Christian:

1. Does not want to avoid one who has sinned.
2. Looks for ways to show love and acceptance.
3. Is usually first to help offender after restoration.

D. How the Gift of Serving Can Be Misused:

1. Neglecting home responsibilities to help others.
2. Accepting too many jobs at one time.
3. Wearing themselves out physically.
4. Being too persistent in giving unrequested help to others.
5. Going around proper authorities to get jobs done.
6. Excluding others from helping on a job.
7. Interfering with God's discipline of others by premature help.
8. Becoming hurt by the ungratefulness of those who were helped.
9. Getting "sidetracked" while working on an assignment.

Appendix

The Gift of Mercy

A. **Commandment:** "He who does acts of mercy with genuine cheerfulness and joyful eagerness" (Amplified). Emphasis in Greek is compassion for the ills and problems of others, which prompts action.

B.

	Characteristics	Illustrations (John)
1.	Ability to sense genuine love Vulnerable to hurts	Primary focus love—Gospel and letters
2.	Need for deep friendship with mutual commitment	Very close relationship with Christ and Peter (John 13:23; 19:26; 20:2; Acts)
3.	Reacts harshly when intimate friends rejected	Luke 9:54
4.	Greater concern over mental joy or distress than physical concerns	Joy, fellowship, hope, confidence, fear, torment (I John 1:3-4, etc.)
5.	Attracts people having mental and emotional distress	Others confide as Christ did (John 13:23-26)
6.	Measures acceptance by closeness and quality time	Closest place (John 13:23)
7.	Desires to remove causes of hurts rather than look for benefits from them	Stop hating and hurting each other (I John 3:11, 15)
8.	Avoids decisions and firmness unless they will eliminate other hurts	Follower, bold not to deny Jesus (Acts 4:13, 19-20)
9.	Attracted to those with motivational gift of prophecy	Spent more time with Peter than others Luke 22:8; Acts 3:1-11; 4:13-19; 8:14)

Appendix

C. Reaction to Discipline of Another Christian:

1. Senses if discipline was done in love.
2. Avoids discipline unless greater hurts will result.
3. Is first to comfort offender when restored.

D. How the Gift of Mercy Can Be Misused:

1. Failing to be firm and decisive when necessary.
2. Taking up offenses for those who have been hurt.
3. Basing decisions on emotions rather than on reason.
4. Prompting improper affections from those of the opposite sex.
5. Cutting off fellowship with those who are insensitive to others.
6. Reacting to God's purposes in allowing people to suffer.
7. Sympathizing with those who are violating God's standards.
8. Establishing possessive friendships with others.

Appendix

The Gift of Exhortation

A. **Commandment:** To give him/herself to this motivation gift. "If our gift be the stimulating of the faith of others let us set ourselves to it" (J. B. Phillips). Always prospective, looking to the future, in contrast to the meaning "to comfort," which is retrospective, having to do with trial experienced.

B.

	Characteristics	Illustrations (Paul)
1.	Urges people to full spiritual maturity	Colossians 1:28-29
2.	Ability to discern where a person is in growth	Corinthians infants (I Corinthians 3:1)
3.	Desires to give precise steps of action urging toward spiritual maturity	Practical counsel on how to grow spiritually
4.	Truth with logical reasoning	Logical reasoning; Resurrection (I Corinthians 15)
5.	Visualizes spiritual achievement	Pictures spiritual goals (Philippians 3:17)
6.	Desires face to face discussion	I Thessalonians 2:17; 3:10; II Timothy 1:4 Personal conferences (II Thessalonians 2:11-12)
7.	Ability to identify	I Corinthians 9:19-23
8.	Motivation for harmony	Resolved conflicts and divisions (I Corinthians 3:3-4; Philippians 2:2; II Corinthians 9:12-14)
9.	Personal tribulation chief motivator	Gloried in infirmities (II Corinthians 1:5; 4:17; 12:9)

Page 276

Appendix

C.   **Reaction to Discipline of Another Christian:**

1.   Visualizes steps of action for restoration.
2.   Sees how offenses can be turned into benefits.
3.   Relates repentance to steps of action.

D.   **How Gift of Exhortation Can Be Misused:**

1.   Raising the expectations of others prematurely.
2.   Taking "family time" to counsel others.
3.   Treating family and friends as "projects" rather than persons.
4.   Sharing private illustrations without permission.
5.   Jumping into new projects without finishing existing ones.
6.   Encouraging others to depend on them rather than God and their authorities.
7.   Trusting visible results rather than a true change of heart.
8.   Neglecting proper emphasis on basic Bible doctrines.
9.   Giving counsel before discerning the type of person or problem.

Appendix

The Gift of Giving

A. **Commandment:** Let him do it with liberality—simplicity, sincerity, unaffectedness, singleness (see Colossians. 3:22—with only a single motive.) I Thessalonians 2:8—Paul speaks of himself and his fellow-ministers as having been well pleased to impart to the new believers both God's Gospel and their own souls, that is, so sharing those with them as to spend themselves and spend out their lives for them.

B.

	Characteristics	Illustrations (Matthew)
1.	Discerns wise investments	More counsel on wise use of money (Matthew 6:19-20; 25:14-30)
2.	Desires to give quietly	Writes to give secretly (Matthew 6:1-4)
3.	Gives unto Lord at his prompting	Give to Christ (Matthew 25:35-46)
4.	Desires to give high quality gifts	Records details of costly gifts given to Jesus: Gold, frankincense, myrrh, precious ointment, new sepulcher
5.	Ability to test faithfulness and wisdom in handling funds	Reveals misuse (Matthew 21:33-34; 25:14-30)
6.	Personal frugality Content with basics	Matthew "left all" (Luke 5:27-32)
7.	Alertness to see what people do with their money	Only Gospel writer to tell of twenty pieces of silver and bribery payment (Matthew 27:3-8; 28:11-15)
8.	See needs others overlook	Condemnation (Matthew 15:3-7) Wages (Matthew 20:1-16)
9.	Use giving as a way to motivate others	Job to motivate people to give (Luke 5:29) See Matthew 18:23-35

Page 278

Appendix

C. Reaction to Discipline of Another Christian:

1. Concerned about legal aspects of discipline.
2. Helps offender get work, if needed.
3. Assists with funds, if true repentance occurs.

D. How the Gift of Giving Can Be Misused:

1. Giving too sparingly to their own family.
2. Causing family to resent gifts to others.
3. Listening to unscriptural counsel on money management.
4. Putting pressure on people who have less to give.
5. Failing to discern God's prompting for a gift.
6. Judging those who misuse funds rather than advising them.
7. Controlling people by giving too much.
8. Corrupting people by giving too much.
9. Investing in projects that do not benefit the lives of people.

Appendix

The Gift of Ruling

A. **Commandment:** Rule "with diligence." "Let the man who wields authority think of his responsibility" (J. B. Phillips).

B.

	Characteristics	Illustrations (Nehemiah)
1.	Ability to visualize final result of major undertaking	Visualized the goal (Nehemiah 1:2-3; 2:5)
2.	Breaks down major goals into smaller, achievable tasks	Many groups worked on smaller sections (Nehemiah 3:1-32)
3.	Knows resources available and needed to reach goal	Requested resources needed to rebuild (Nehemiah 2:6-8)
4.	Removes himself from distracting details	Did not build but removed obstacles (Nehemiah 5:1-13)
5.	Willing to endure reaction from insiders and outsiders	Had opposition from within and without (Nehemiah 4:8-18)
6.	Needs loyalty and confidence from those being directed	Required oaths of cooperation (Nehemiah 5:1-13)
7.	Knows what and what not to delegate to others	Delegated work on walls; retained responsibility of dealing with enemies and guarding walls
8.	Inspires and encourages with cheerfulness and challenges	Cheerful (Nehemiah 2:1) Challenge, encouragement (4:14)
9.	Joy in seeing finished product	Expressed joy in completed task—singers, celebration (Nehemiah 7:1-2; 8:1-18)

Appendix

C. Reaction to Discipline of Another Christian:

1. Is most skillful in finding out all the facts.
2. Sees dangers, if discipline is inconsistent.
3. Knows what is necessary to carry out discipline.

D. How the Gift of Ruling Can Be Misused:

1. Viewing people as "human resources" rather than human beings.
2. Using people to accomplish personal ambitions.
3. Showing favoritism to those who appear to be more loyal.
4. Taking charge of projects that were not God's direction.
5. Delegating too much work to others.
6. Overlooking serious character faults in valuable workers.
7. Being unresponsive to suggestions and appeals.
8. Failing to give proper explanations and praise to workers.

Appendix

How Can We Discover Our Motivational Gift?

A. Make Sure You Are a Christian.

B. Break Sin's Power.

C. Concentrate on Others.

D. Discern Your Motives.

E. Examine Your Irritations.

F. Find Your Characteristics.

G. Give Adequate Time.

H. Humble Your Heart.

I. Identify Gift Misuses.

Appendix

Hindrances to Discovering Your Gift

There may be many reasons why a person is not able to discern his motivational spiritual gift. Here are a few:

A. Unresolved Root Problems in Personal Living.

It is significant that the gifts of Romans 12 are not mentioned until the moral conflicts of Romans 1 through 11 are dealt with.

B. Lack of Involvement with the Needs of Others.

Our gifts are stirred up and discovered as we focus on the needs of others rather than what our ministry is to be. A servant's heart is essential to discover our motivational gift.

C. Attempts to Imitate Motivations of Others.

If a Christian is caught up in trying to imitate the ministry of other Christians, he will not be free to discover his own motivation.

D. Failure to Analyze Why Certain Activities Appeal to Us.

It is important for us to understand what basic motivation is for our present Christian activities. Many activities will be the means of fulfilling our basic motivation.

E. Confusion between Motivational Gift and Ministry Gift.

A person with the motivation of teaching may, for example, have a ministry of prophecy that he thoroughly enjoys. This may cause him to questions which one is his actual motivational gift.

(From "Motivational Gifts" by Dr. Graham B. Truscott. Copyrighted. Mission Bay Christian Fellowship, School of Christian Ministries. Used by permission.)

Bibliography

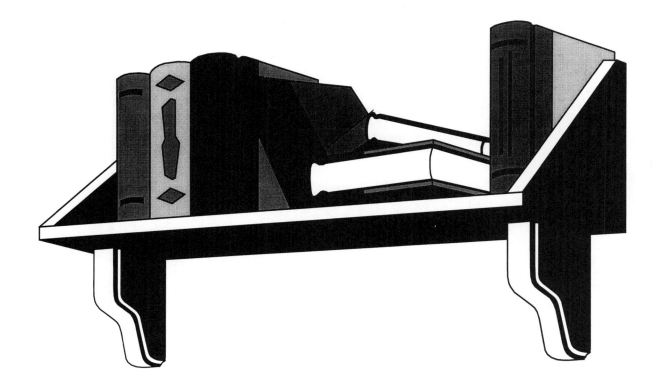

Bibliography
for the "Hard" to Obtain Resources

As much as possible, it is recommended for cost containment to use the library as the primary source for materials. Comparable books and sources are fine to use. All libraries contain The "Little House" Series. Therefore, it may be possible to even use the library for these books. Generally check out time is one month and the study done at the suggested pace will take a month. Unfortunately, your study becomes limited to the availability of the book. Because of this, it is recommended that the series be purchased. The <u>Primer</u>'s pages correspond with the paperback edition, illustrated by Garth Williams, published in 1953.

**** Books or materials that are to be used several times during the series.

*** Books or materials that are used during the study of only one book.

** Books or materials that are used only for a single day's assignment in one book.

* References of interest for parental use, but not necessary for study by child.

Cadron Creek Christian Curriculum
51 West Cadron Ridge Road
Greenbrier, AR 72058
Phone: 1-501-679-5142
**** <u>American Dictionary of the English Language</u> (the 1828 edition by Noah Webster). *This is an expensive resource, but it will add a different depth to some of the word studies.*
*** "Historical Timetable" by Jane Williams. *This is an excellent, inexpensive source for making timelines.*
**** <u>The Little House Cookbook</u> by Barbara M. Walker hardback or paperback
**** <u>The Laura Ingalls Wilder Songbook</u> (63 songs:words with score)-presentlly out of print
**** <u>Musical Memories</u> (book and tape set)

Christian Teaching Materials
P. O. Box 639
Glenpool, OK 74033-0639
Phone: 1-918-322-3420
(They carry additional 1800's curriculum:)
* <u>Ray's Arithmetic</u>
* <u>Spencerian System of Practical Penmanship</u> (Mott Media)

Color the Classics
P.O. Box 440
Silver Springs, NY 14550
** Color the Patriotic Classics

Bibliography

CPSI
Suite 300
1875 Connecticut Ave., NW
Washington, DC 20009
Phone: 1-202-667-7483
    ** "CPSI's Eating Smart Fat Guide"
    ** "CPSI's Sugar Scoreboard"
    ** "CPSI's Rate Your Plate"

The Elijah Co.
Route 2, Box 100-B
Fred Ford Road
Crossville, TN 38555
Phone: 1-615-456-6284
    Also has assorted biographies available.
    ** <u>Going Home to School</u> by Llewellyn Davis
    *** <u>The Indian How Book</u> by Arthur Parker
    *** <u>Tracking and the Art of Seeing</u> by Paul Rezendes
    *** <u>My Indian Boyhood</u> by Luther Standing Bear
    *** <u>The Weather Report</u> by Mike Graf

Family Learning Center
Route 2, Box 264
Hawthorne, FL 32640
    *** <u>Pocket Science: Tools and Machines</u> by Dinah Zike and Jan Hutchings

---

Family Research Council
Suite 500
700 Thirteenth Street, NW
Washington, DC 20005-3960
Phone: 1-800-A-FAMILY
    ** "Washington Watch" (You might obtain this from a friend that is interested in political action; they may have this resource.)

Farm Country General Store
412 North Fork Rd
Metamora, IL 61548
1-800-551-FARM
    * <u>God's Key to Health and Happiness</u> by Elmer Josephson
    * <u>Foods that Heal</u> by Maureen Salaman
    * <u>The Diet Bible</u> by Maureen Salaman

Bibliography

Focus on the Family
P.O. Box 35500
Colorado Springs, CO 80935-3550
Phone: 1-800-A-FAMILY
   ** "Citizen" (You might obtain this from a friend that is interested in political action; they may have this resource.)

Home School Supply House
P.O. Box 2000
Beaver, UT 84713
Phone: 1-800-772-3129 or 1-801-438-1254
   *** Andrew Jackson and the New Populism by William Gutman
   ** Moccasin Making Kit
   *** Thomas Jefferson and the American Ideal by Russell Shorto
  **** The Young Scientist book of the Human Body (Usborne)
   *** The Young Scientist Book of Medicine, Doctors, and Health (Usborne)

In His Steps
PO 268
Ponder, TX 76259-0268
Phone:1-800-583-1336
   *** Trailblazer series
   *** Pioneer Crafts for Kids compiled by Neva Henderson
   *** The Little Kid's Americana Craft Book by Jackie Vermeer
   *** Louis Braille: Boy Who Invented Books for the Blind
   *** Weeds A Golden Guide

Institute in Basic Life Principles
Box One
Oak Brook, IL 60522-3001
Phone: 1-708-323-9800
 **** Basic Care Bulletin, Medical Training Institute of America. *This is rather expensive, but a good resource. If possible, preview one from a friend. One must be an alumni of Basic Youth Conflicts Seminar to purchase.*
  *** Dwight L. Moody Heros of Faith
   ** Pineapple Story. *An excellent story on yielding one's rights.*

Bibliography

Lifetime Books and Gifts, The Always Incomplete Catalog
3900 Chalet Suzanne Drive
Lake Wales, FL 33853-7763
Phone: 1-800-377-0390

  *** Assorted biographies recommended in the Primer by various authors and publishers with differing reading difficulty:
     Abe Lincoln
     Clara Barton
     Thomas Jefferson
     Samuel B. Morse
     Louis Pasteur
     George Washington
     Noah Webster

   ** Blood and Guts by Linda Allison
  *** Confederate Trilogy for Young Readers by Williamson
    * Dating with Integrity by Holzmann
   ** Facts the Historians Leave Out: A Confederate Primer by Tilly
   ** Favorite Little House Songs by Waring (cassette)
    * If You Are Trying to Teach Kids How to Write, You've Got to Have This Book by Marjorie Frank
 **** Laura Ingalls Wilder Country by William Anderson. *Many libraries have this book, but it will be used at the conclusion of each Book and is a beautiful reference.*
    * Learning Grammar through Writing
 **** Little House Cookbook by Barbara M. Walker
    * Ray's Arithmetic
  *** The Right Choice—Home Schooling by Christopher Klicka
   ** "South Speaks Out" video
  *** Southern by the Grace of God by Michael Grissom (This is adult reading)
   ** Wonderful Way Babies Are Made by Larry Christenson
    * You CAN Teach Your Child Successfully Grades 4-8 by Ruth Beechick

Jonathan Lindvall
P.O. Box 820
Springville, CA 93265
Phone: 1-209-539-0500
Various cassette tapes on dating, including:
    * "Preparing for Romance" and "A Talk to Godly Teens About Sex and Romance"

Little House Bookstore
Route 1, Box 24
Mansfield, MO 65704
Phone: 1-417-924-3626

 **** Laura Ingalls Wilder Country by William Anderson
   ** The Story of the Ingalls by William Anderson

Bibliography

Mantle Ministries
"Little Bear Wheeler"
228 Stillridge
Bulberde, TX 78163
830-438-3777
    *** <u>1861-1865 A.D.</u> (Volume 7) cassette series
     ** <u>Songs Than Made America Great</u>
      * <u>Warning: Dating is No Game</u>

Milliken
1100 Research Blvd.
St. Louis, MO 63132
Phone: 1-800-325-4136
    *** <u>Solids, Liquids, and Gases</u> (Milliken)
     ** <u>Studying Plants</u> (Milliken)
    *** <u>Work and Machines</u> (Milliken)
        (all reproducible)

National Fire Protection Association
One Batterymarch Park
Quincy, MA 02269-9101
    *** "Fire in Your Home: Prevention and Survival." (This is available only in quantities greater than 100. Unless your support group or a local business wants to purchase, this is impractical.)

The Sycamore Tree
2179 Meyer Place
Costa Mesa, CA 92627
Phone: 1-714-650-4466
     ** American Indian Moccasins
        Assorted Biographies
     ** <u>Blood and Guts</u> by Linda Allison
      * <u>If You're Trying to Teach Kids How to Write You've Gotta Have This Book</u> by Marjorie Frank
     ** <u>Lap loom</u>
  **** <u>The Little House Cookbook</u> by Barbara M. Walker
      * <u>Ray's Arithmetic</u>
      * <u>Spencerian System of Practical Penmanship</u> (Mott Media)
      * "Songs from the Little House" cassette tape
     ** <u>The Thomas Edison Book of Easy and Incredible Experiments</u>
   *** <u>The Weather Report</u> by Mike Graf
      * <u>You Can Teach Your Child Successfully</u> by Ruth Beechick

---

SOLD TO: (PLEASE PRINT)

Name: _____
Address: _____
City: _____ State: _____
Zip Code: _____ Phone: _____

PLEASE MAKE CHECK OR MONEY ORDER PAYABLE TO:

Cadron Creek Christian Curriculum or CCCC
4329 Pinos Altos RD
Silver City, New Mexico 88061
(505)534-1496
Website: CadronCreek.com

QUANTITY	ITEM	PRICE	TOTAL
	The Prairie Primer (290 Pages)	$45.00	
	The Little House Cookbook (Hardback 15.95) (Paperback 7.95)		
	The Laura Ingalls Wilder Songbook (63 Songs;Words With Score) Presently Out Of Print		
	Laura Ingalls Wilder Historical Timetable (Shipping Included)	2.35	
	Musical Memories (Book & Tape Set)	24.95	
	The World Of Little House	19.95	
	Laura Ingalls Wilder Country	22.50	
	My Little House Sewing Book	10.95	
	My Little House Craft Book	8.95	
	American Dictionary of The English Language(1828 Edition By Noah Webster)	55.00	
	Academics &Anne	30.00	
	Anne's Anthology (Coming Soon)		
	Annotated Anne Of Green Gables (Hardback)	35.00	
	What In The World's Going on Here? (Circle One)vol. I , II (Cassette Tape)	19.95 ea.	
	World Leaders Past & Present: Queen Victoria (Hardback)	19.99	
	Are You Liberal, Conservative, or Confused?	9.95	
	Spelling Power	49.95	
	Spelling Power Activity Task Cards	29.95	
	Spelling Power Workbook (Red, Blue, Green, Yellow)	5.95	
	Things We Wish We'd Known	12.99	
	TAX (NM RESIDENTS 5.8125%)		
	SHIPPING 10% (MINIMUM $2.50)		
			TOTAL DUE